The Complete Book of
Modern Classics

Editorial director Susan Tomnay
Creative director Hieu Chi Nguyen
Editor Stephanie Kistner
Feature writer Meg Thomason
Designer Sylvia Weimer/Spacelab Design
Food director Pamela Clark
Food editor Cathie Lonnie
Nutritional information Angela Muscat

Sales director Brian Cearnes
Marketing director Matt Dominello
Marketing manager Bridget Cody
Production manager Cedric Taylor
Business analyst Ashley Davies

Chief executive officer Ian Law
Group publisher Pat Ingram
General manager Christine Whiston
Editorial director (AWW) Deborah Thomas

The publishers would like to thank the
following for props used in photography:
Accoutrement, Mosman;
Orson and Blake, Woollahra.

Photographers Alan Benson, Steve Brown,
Chris Chen, Gerry Colley, Joshua Dasey,
Ben Dearnley, Joe Filshie, Louise Lister,
Andre Martin, Con Poulos, Prue Ruscoe,
Stuart Scott, Brett Stevens, Ian Wallace,
Andrew Young, Tanya Zouev
Stylists Wendy Berecry, Julz Beresford,
Janelle Bloom, Margot Braddon, Kate Brown,
Kirsty Cassidy, Marie-Helene Clauzon, Jane
Hann, Sarah O'Brien, Michaela Le Compte,
Louise Pickford, Christine Rooke, Suzie Smith

Step photography
Photographer Phillip Castleton
Food preparation Sharon Reeve

Cover and chapter opener photography
Photographer Joshua Dasey
Stylist Margot Braddon
Food preparation Nicole Jennings

Produced by ACP Books, published by ACP Books, a division of ACP Magazines Ltd.
54 Park St, Sydney NSW Australia 2000. GPO Box 4088, Sydney, NSW 2001.
Phone +61 2 9282 8618 Fax +61 2 9267 9438
acpbooks@acpmagazines.com.au www.acpbooks.com.au
To order books, phone 136 116. Send recipe enquiries to recipeenquiries@acpmagazines.com.au
Printed in China through Phoenix Offset

Rights enquiries Laura Bamford, Director ACP Books. lbamford@acpuk.com

Australia Distributed by Network Services, GPO Box 4088, Sydney, NSW 2001.
Phone +61 2 9282 8777 Fax +61 2 9264 3278 networkweb@networkservicescompany.com.au
United Kingdom Distributed by Australian Consolidated Press (UK),
10 Scirocco Close, Moulton Park Office Village, Northampton, NN3 6AP.
Phone +44 1604 642 200 Fax +44 1604 642 300 books@acpuk.com www.acpuk.com
New Zealand Distributed by Netlink Distribution Company, ACP Media Centre, Cnr Fanshawe and
Beaumont Streets, Westhaven, Auckland. PO Box 47906, Ponsonby, Auckland, NZ.
Phone +64 9 366 9966 Fax 0800 277 412 ask@ndc.co.nz
South Africa Distributed by PSD Promotions, 30 Diesel Road Isando, Gauteng Johannesburg.
PO Box 1175, Isando 1600, Gauteng Johannesburg.
Phone +27 11 392 6065/6/7 Fax +27 11 392 6079/80 orders@psdprom.co.za

Clark, Pamela.
The Australian women's weekly the complete book of modern classics.
Includes index.
ISBN 978-1-86396-510-1.
1. Cookery. I. Title. II. Title: Australian women's weekly.
641.5

© ACP Magazines Ltd 2005
ABN 18 053 273 546

THE AUSTRALIAN
Women's Weekly

The Complete Book of
Modern Classics

400+ essential recipes for today's cook

acp
books

contents

Recipes come and go, but some stay to become part of our lives. As the trusted companion to generations of Australian cooks, *The Australian Women's Weekly* has seen them all. Over the years, we've seen Australian tastes change as our population has grown and become more pluralist. We're now a nation of spice lovers, having embraced Asian and Middle-Eastern cooking in recent years just as we embraced Mediterranean food earlier. Today, our most popular quick and easy meals to make at home are pasta or a stir-fry — familiar, everyday ideas now, yet not so very long ago they were excitingly new. There has also been a wonderful increase in the range of ingredients we can buy. From tofu to Thai basil, Atlantic salmon to arborio, haloumi to harissa, we have made them a part of our day-to-day cooking.

This book is a treasury of Australian Women's Weekly recipes that have proved their staying power. Some are time-honoured friends: we'll always want to make mayonnaise, a good meat pie or steamed pudding. Many are newer, reflecting the way we cook now. All have the Weekly's hallmark of inspiration allied to commonsense. We hope you will enjoy cooking these modern classics.

introduction

essential
ingredients

black
beans

AIOLI An addictive garlic mayonnaise, aïoli has inflamed the passions of so many people around the world that local aïoli festivals are held at garlic harvest time every year. With 'ail' meaning garlic and 'oli' meaning oil, this Provençal classic marries well with fish, meats and vegetables. **BEANS Black beans** Also known as turtle beans, black beans are a common ingredient in Caribbean and Latin American soups, salsas and salads. They are available from health food stores and gourmet food outlets. **Broad beans** Also known as fava, windsor or horse beans, broad beans are available dried, fresh, canned and frozen. Fresh and frozen, they

are best peeled twice (discarding both the outer long green pod and beige-green tough inner shell).
BETEL LEAVES Grown and consumed in India and throughout South-East Asia, betel leaves are used raw as a wrap, cooked as a vegetable, or chopped and used both as a herb and medicine. They are available at some greengrocers and most Asian food stores, especially those specialising in Vietnamese produce.
CAPERBERRIES The fruit formed after caper buds have flowered, caperberries are milder in taste than capers. They marry well with seafood dishes and look fantastic on an antipasto platter. Sold pickled with stalks

betel
leaves

broad
beans

caperberries

daikon

intact, they can be purchased from most delicatessens. **CHERMOULLA** A Moroccan blend of fresh herbs, spices and condiments, chermoulla is traditionally used for preserving or seasoning meat and fish. **CHINESE WATER SPINACH** Also known as swamp spinach, chinese water spinach has arrowhead-shaped leaves and hollow stems. Used like spinach in soups and stir-fries, sometimes the stems are sold separately in Asian food stores. **CHIPOTLE** Chipotle is the name used for jalapeño chillies once they've been dried and smoked. Having a deep, intensely smoky flavour rather than a searing heat, chipotles are dark brown in colour. They

are available from specialty spice stores and gourmet delicatessens. **CHOY SUM** also known as pakaukeio or flowering cabbage, choy sum is a member of the bok choy family. Easy to identfy with its long stems, pale green leaves and yellow flowers, it's eaten, stems and all, steamed or sitr-fried. **DAIKON** White radish used extensively in Japanese cooking. Possessing a sweet, fresh flavour without the bite of the common red radish, it can be used raw in salads, as a garnish or in stews. **DASHI** Dashi is the basic stock used in nearly every Japanese dish. Either vegetarian or seafood-based, with the most common dashi being a combination of

choy
sum

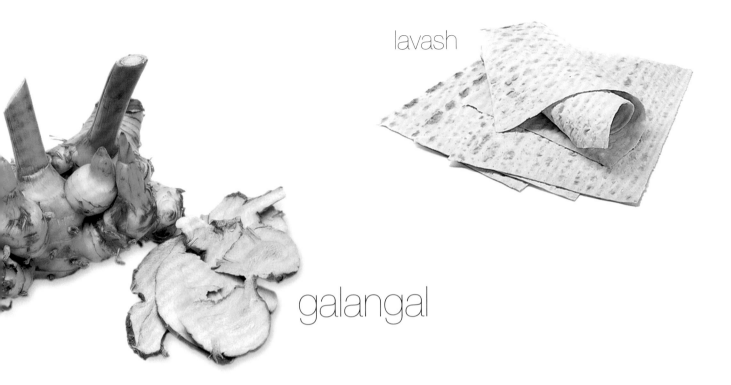

lavash

galangal

both kelp and smoked dried bonito flakes. Available in concentrated liquid as well as granule or powdered form from most Asian food stores. **GAI LARN** Also known as gai lum, chinese broccoli and chinese kale, this vegetable is prized more for its stems than its coarse leaves. Can be eaten stir-fried on its own or tossed into various soups and noodle dishes. Available from most supermarkets, Asian food stores and greengrocers. **GALANGAL** Also known as ka, galangal is a rhizome with a hot ginger-citrusy flavour that is used similarly to ginger as a seasoning and as an ingredient. Fresh ginger can be substituted for fresh galangal but the

flavour of the dish will not be exactly the same. Available from some greengrocers and Asian food stores. **HARISSA** A North African paste made from dried red chillies, garlic, olive oil and caraway seeds, can be used as a rub for meat and as an ingredient in sauces and dressings. It is available ready-made from some supermarkets and Middle Eastern food stores. **KAFFIR LIME LEAVES** They are used, fresh or dried, as a flavouring, like bay leaves, throughout Asia. Sold fresh, dried or frozen, the dried leaves are less potent so double the number called for in a recipe if you substitute them for fresh leaves. Available from most

kaffir lime leaves

gai larn

nashi

greengrocers and Asian food stores. **LAVASH** A soft, thin, flat, unleavened bread of Mediterranean origin, lavash can be used for wraps or be cut into triangles, toasted and used as a dipper. Available from most supermarkets. **LEMON GRASS** A tall, clumping, sharp-edged aromatic tropical grass that both smells and tastes of lemon. Generally only the stem end of the plant is used in cooking. It is sold fresh in most supermarkets, greengrocers and Asian food stores. **LYCHEES** Originating in China over 1000 years ago, lychees are a delicious fresh fruit with a light texture and flavour. Peel away rough skin, remove seed and

they're ready to eat. Available, fresh and canned, from most supermarkets and greengrocers. **MISO** A fermented soybean paste commonly used in Japanese cooking. There are many types of miso, each with its own aroma, flavour, colour and texture. Generally, the darker the miso, the saltier the taste and denser the texture. Available from Asian food stores. **NASHI** Also called Japanese or Asian pear, nashi is a member of the pear family but similar in appearance to an apple. Great poached or in salads, nashi are available from autumn to spring from some supermarkets and greengrocers.

lemon grass

lychees

rice
noodles

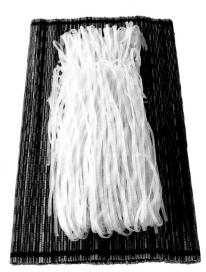

soba
noodles

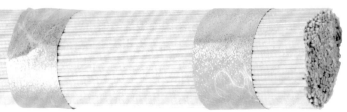

NOODLES **Bean thread noodles**, also known as bean thread vermicelli, cellophane noodles or glass noodles. **Rice noodles** are a common form of noodle used throughout South East Asia. Chewy and pure white, they do not need pre-cooking before use. **Soba noodles**, also known as buckwheat noodles, are made from various proportions of buckwheat flour. Usually available dried, but can be purchased fresh from local noodle makers. **NUTMEG** Whole nutmeg can be shaved or grated over dishes. With an aromatic, full-bodied flavour, nutmeg goes well with pumpkin, kumara, cheese sauces, and sweet spicy cakes. Available in ground form or whole, from most supermarkets and specialty spice stores. **PITTA BREAD** Round, dinner-plate sized Lebanese bread eaten on its own; roughly torn and used to scoop up dips and salads; or filled with a combination of meats and salad vegetables and rolled into a substantial sandwich. **POLENTA** A flour-like cereal made from dried corn (maize) sold ground in several different textures and available at most supermarkets. Can be eaten soft and creamy, or chilled and grilled. **SAFFRON** One of the most expensive spices in the world, true saffron comes only from the saffron crocus, that can produce several flowers a year.

nutmeg

polenta

saffron

sambal
oelek

Available from supermarkets and specialty spice stores. **SAMBAL OELEK** Also spelt ulek or olek, this spicy Indonesian condiment is usually made of chillies, shrimp paste, sugar and salt. Available from most supermarkets and Asian food stores. **SEAWEED Wakame** is a dark green vegetable that grows in cool to cold sea waters. Dried wakame can be shredded and used in many different ways in soups, salads and other dishes, or as a seasoning. **Kombu** is the deep-green seaweed which is used as the basis for one of the main types of dashi; it is sold dry in hard sheets or in powdered form. The dried product is very rich in

sodium, calcium and phosphorous, and contains a high percentage of protein. Kombu is a basic ingredient in most traditional one-pot dishes such as shabu-shabu and in many macrobiotic recipes. **Nori** is the most popular seaweed in Japan and especially rich in vitamin A. Koyo-nori is selected from the finest grades available for its rich, shiny colour, fine texture and delicious flavour. It is ideal for making 'nori-maki' sushi rolls, or for wrapping 'onigiri' rice balls. Also an excellent garnish for brown rice, tofu and vegetable dishes, as well as soups and noodles. Available from supermarkets and Asian food stores.

pitta bread

kombu

wakame

seaweed

nori

sichuan
peppercorns

shiitake

SICHUAN PEPPERCORNS Also known as szechuan or chinese pepper, a mildly hot spice that comes from the prickly ash tree. Although it is not related to the peppercorn family, small, red-brown aromatic sichuan berries look like black peppercorns and have a distinctive peppery-lemon flavour and aroma. Available from Asian food stores and specialty spice stores.

SHIITAKE MUSHROOMS Called the king of mushrooms in their native Japan; available both fresh and dried. Fresh shiitake need to have their woody stems removed before they're used; their rich flavour and dense, substantial texture are shown to best advantage when braised or fried then eaten on their own. When dried, shiitake must be reconstituted by being soaked in water before use in stir-fries and various one-pot dishes. **STAR ANISE** The dried, star-shaped seed pod can be used whole as a flavouring and the seeds used alone as a spice; both can be used ground. While it does have a slight liquorice-like taste, it should not be compared to or confused with anise, being far more spicily pungent, with overtones of clove and cinnamon. Available from supermarkets and Asian food stores. **SUMAC** A deep-purple-red astringent spice coarsely ground from berries growing on shrubs that

sumac

star
anise

tat soi

tofu

flourish wild around the Mediterranean, sumac adds a tart, lemony flavour to dips and dressings and goes well with poultry, fish and meat. Available from Middle Eastern food stores and specialty spice stores. **TAHINI** A sesame seed paste most often used in hummus, baba ghanoush and other Lebanese recipes. Available from Middle Eastern food stores and health food stores. **TAMARIND** Tamarind is the product of a native tropical African tree. Dried tamarind is reconstituted in a hot liquid which gives a sweet-sour, astringent taste to food. **TAT SOI** Also known as pak choy and chinese flat cabbage, tat soi is a variety of bok choy. Its dark green leaves are cut into sections rather than separated and used in soups, braises and stir-fries. Available from some supermarkets and greengrocers. **THAI BASIL** Also known as horapa, Thai basil has smallish leaves and purple stems, a sweet licorice aniseed taste and is one of the basic flavours that typify Thai cuisine. Available from greengrocers. **TOFU** Also known as bean curd, tofu is an off-white, custard-like product made from the milk of crushed soy beans. Available fresh as soft or firm, and processed as fried or pressed dried sheets. Silken tofu refers to the method by which it is made – where it is strained through silk. Available

tamarind

thai basil

turmeric

vanilla
bean

from supermarkets and Asian food stores. **TURMERIC** A member of the ginger family, turmeric is a root that is dried and ground, resulting in the rich yellow powder used in most Asian cuisines. It is intensely pungent in taste but not hot. Available from supermarkets and Asian or Indian food stores. **VANILLA BEAN** Dried long, thin pod from a tropical golden orchid grown in Central and South America and Tahiti. The black seeds inside the bean are used to impart a luscious vanilla flavour in baking and desserts. **VIETNAMESE MINT** Not a mint at all, but a pungent, peppery narrow-leafed member of the buckwheat family. It is a common ingredient in Thai foods. Available from most

greengrocers. **VINEGAR Raspberry** There are many white wine vinegars available that have had fruit or herbs macerated in them. Raspberry is one of the most common varieties, and it can be used in a great many ways other than as part of a vinaigrette. Sprinkle it over a bowl of cooked vegetables or a fresh fruit salad to bring up the flavours and add a note of piquancy, or use it in a marinade or sauce for meat, poultry or game — it's particularly suited to duck. **Rice** Also known as seasoned rice vinegar, rice vinegar is a colourless vinegar made from fermented rice and flavoured with sugar and salt. **WASABI** An Asian horseradish used to make the pungent, green-coloured paste traditionally

water
chestnut

vietnamese
mint

wild
rice

watercress

wasabi
paste

served with Japanese raw fish dishes. Available, in powdered or paste form, from supermarkets and Asian food stores. **WATER CHESTNUTS** Resemble chestnuts in appearance, hence the English name. They are small brown tubers with a crisp, white, nutty-tasting flesh. Their crunchy texture is best experienced fresh, however, canned water chestnuts are more easily obtained and can be kept about a month, once opened, under refrigeration. **WATERCRESS** One of the cress family, a large group of peppery greens used raw in salads, dips and sandwiches, or cooked in soups. Highly perishable, so must be used as soon as possible after purchase. **WILD RICE** Not a true member of the rice family, this blackish-brown North American seed has a distinctive nutty flavour. It is fairly expensive as it is difficult to cultivate and hence, is often blended with white rice. **WITLOF** Sometimes spelled witloof, and in some countries known as Belgian endive or chicory, witlof has a distinctively bitter flavour; this versatile vegetable can be eaten cooked or raw. Available all year round from most supermarkets and greengrocers. **ZA'ATAR** A blend of roasted herbs and spices such as thyme, sumac, sesame seeds and marjoram sprinkled over cheese, toast or grilled meats. Za'atar is easy to make but is also sold in Middle Eastern food stores.

witlof

za'atar

essential equipment

flan tin

baba pan

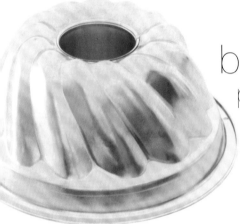

silicon muffin pan

BABA PAN A tall, cylindrical, ring-shaped fluted cake pan. **BLENDER, HAND-HELD STICK** This simple electric mixer can do almost everything a food processor does and is easier to clean and store. **CANDY THERMOMETER** A necessity when making sweets such as nougat and fudge. Most thermometers can reach temperatures between 30°C (60°F) and 200°C (400°F) and are a cheap yet crucial tool when making anything that requires a specific degree of heat. **CHAN** The Chinese invented this form of spatula to use on woks. Use for stir-frying as it can easily turn large quantities of food. **CHINOIS** Used for straining or pureeing, a chinois is a conical sieve made of stainless steel. **FLAN TIN** A round shallow or deep tin made from metal with a removable base for making quiches

and pastry flans. **FRIAND PAN** Similar to a muffin pan, but the holes are either rectanglular or oval in shape. **MEZZALUNA** Chopping herbs like chervil, parsley and coriander to the finest of minces without crushing the leaves into a blackened wet slush is accomplished easily and effectively with a mezzaluna. Shaped like a half (mezza)-moon (luna), this sturdy kitchen tool has been used for centuries by Italian cooks and has over the years gained in popularity among other nations' kitchens too. **MORTAR AND PESTLE** Investing in a good mortar and pestle is one of the wisest kitchen moves you'll ever make if you're serious about preparing authentic Thai food. **MUFFIN PANS** Sold in a plethora of shapes and sizes, there are three standard sizes – mini, regular and Texas – that are readily available.

candy thermometer

chinois

mezzaluna

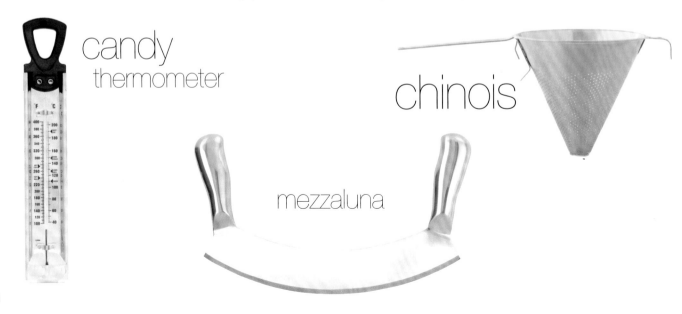

salad
spinner

chan

tagine

olive
pipper

OLIVE PIPPER An olive pipper can pop the seeds out of cherries as well as olives, plus it can be used to perform the reverse task of stuffing olives with bits of anchovy, fetta or sun-dried tomato. **SALAD SPINNER** The best spinner model incorporates a heat-resistant colander-like basket which fits snugly inside a bowl, with a tight-fitting lid housing an operating draw cord. **SILICON PRODUCTS** The rubber-like material is man-made and does not retain odours or flavours. Oven trays, muffin pans and biscuit trays are just some of the items made from it; these can be found in kitchen specialty shops and some department stores. Silcone can stand temperatures anywhere between -50°C to 220°C, but keep in mind that some domestic ovens can go up to 250°C. **TAGINE** Originally from Moroccan kitchens and now found in many of ours, a tagine is the earthenware, cone-lidded vessel in which the spicy, fragrant North African stew of the same name is cooked. **WHISK** In this age of electronic wizardry, it's interesting that the common hand-operated whisk still plays such an important part in the drama of a kitchen, for its superb aerating qualities – nothing incorporates air into egg whites and cream, sauces and batters, better. **ZESTER** A small handheld tool with one end slightly bevelled and housing four or five tiny grater-like holes, angled precisely to remove nothing but long strands of citrus peel, leaving the bitter-tasting white pith beneath unscathed. Zesting the rind of a citrus is generally better than chopping the rind because it helps release the aromatic oils contained within the rind.

mortar
and pestle

zester

Finger Food
and Drinks

Think real food, then take the
size down, for great party food.
One mouthful, or at the most two
(provided it's not something that
will drip or shatter), is the scale
to keep in mind. Don't worry
about striving for a large variety
of offerings – just a few kinds
of appetising little somethings
will keep your guests very happy.
Professional caterers allow
seven to 10 'bites' per person,
so calculate what you will
need accordingly.

fish cakes with mirin dipping sauce

fig and fetta canapés

mini prawn cocktail

mini zucchini frittatas

fish cakes with mirin dipping sauce

preparation time 20 minutes (plus refrigeration time)
cooking time 20 minutes
makes 56

1kg boneless skinless fish fillets
3 green onions, chopped finely
2 cloves garlic, crushed
¼ cup coarsely chopped fresh coriander
2 tablespoons red curry paste
1 egg
¼ cup (60ml) coconut milk
100g green beans, sliced thinly
peanut oil, for shallow-frying
⅔ cup (160ml) mirin
⅓ cup (80ml) salt-reduced soy sauce
2 green onions, chopped finely, extra

1 Blend or process fish, onion, garlic, coriander, paste, egg and coconut milk until just combined. Stir beans into mixture.
2 Using hands, shape level tablespoons of fish mixture into cakes, place on tray, cover; refrigerate 30 minutes.
3 Heat oil in large frying pan; shallow-fry fish cakes, in batches, about 3 minutes or until lightly browned both sides and cooked through (do not overcook or cakes will become rubbery). Drain on absorbent paper.
4 Combine mirin, sauce and extra onion in small serving bowl.
5 Serve hot fish cakes with mirin sauce.
per fish cake 2.2g total fat (0.6g saturated fat); 163kJ (39 cal); 0.3g carbohydrate; 4g protein; 0.2g fibre
TIP Uncooked fish cakes can be prepared and dipping sauce made a day ahead. Cover; refrigerate until required.

fig and fetta canapés

preparation time 10 minutes
makes 24

125g marinated fetta
1 tablespoon finely chopped fresh chives
24 melba toasts
3 medium fresh figs (180g)

1 Using fork, mash cheese with chives in small bowl; spread on one side of each toast.
2 Cut each fig into eight wedges; place one wedge on each toast. Sprinkle with coarsely ground black pepper, if desired.
per canapé 1.4g total fat (0.8g saturated fat); 151kJ (36 cal); 4.2g carbohydrate; 1.7g protein; 0.4g fibre

mini prawn cocktail

preparation time 30 minutes
makes 32

32 medium cooked prawns (800g)
⅓ cup (100g) whole egg mayonnaise
2 tablespoons cream
1 tablespoon tomato sauce
1 teaspoon worcestershire sauce
½ teaspoon Tabasco sauce
1 teaspoon prepared horseradish
2 baby cos lettuces
1 tablespoon coarsely chopped fresh chives
1 tablespoon finely grated lemon rind

1 Shell and devein prawns.
2 Whisk mayonnaise, cream, sauces and horseradish in small bowl.
3 Trim ends from lettuces; separate leaves (you need 32 leaves). Top each leaf with one prawn; divide cocktail sauce over prawns then sprinkle with chives and rind.
4 Serve immediately.
per cocktail 1.7g total fat (0.5g saturated fat); 125kJ (30 cal); 1.1g carbohydrate; 2.8g protein; 0.3g fibre
TIP Cocktail sauce can be made up to 2 days ahead. Cover; refrigerate until required.

mini zucchini frittatas

preparation time 20 minutes
cooking time 15 minutes
makes 48

8 eggs
1 cup (240g) sour cream
¼ cup finely chopped fresh chives
1 large yellow zucchini (150g), grated coarsely
1 large green zucchini (150g), grated coarsely
⅓ cup (25g) finely grated parmesan
2 tablespoons coarsely chopped fresh chives, extra

1 Preheat oven to moderate (180°C/160°C fan-forced). Lightly oil four 12-hole mini (1 tablespoon/20ml) muffin pans.
2 Whisk eggs with two-thirds of the sour cream in large bowl until smooth; stir in chives, zucchini and cheese.
3 Divide mixture among holes of prepared pans. Bake, uncovered, 15 minutes. Turn onto wire rack to cool.
4 Serve at room temperature, topped with remaining sour cream and extra chives.
per frittata 3.1g total fat (1.7g saturated fat); 142kJ (34 cal); 0.3g carbohydrate; 1.5g protein; 0.1g fibre
TIP Frittata mixture can be prepared up to 2 hours ahead and baked in batches, if you don't have enough muffin pans. Cover; refrigerate until required. Bake frittatas just before serving.

peking duck rolls

preparation time 20 minutes
makes 12

½ **chinese barbecued duck**
2 **green onions**
12 x 17cm-square rice paper sheets
2 **tablespoons hoisin sauce**
1 **tablespoon plum sauce**
1 **lebanese cucumber (130g), seeded,**
   cut into batons

1 Remove skin and meat from duck. Discard bones; slice meat and skin thinly.
2 Cut each onion crossways into three equal pieces; slice pieces thinly lengthways.
3 To assemble rolls, place 1 sheet of rice paper in medium bowl of warm water until just softened. Lift sheet from water carefully; place, with one point of the square sheet facing you, on board covered with tea towel. Spread 1 teaspoon of combined sauces vertically along centre of sheet; top with a little of the cucumber, a little of the onion and a little of the duck meat. Fold top and bottom corners over filling, then roll sheet from side to side to enclose filling. Repeat with remaining rice paper sheets, combined sauces, cucumber, onion and duck.
per roll 12.7g total fat (3.8g saturated fat); 736kJ (176 cal); 5.7g carbohydrate; 10.1g protein; 0.7g fibre

After placing a little of the sauces, cucumber, onion and duck on a softened rice paper sheet, fold two opposing corners inwards, then roll to enclose filling.

gyoza with soy vinegar sauce

preparation time 40 minutes (plus refrigeration time)
cooking time 15 minutes
makes 40

300g pork mince

2 tablespoons kecap manis

1 teaspoon sugar

1 tablespoon sake

1 egg, beaten lightly

2 teaspoons sesame oil

3 cups (240g) finely shredded chinese cabbage

4 green onions, sliced thinly

40 gyoza or gow gee wrappers

1 tablespoon vegetable oil

SOY VINEGAR SAUCE

½ cup (125ml) light soy sauce

¼ cup (60ml) red vinegar

2 tablespoons white vinegar

2 tablespoons sweet chilli sauce

1 Combine pork, kecap manis, sugar, sake, egg, sesame oil, cabbage and onion in large bowl. Cover; refrigerate 1 hour.

2 Combine ingredients for soy vinegar sauce in small bowl.

3 Place 1 heaped teaspoon of the pork mixture in centre of one wrapper; brush one edge of wrapper with a little water. Pleat damp side only of wrapper, fold other side over to enclose filling; pinch sides together to seal. Repeat with remaining pork mixture and wrappers.

4 Cover base of large frying pan with water; bring to a boil. Add gyoza, in batches; reduce heat, simmer, covered, 3 minutes. Using slotted spoon, remove gyoza from pan. Drain pan; dry thoroughly.

5 Heat vegetable oil in same pan; cook gyoza, in batches, unpleated side and base only, until golden brown. Serve hot with soy vinegar sauce.

per gyoza 1.5g total fat (0.4g saturated fat); 192kJ (46 cal); 5.1g carbohydrate; 2g protein; 0.2g fibre
TIP Gyoza filling can be prepared up to 4 hours ahead. Cover; refrigerate until required.

mixed berry punch

preparation time 15 minutes (plus refrigeration time)
serves 8

1 teabag

1 cup (250ml) boiling water

120g raspberries

150g blueberries

125g strawberries, halved

¼ cup loosely packed fresh mint leaves

750ml chilled sparkling apple cider

2½ cups (625ml) chilled lemonade

1 Place teabag in mug, cover with the boiling water; stand 10 minutes. Squeeze teabag over mug, discard teabag; cool tea 10 minutes.

2 Using fork, crush raspberries in punch bowl. Add blueberries to bowl with strawberries, mint and cooled tea; stir to combine. Cover; refrigerate 1 hour.

3 Just before serving, stir cider and lemonade into punch; sprinkle with extra mint leaves, if desired.

coconut chicken salad in crisp wonton cups

preparation time 25 minutes
cooking time 25 minutes (plus cooling time)
makes 40

350g chicken breast fillets
¾ cup (180ml) chicken stock
1 cup (250ml) coconut cream
4 fresh kaffir lime leaves, shredded finely
1 tablespoon brown sugar
1 tablespoon fish sauce
1 clove garlic, crushed
1 fresh small red thai chilli, chopped finely
40 square wonton wrappers
cooking-oil spray
100g snow peas, trimmed, sliced thinly
½ cup finely chopped fresh coriander

1 Preheat oven to moderately hot (200°C/180°C fan-forced). Lightly oil four 12-hole mini (1 tablespoon/20ml) muffin pans.
2 Combine chicken, stock, coconut cream and lime leaves in medium saucepan; bring to a boil. Reduce heat; simmer, uncovered, about 10 minutes or until chicken is cooked through. Cool chicken in coconut mixture 10 minutes.
3 Remove chicken from coconut mixture; chop finely. Bring coconut mixture to a boil. Reduce heat; simmer, uncovered, until mixture reduces by half. Strain into medium bowl; stir sugar, fish sauce, garlic and chilli into dressing. Cool to room temperature.
4 Meanwhile, push wonton wrappers into holes of prepared pans; spray lightly with oil. Bake, uncovered, about 7 minutes or until cups are browned lightly. Stand in pans 2 minutes; turn onto wire racks to cool.
5 Stir chicken, snow peas and coriander into dressing in bowl; divide chicken mixture among wonton cups.
per cup 1.7g total fat (1.2g saturated fat); 205kJ
(49 cal); 5.2g carbohydrate; 3.2g protein; 0.2g fibre

Gently push one wonton wrapper into each lightly oiled muffin hole.

cosmopolitan

10ml citron vodka
20ml vodka
30ml Cointreau
60ml cranberry juice
10ml fresh lime juice
1 cup ice cubes

1 Combine ingredients in a cocktail shaker.
2 Shake vigorously; strain into chilled glass.
glass 150ml cocktail
garnish twist of lime rind

caipiroska

1 lime, cut into 8 wedges
1 tablespoon palm sugar or brown sugar
60ml vodka
10ml sugar syrup (see recipe following)
½ cup ice cubes
½ cup crushed ice

1 Using a mortar and pestle (or muddler), crush 6 lime wedges with sugar.
2 Combine lime mixture in a cocktail shaker with vodka, sugar syrup and ice cubes. Shake vigorously; pour into glass with crushed ice; do not strain.
glass 180ml old-fashioned
garnish remaining lime wedges and two straws

SUGAR SYRUP (makes about 350ml)
Combine 1 cup (220g) sugar and 1 cup (250ml) water in small saucepan; stir over low heat until sugar dissolves. Bring to a boil; reduce heat, simmer, uncovered, without stirring, 5 minutes. Remove from heat; cool.
TIP Refrigerate in airtight container for up to 2 months.

long island iced tea

1 cup ice cubes
30ml vodka
30ml tequila
30ml Bacardi
30ml gin
15ml Cointreau
15ml fresh lemon juice
15ml sugar syrup (see page 34)
30ml cola

1 Place ice in glass; add vodka, tequila, Bacardi, gin and Cointreau, one after the other.
2 Add juice and syrup, top with cola; stir.
glass 300ml highball
garnish twist of lemon rind, mint leaves, swizzle stick and a straw

margarita

45ml tequila
30ml fresh lime juice
30ml Cointreau
1 cup ice cubes

1 Combine ingredients in a cocktail shaker.
2 Shake vigorously; strain into a salt-rimmed glass.
glass 150ml margarita
garnish a slice of a lemon
TIP You can use triple sec or white curacao instead of Cointreau, if you prefer.

Starters
and Light Meals

The recipes in this chapter can operate as elegant first courses, or as perfect ideas for all those times when a serious meal is not indicated but something interesting is. They're the equivalent of the café food we all like so much – light, stylish, not too filling. Some can be completely prepared ahead, others can be taken to the last stage then finished with just a little attention when needed.

goat cheese soufflé with creamed spinach sauce

oysters with leek confit and salmon roe

radicchio with thai crab salad

duck liver parfait with red onion jam

goat cheese soufflé with creamed spinach sauce

preparation time 15 minutes
cooking time 25 minutes (plus cooling time)
serves 6

cooking-oil spray
¼ cup (25g) packaged breadcrumbs
30g butter
2 tablespoons plain flour
1 cup (250ml) milk
4 eggs, separated
¼ teaspoon cayenne pepper
150g firm goat cheese, crumbled

CREAMED SPINACH SAUCE
180g baby spinach leaves
⅔ cup (160ml) cream, warmed

1 Preheat oven to moderately hot (200°C/180°C fan-forced). Spray six 1-cup (250ml) soufflé dishes with cooking-oil spray, sprinkle with breadcrumbs; place on oven tray.
2 Melt butter in small saucepan, add flour; cook, stirring, until mixture bubbles and thickens. Gradually add milk; stir until mixture boils and thickens. Transfer to large bowl; stir in egg yolks, pepper and cheese; cool 5 minutes.
3 Beat egg whites in small bowl with electric mixer until soft peaks form; gently fold whites, in two batches, into cheese mixture.
4 Divide mixture among prepared dishes; bake, uncovered, about 15 minutes or until soufflés are puffed and browned lightly.
5 Meanwhile, make creamed spinach sauce.
6 Serve soufflés with sauce.
CREAMED SPINACH SAUCE
Boil, steam or microwave spinach until just wilted; drain. Using hand, squeeze out excess liquid. Blend or process spinach until almost smooth. With motor operating, gradually add cream; process until smooth.
per serving 26.1g total fat (15.3g saturated fat); 1304kJ (312 cal); 8.8g carbohydrate; 11.4g protein; 1.1g fibre

oysters with leek confit and salmon roe

preparation time 30 minutes (plus standing time)
cooking time 45 minutes (plus cooling time)
serves 4

3 small leeks (600g), sliced thinly
2 teaspoons salt
24 oysters, on the half shell (600g)
50g butter
¼ cup (60ml) water
2 tablespoons salmon roe

1 Combine leek and salt, place in sieve over medium bowl; stand 1 hour.
2 Meanwhile, remove oysters from shells; wash shells, dry thoroughly, reserve. Refrigerate oysters until required.
3 Rinse leek under cold water; drain. Pat dry with absorbent paper.
4 Melt butter in medium frying pan, add leek and the water; cook, uncovered, stirring occasionally, over low heat about 45 minutes or until leek breaks down and is almost pulpy. Cool 10 minutes.
5 Divide shells among serving plates; divide leek confit among shells. Place one oyster on leek mixture; top with roe.
per serving 12.8g total fat (7.5g saturated fat); 723kJ (173 cal); 4g carbohydrate; 11g protein; 2.7g fibre

radicchio with thai crab salad

preparation time 20 minutes (plus refrigeration time)
cooking time 5 minutes
makes 64

¼ cup (60ml) water
¼ cup (60ml) lime juice
2 tablespoons sugar
2 red thai chillies, seeded, chopped finely
500g fresh crab meat
1 lebanese cucumber (130g), seeded,
  chopped finely
1 small red capsicum (150g), chopped finely
2 green onions, sliced thinly
6 radicchio

1 Combine the water, juice, sugar and chilli in small saucepan; stir over heat, without boiling, until sugar dissolves. Bring to a boil; remove from heat, cool. Cover; refrigerate dressing until cold.
2 Combine crab, cucumber, capsicum, onion and dressing in medium bowl.
3 Trim ends from radicchio; separate leaves (you need 64 leaves). Place 1 heaped teaspoon of the crab salad on each leaf. Serve cold.
per leaf 0.1g total fat (0g saturated fat); 42kJ (10 cal); 1g carbohydrate; 1.3g protein; 0.4g fibre
TIP Dressing can be made a day ahead. Cover; refrigerate until required. Crab salad can be assembled up to 4 hours ahead. Cover; refrigerate until required.

duck liver parfait with red onion jam

preparation time 25 minutes
cooking time 40 minutes (plus refrigeration time)
serves 8

30g butter
6 shallots (150g), chopped finely
2 cloves garlic, crushed
½ teaspoon ground allspice
1 tablespoon finely chopped fresh thyme
1 teaspoon cracked black pepper
⅔ cup (160ml) brandy
400g duck livers, trimmed
¾ cup (180ml) cream
4 eggs
150g butter, melted, cooled
2 bay leaves, halved
2 sprigs thyme, halved
100g butter, extra

RED ONION JAM
50g butter
4 medium red onions (680g), sliced thinly
¼ cup (55g) sugar
¾ cup (180ml) dry red wine
¼ cup (60ml) port
¼ cup (60ml) red wine vinegar

1 Preheat oven to slow (150°C/130°C fan-forced). Oil 1.5-litre (6-cup) ovenproof terrine dish.
2 Melt butter in small frying pan; cook shallot and garlic, stirring, until shallot softens. Add allspice, thyme, pepper and brandy; bring to a boil. Reduce heat; simmer, uncovered, about 2 minutes or until liquid is reduced to about 1 tablespoon.
3 Blend or process shallot mixture with livers, cream, eggs and melted butter until mixture is smooth. Push parfait mixture through fine sieve into medium bowl; repeat process through same cleaned sieve.
4 Pour parfait mixture into prepared terrine dish; place terrine in baking dish. Pour enough boiling water into baking dish to come halfway up sides of terrine; cover terrine with foil. Bake, covered, about 40 minutes or until just set. Remove terrine from baking dish; cool parfait 10 minutes.
5 Meanwhile, make red onion jam.
6 Decorate parfait with bay leaves and thyme. Melt extra butter in small pan; cool 2 minutes then carefully pour butter fat over parfait, leaving milk solids in pan. Cover parfait in terrine; refrigerate 3 hours or overnight.
7 Turn parfait onto board. Using hot, wet knife, cut into eight slices; serve with red onion jam and, if desired, toasted brioche.
RED ONION JAM
Melt butter in large frying pan; cook onion and sugar, stirring occasionally, over medium heat, about 20 minutes or until onion starts to caramelise. Add wine, port and vinegar; bring to a boil. Reduce heat; simmer, uncovered, about 30 minutes or until jam thickens.
per serving 48.4g total fat (30.2 saturated fat); 2537kJ (607 cal); 14.7g carbohydrate; 14.6g protein; 1.4g fibre

white wine risotto cakes with smoked chicken

preparation time 20 minutes
cooking time 45 minutes
  (plus cooling and refrigeration time)
serves 4

2¾ cups (680ml) chicken stock
10g butter
1 tablespoon olive oil
1 small brown onion (80g), chopped finely
1 clove garlic, crushed
⅔ cup (130g) arborio rice
¼ cup (60ml) dry white wine
¼ cup (20g) coarsely grated parmesan
2 tablespoons finely shredded fresh basil
1 tablespoon dijon mustard
1 tablespoon sour cream
2 tablespoons vegetable oil
32 baby rocket leaves
170g smoked chicken breast, shredded coarsely

1 Place stock in medium saucepan; bring to a boil. Reduce heat; simmer, covered.

2 Meanwhile, heat butter and half of the olive oil in medium saucepan; cook onion and garlic, stirring, until onion just softens. Add rice; stir to coat in onion mixture. Add wine; cook, stirring, until wine is almost evaporated. Stir in ½ cup simmering stock; cook, stirring, over low heat until liquid is absorbed. Continue adding stock, in ½-cup batches, stirring until liquid is absorbed after each addition. Total cooking time should be about 30 minutes or until rice is tender. Gently stir in cheese and basil; cool 20 minutes.

3 Divide risotto into four portions. Using hands, shape portions into 1cm-deep patty-shaped cakes. Cover; refrigerate 30 minutes.

4 Meanwhile, combine mustard and sour cream in small bowl.

5 Heat vegetable oil in large frying pan; cook risotto cakes, uncovered, until browned both sides and heated through.

6 Place a risotto cake on each serving plate; top each cake with 8 rocket leaves, a quarter of the chicken and 2 teaspoons of the mustard mixture. Drizzle with remaining olive oil.

per serving 22.2g total fat (6.4g saturated fat); 1563kJ (374 cal); 28.2g carbohydrate; 13.3g protein; 0.9g fibre
TIP Wine is stirred into a risotto both to enhance flavour and to impart depth to the finished dish. Add it before the stock so that the alcohol burns off when the wine hits the base of the pan. A clean, dry white wine is best, although some cooks like red wine risottos. Finish the bottle of chilled wine with dinner.

quail, fig and orange salad

preparation time 15 minutes
cooking time 20 minutes
serves 4

6 quails (1.2kg)
3 medium oranges (720g)
4 medium fresh figs (240g), quartered
100g mizuna
½ cup (60g) coarsely chopped toasted pecans

MAPLE ORANGE DRESSING
⅓ cup (80ml) orange juice
¼ cup (60ml) olive oil
2 tablespoons pure maple syrup
1 clove garlic, crushed

1 Place ingredients for maple orange dressing in screw-top jar; shake well.
2 Rinse quails under cold water; pat dry with absorbent paper. Discard neck from quails. Using kitchen scissors, cut along each side of each quail's backbone; discard backbones. Halve each quail along breastbone; brush quail halves with half of the dressing. Cook quail on heated oiled grill plate (or grill or barbecue), uncovered, until cooked through.
3 Meanwhile, segment oranges over large bowl; add remaining ingredients and remaining dressing, toss gently to combine.
4 Divide salad among serving plates; top with quails.
per serving 41.4g total fat (7g saturated fat); 2504kJ (599 cal); 26.2g carbohydrate; 31.9g protein; 5.7g fibre

mediterranean vegetables and haloumi bruschetta

preparation time 15 minutes
cooking time 10 minutes
serves 4

1 small french breadstick
1 tablespoon olive oil
1 small eggplant (230g), sliced thinly
200g haloumi cheese, sliced thinly
2 tablespoons plain flour
2 medium egg tomatoes (150g), sliced thinly
2 tablespoons fresh baby basil leaves
1 tablespoon baby capers, rinsed, drained

1 Preheat oven to hot (220°C/200°C fan-forced).
2 Cut bread, on an angle, into eight slices; brush both sides with half of the oil, place on oven tray. Toast, uncovered, about 5 minutes.
3 Meanwhile, cook eggplant on heated oiled grill plate (or grill or barbecue) until just tender.
4 Coat haloumi in flour; cook on heated oiled grill plate (or grill or barbecue) until browned lightly.
5 Divide eggplant, haloumi, tomatoes, basil and capers evenly among bruschetta. Drizzle with remaining oil.
per serving 14.6g total fat (6.3g saturated fat); 1204kJ (288 cal); 24.2g carbohydrate; 15.1g protein; 3.3g fibre

risotto-filled zucchini flowers

preparation time 50 minutes
cooking time 50 minutes
makes 48

1 cup (250ml) dry white wine
2 cups (500ml) vegetable stock
½ cup (125ml) water
1 tablespoon olive oil
1 small brown onion (80g), chopped finely
1 clove garlic, crushed
1 cup (200g) arborio rice
150g mushrooms, sliced thinly
2 trimmed silverbeet leaves (160g), chopped finely
¼ cup (20g) finely grated parmesan
48 tiny zucchini with flowers attached
cooking-oil spray

1 Combine wine, stock and the water in large saucepan; bring to a boil. Reduce heat; simmer, covered, to keep hot.

2 Meanwhile, heat oil in large saucepan; cook onion and garlic, stirring, until onion softens. Add rice; stir to coat in onion mixture. Stir in 1 cup of the hot stock mixture; cook, stirring, over low heat until liquid is absorbed. Continue adding hot stock mixture, in 1-cup batches, stirring, until liquid is absorbed after each addition. Total cooking time should be about 35 minutes or until rice is tender.

3 Add mushrooms and silverbeet; cook, stirring, until mushrooms are just tender. Stir in cheese.

4 Remove and discard stamens from centre of flowers; fill flowers with risotto, twist petal tops to enclose filling.

5 Cook zucchini with flowers, in batches, on heated oiled grill plate (or grill or barbecue) until zucchini are just tender and risotto is heated through. Serve hot.

per zucchini 0.8g total fat (0.2g saturated fat); 125kJ (30 cal); 3.9g carbohydrate; 1g protein; 0.6g fibre
TIP Risotto can be prepared a day ahead. Spread risotto on oven tray. Cover; refrigerate until required.

Gently remove and discard the stamen from the centre of each zucchini flower.

Fill zucchini flowers with spoonfuls of filling, twisting petals together to enclose.

ocean trout sashimi rolls with lemon dipping sauce

preparation time 25 minutes (plus standing time)
cooking time 5 minutes
makes 16

200g sashimi ocean trout
¼ medium red capsicum (50g)
½ lebanese cucumber (65g)
1 green onion, trimmed

LEMON DIPPING SAUCE
½ cup (125ml) rice vinegar
¼ cup (55g) caster sugar
2 teaspoons light soy sauce
½ teaspoon finely grated lemon rind

1 Make lemon dipping sauce.
2 Using sharp knife, cut trout into paper-thin slices (you need 16 slices).
3 Remove and discard seeds and membranes from capsicum; halve cucumber lengthways, scoop out seeds. Halve onion lengthways. Slice capsicum, cucumber and onion into 8cm-long pieces.
4 Lay trout slices on board in single layer; divide capsicum, cucumber and onion among trout slices, mounding at one of the narrow edges. Roll slices around filling; place, seam-side down, on serving platter.
5 Serve immediately with lemon dipping sauce.
LEMON DIPPING SAUCE
Heat vinegar, sugar and sauce in small saucepan, stirring, until sugar dissolves. Remove from heat, add rind; stand 10 minutes. Strain sauce into serving bowl; discard rind.
per roll 0.5g total fat (0.1g saturated fat); 125kJ (30 cal); 3.7g carbohydrate; 2.5g protein; 0.1g fibre

braised leek and witlof salad with poached eggs and roasted kipflers

preparation time 20 minutes
cooking time 50 minutes
serves 4

1kg kipfler potatoes, halved lengthways
2 teaspoons sea salt
½ teaspoon cracked black pepper
2 cloves garlic, crushed
olive oil cooking-spray
1 tablespoon olive oil
20 pencil leeks (1.6kg), trimmed to 15cm in length
6 white witlof (750g), halved lengthways
⅔ cup (160ml) dry white wine
1 cup (250ml) vegetable stock
1 teaspoon sugar
8 eggs

CREAMY CHERVIL DRESSING
2 tablespoons lemon juice
1 tablespoon wholegrain mustard
⅔ cup (160ml) cream
¼ cup loosely packed fresh chervil leaves

1 Preheat oven to moderately hot (200°C/180°C fan-forced).
2 Place ingredients for creamy chervil dressing in screw-top jar; shake well.
3 Toss potato with salt, pepper and garlic in large baking dish; spray lightly with cooking-oil spray. Roast, uncovered, about 50 minutes or until tender and crisp.
4 Meanwhile, heat oil in large flameproof baking dish; cook leeks and witlof, cut-side down, in single layer, for 1 minute. Add wine, stock and sugar; bring to a boil. Reduce heat; simmer, uncovered, 2 minutes. Transfer to oven; bake, covered tightly, for last 20 minutes of potato cooking time.
5 With 10 minutes left of potato cooking time, half-fill a large shallow frying pan with water; bring to a boil. One at a time, break eggs into cup and slide into pan. When all eggs are in pan, allow water to return to a boil. Cover pan, turn off heat; stand about 4 minutes or until a light film of egg white sets over yolks. One at a time, remove eggs, using slotted spoon, and place on absorbent-paper-lined saucer to blot poaching liquid.
6 Divide potato and witlof among serving plates; top with leeks and 2 eggs each, drizzle with dressing.
per serving 35g total fat (15.7g saturated fat); 2587kJ (619 cal); 42.5g carbohydrate; 26.9g protein; 14.2g fibre

pumpkin and spinach frittata

preparation time 20 minutes (plus refrigeration time)
cooking time 45 minutes
serves 6

900g pumpkin, sliced thinly
2 cloves garlic, crushed
1 tablespoon olive oil
6 eggs
½ cup (125ml) cream
40g baby spinach leaves
¼ cup (20g) coarsely grated parmesan

1 Preheat oven to moderately hot (200°C/180°C fan-forced).
2 Place pumpkin, in single layer, on baking trays; brush with combined garlic and oil. Roast, uncovered, about 20 minutes or until tender.
3 Oil deep 20cm-square cake pan; line base and sides with baking paper.
4 Whisk eggs with cream in medium jug. Layer half of the pumpkin in prepared pan; pour half of the egg mixture over pumpkin. Top with spinach and remaining pumpkin then pour in remaining egg mixture; sprinkle with cheese.
5 Bake, uncovered, about 25 minutes or until firm. Stand 5 minutes before cutting into triangles.
per serving 19g total fat (9.1g saturated fat); 1037kJ (248 cal); 8.8g carbohydrate; 11.1g protein; 1.8g fibre

crying tiger

preparation time 20 minutes (plus refrigeration time)
cooking time 10 minutes (plus standing time)
serves 4

50g dried tamarind
1 cup (250ml) boiling water
400g beef eye fillet
2 cloves garlic, crushed
2 teaspoons dried green peppercorns, crushed
1 tablespoon peanut oil
2 tablespoons fish sauce
2 tablespoons soy sauce
10cm stick (20g) finely chopped fresh lemon grass
2 fresh small red thai chillies, chopped finely
1 large carrot (180g)
1 cup (80g) thinly sliced chinese cabbage

CRYING TIGER SAUCE
¼ cup (60ml) fish sauce
¼ cup (60ml) lime juice
2 teaspoons grated palm sugar
1 teaspoon finely chopped dried red thai chilli
1 green onion, sliced thinly
2 teaspoons finely chopped fresh coriander

1 Soak tamarind in the water for 30 minutes. Pour into fine strainer set over small bowl; push as much tamarind pulp through strainer as possible, scraping underside of strainer occasionally. Discard any tamarind solids left in strainer; reserve ½ cup of pulp for crying tiger sauce.
2 Halve beef lengthways. Combine remaining tamarind pulp, garlic, peppercorns, oil, sauces, lemon grass and chilli in large bowl; add beef, stir to coat in marinade. Cover; refrigerate 3 hours or overnight.
3 Place reserved tamarind pulp and ingredients for crying tiger sauce in bowl; whisk until sugar dissolves.
4 Cook beef on heated oiled grill plate (or grill or barbecue) about 10 minutes or until browned all over and cooked as desired. Cover beef; stand 10 minutes, slice thinly.
5 Meanwhile, cut carrot into 10cm lengths; cut slices into thin matchsticks.
6 Place sliced beef on serving dish with carrot and cabbage; serve crying tiger sauce separately.
per serving 10.8g total fat (3.3g saturated fat); 953kJ (228 cal); 7.7g carbohydrate; 24.4g protein; 2.5g fibre
TIPS When you use fresh lemon grass, start chopping from the white end, going up only until you just reach the green upper part of the stalk. Discard the tough top green section. Lemon or lime rind can be substituted for the lemon grass in this recipe. Chilling the carrot sticks by immersing them in a bowl of iced water makes them crisp and crunchy.

corn fritters with rocket and avocado salad

preparation time 10 minutes
cooking time 20 minutes
serves 4

1 cup (150g) self-raising flour
½ teaspoon bicarbonate of soda
1 cup (250ml) milk
2 eggs
2 cups (330g) fresh corn kernels
4 green onions, chopped finely
1 fresh small red thai chilli, seeded, chopped finely

TOMATO CHILLI SAUCE
425g can crushed tomatoes
1 tablespoon brown sugar
⅓ cup (80ml) sweet chilli sauce
2 tablespoons malt vinegar

ROCKET AND AVOCADO SALAD
¼ cup (60ml) balsamic vinegar
1 tablespoon olive oil
100g baby rocket leaves
1 medium avocado (250g), sliced thinly
1 medium red onion (170g), sliced thinly

1 Make tomato chilli sauce.
2 Meanwhile, sift flour and soda into medium bowl. Make well in centre of flour mixture; gradually whisk in combined milk and egg until batter is smooth. Stir corn, onion and chilli into batter.
3 Pour ¼-cup of the batter onto heated oiled flat plate; using spatula, spread batter into a round. Cook, uncovered, about 2 minutes each side or until fritter is browned lightly and cooked through. Remove from flat plate; cover to keep warm. Repeat with remaining batter.
4 Meanwhile, make rocket and avocado salad. Serve corn fritters with salad and sauce.
TOMATO CHILLI SAUCE
Combine ingredients in medium frying pan; bring to a boil. Reduce heat; simmer, uncovered, about 10 minutes or until sauce thickens.
ROCKET AND AVOCADO SALAD
Place vinegar and oil in screw-top jar; shake well. Place rocket, avocado, onion and dressing in large bowl; toss gently to combine.
per serving 26g total fat (6.4g saturated fat); 2232kJ (534 cal); 58.9g carbohydrate; 15.2g protein; 8.3g fibre

salt and pepper squid

preparation time 15 minutes
cooking time 5 minutes
serves 4

500g squid hoods
¾ cup (110g) plain flour
2 tablespoons salt
2 tablespoons freshly ground black pepper
vegetable oil, for deep-frying
150g mesclun

CHILLI DRESSING
½ cup (125ml) sweet chilli sauce
1 teaspoon fish sauce
¼ cup (60ml) lime juice
1 clove garlic, crushed

1 Cut squid in half lengthways; score inside surface of each piece. Cut into 2cm-wide strips.
2 Combine flour, salt and pepper in large bowl; add squid, toss to coat in flour mixture. Shake off excess.
3 Heat oil in wok or large saucepan; deep-fry squid, in batches, until tender and browned all over. Drain on absorbent paper.
4 Place ingredients for chilli dressing in screw-top jar; shake well.
5 Serve squid on mesclun with chilli dressing.
per serving 11.3g total fat (1.8g saturated fat); 1329kJ (318 cal); 27.7g carbohydrate; 25.1g protein; 4.3g fibre

pizza trio

preparation time 40 minutes (plus standing time)
cooking time 10 minutes
makes 3 thin pizzas (5 slices per pizza)

2 teaspoons (7g) dry yeast
½ teaspoon caster sugar
¾ cup (180ml) warm water
2 cups (300g) plain flour
1 teaspoon salt
2 tablespoons olive oil
3 teaspoons olive oil, extra

PANCETTA TOPPING

2 teaspoons olive oil
⅓ cup (80ml) tomato sauce
2 cloves garlic, sliced thinly
½ cup (40g) parmesan flakes
6 thin slices chilli pancetta

ANCHOVY OLIVE TOPPING

2 teaspoons olive oil
⅓ cup (80ml) tomato sauce
7 anchovy fillets, halved
¼ cup (30g) black olives, pitted, halved
12 fresh basil leaves

SPICY SAUSAGE TOPPING

2 teaspoons olive oil
⅓ cup (80ml) tomato sauce
175g cooked spicy italian sausage
1 long red thai chilli, sliced thinly
¼ cup (30g) olives, pitted, halved
100g bocconcini or mozzarella cheese, sliced
2 tablespoons fresh oregano

1 Combine yeast, sugar and water in small bowl; cover, stand in warm place for 10 minutes or until frothy.
2 Sift flour and salt in large bowl; stir in yeast mixture and oil, mix to a soft dough. Bring dough together with hands and add a little extra water, if needed, until ingredients are combined.
3 Knead on lightly floured surface 10 minutes or until smooth and elastic, pushing dough with heel of your hand and giving it a quarter turn each time. Place dough in lightly oiled large bowl; cover, stand in warm place about 1 hour or until doubled in size.
4 Preheat covered barbecue.
5 Punch dough down with your fist, knead on lightly floured surface until smooth. Divide into three portions; roll each portion on a wooden or marble board to about 16cm x 40cm rectangle.
6 Layer two pieces of aluminium foil large enough to fit one rectangle of dough. Brush foil with 1 teaspoon of the extra oil. Place one portion of dough on top; repeat with extra foil and remaining oil and dough.
7 Turn off burners underneath middle grill plate, leaving outer burners on to cook by indirect heat. Place pizzas on foil on grill plate, cover barbecue, cook 4 minutes or until underneath is browned. (If dough puffs up, flatten quickly with a lifter.)
8 Carefully remove pizzas from barbecue, close cover. Turn pizzas over on foil, brush cooked side with oil, then spread with tomato sauce; top with topping ingredients except fresh herbs. Return pizzas to barbecue on foil; cover barbecue, cook 5 minutes or until well browned underneath and crisp. Sprinkle pizzas with herbs.
pizza per slice (5)
pancetta 10.7g total fat (3.4g saturated fat); 832kJ (199 cal); 16.7g carbohydrate; 9.2g protein; 1.5g fibre
anchovy olive 6.1g total fat (0.9g saturated fat); 598kJ (143 cal); 17.8g carbohydrate; 4.1g protein; 1.4g fibre
spicy sausage 18.4g total fat (6.4g saturated fat); 1166kJ (279 cal); 18.3g carbohydrate; 10.2g protein; 1.5g fibre

After the yeast mixture has become frothy, it can be mixed into the flour and salt.

Before kneading, punch the dough down with your fist once it has doubled in size.

Knead the dough gently, pushing it away from you, on a lightly floured surface.

prosciutto and roast capsicum rösti stacks

preparation time 15 minutes
cooking time 30 minutes
serves 4

1 small red capsicum (150g)
1 small yellow capsicum (150g)
⅓ cup (90g) tomato relish
1kg russet burbank potatoes, peeled
80g unsalted butter
2 teaspoons olive oil
8 slices prosciutto (120g)
20g baby spinach leaves
50g parmesan, shaved

1 Quarter capsicums; remove and discard seeds and membranes. Roast capsicum under grill or in very hot oven, skin-side up, until skin blisters and blackens. Cover capsicum with plastic or paper 5 minutes. Peel away skin; slice capsicum thinly. Combine capsicum and relish in small bowl.

2 Meanwhile, grate potatoes coarsely; squeeze excess moisture from potato with hands, transfer to large bowl. Divide into eight portions.

3 Heat 10g of the butter in 20cm non-stick frying pan; spread one portion of the potato mixture over base of pan, flatten with spatula to form a firm pancake. Cook, uncovered, over medium heat, until golden brown on underside; shake pan to loosen rösti, then invert onto large plate. Gently slide rösti back into pan; cook, uncovered, until other side is golden brown and potato centre is tender. Drain on absorbent paper; cover to keep warm. Repeat with remaining butter and potato mixture.

4 Heat oil in same frying pan; cook prosciutto until crisp. Place one rösti on each serving plate, top with spinach, prosciutto, capsicum mixture and cheese; top with second rösti.

per serving 123g total fat (79.1g saturated fat); 5463kJ (1307 cal); 36.1g carbohydrate; 17.7g protein; 4.5g fibre

carpaccio with fennel salad

preparation time 10 minutes (plus freezing time)
serves 4

400g piece eye fillet
2 medium fennel bulbs (600g)
2 trimmed celery stalks (200g)
2 tablespoons finely chopped fresh
   flat-leaf parsley
2 tablespoons lemon juice
1 clove garlic, crushed
¼ teaspoon sugar
½ teaspoon dijon mustard
⅓ cup (80ml) olive oil
⅔ cup (160ml) cream, warmed

1 Remove any excess fat from fillet, wrap tightly in plastic wrap; freeze about 1 hour or until partially frozen. Using sharp knife, slice fillet as thinly as possible.

2 Meanwhile, slice fennel and celery finely. Toss in medium bowl with remaining ingredients.

3 Arrange carpaccio slices in single layer on serving plates; top with fennel salad. Serve accompanied with sliced Italian bread.

per serving 24.4g total fat (5.1g saturated fat); 1354kJ (324 cal); 4.2g carbohydrate; 22.3g protein; 3.3g fibre

caramelised onion and goat cheese tartlets

preparation time 25 minutes (plus refrigeration time)
cooking time 45 minutes
serves 4

1 cup (150g) plain flour
80g cold butter, chopped
1 egg yolk
2 tablespoons cold water
100g soft goat cheese
2 tablespoons coarsely chopped fresh chives

CARAMELISED ONION
2 tablespoons olive oil
4 large brown onions (800g), sliced thinly
⅓ cup (80ml) port
2 tablespoons red wine vinegar
2 tablespoons brown sugar

1 Blend or process flour and butter until mixture is crumbly. Add egg yolk and the water; process until ingredients come together. Enclose in plastic wrap; refrigerate 30 minutes.
2 Meanwhile, make caramelised onion.
3 Preheat oven to moderately hot (200°C/180°C fan-forced). Oil four 10.5cm loose-based flan tins.
4 Divide pastry into four portions. Roll one portion of pastry between sheets of baking paper until large enough to line prepared tin. Lift pastry into tin; press into side, trim edge, prick base all over with fork. Repeat with remaining pastry.
5 Place tins on oven tray; cover pastry with baking paper, fill with dried beans or rice. Bake, uncovered, 10 minutes. Remove paper and beans carefully; bake, uncovered, further 5 minutes or until tartlet shells brown lightly.
6 Divide onion mixture and cheese among tartlets. Bake, uncovered, 5 minutes or until heated through. Sprinkle tartlets with chives.
CARAMELISED ONION
Heat oil in large frying pan; cook onion, stirring, until onion softens. Add port, vinegar and sugar; cook, stirring occasionally, about 25 minutes or until onion caramelises.
per serving 31.5g total fat (15.2g saturated fat); 2169kJ (519 cal); 43.8g carbohydrate; 11.1g protein; 4.1g fibre

gnocchi with burnt butter and sage

preparation time 25 minutes (plus refrigeration time)
cooking time 25 minutes
serves 4

3 large desiree potatoes (900g), unpeeled
1 clove garlic, crushed
2 tablespoons milk
2 egg yolks
⅓ cup (25g) grated parmesan
1 cup (150g) plain flour, approximately
125g butter, chopped coarsely
12 fresh sage leaves
¼ cup (20g) parmesan flakes, extra

1 Steam or boil whole potatoes until tender; drain. Cool slightly; peel. Mash potatoes with a ricer, mouli or masher until smooth; stir in garlic and milk. Stir in egg yolks, grated parmesan and enough of the flour to form a firm dough.

2 Roll a quarter of the dough on lightly floured surface into a 2cm-thick sausage. Cut into 2cm lengths; roll into gnocchi-shaped ovals. Place each oval in palm of hand; press with inverted floured fork tines to flatten gnocchi slightly and make a grooved imprint. Place on lightly floured tray in single layer. Cover; refrigerate 1 hour.

3 Cook gnocchi, in batches, in large saucepan of boiling water about 3 minutes or until gnocchi float to the surface. Remove from pan with slotted spoon; drain.

4 Meanwhile, cook butter in small shallow frying pan until just browned. Add sage; immediately remove from heat. Divide gnocchi among serving plates; drizzle with sage butter. Serve topped with parmesan flakes and freshly ground black pepper.

per serving 33.2g total fat (20.4g saturated fat); 2399kJ (574 cal); 53.7g carbohydrate; 15.2g protein; 4.7g fibre
TIP Gnocchi can be made a day ahead up to the end of step 2; cover, refrigerate, or freeze for up to 3 months. Just before serving, cook in boiling water.

pork and chicken sang choy bow

preparation time 20 minutes
cooking time 45 minutes
serves 4

500g pork fillets
⅓ cup (80ml) char siu sauce
1 tablespoon peanut oil
150g chicken mince
1 clove garlic, crushed
100g fresh shiitake mushrooms, chopped finely
190g can water chestnuts, rinsed, drained, chopped finely
2 green onions, chopped finely
2 tablespoons oyster sauce
1 tablespoon soy sauce
1 teaspoon sesame oil
1½ cups (120g) bean sprouts
8 large iceberg lettuce leaves
2 green onions, sliced thinly

1 Preheat oven to moderate (180°C/160° fan-forced).

2 Place pork on wire rack in large shallow baking dish; brush all over with ¼ cup of the char siu sauce. Roast, uncovered, about 40 minutes or until cooked as desired, brushing occasionally with pan drippings. Cool 10 minutes; chop pork finely.

3 Meanwhile, heat peanut oil in wok; stir-fry chicken, garlic and mushrooms, 5 minutes. Add water chestnuts, chopped onion, sauces, sesame oil, pork and remaining char siu sauce; stir-fry until chicken is cooked through. Remove from heat; add sprouts, toss gently to combine.

4 Divide lettuce leaves among serving plates; spoon sang choy bow into leaves, sprinkle with sliced onion.

per serving 13.4g total fat (3.1g saturated fat); 1434kJ (343 cal); 17.5g carbohydrate; 38g protein; 6.2g fibre
TIP An easy way to remove whole lettuce leaves is to rap the head, stem-end down, on a hard surface to loosen the core. Discard the core, and run a strong stream of cold water into the cavity – leaves will fall away, intact. Submerge leaves in iced water until ready to serve; use lettuce centre for a salad.

Soups

Nothing beats the long-simmered, rich and warming soups of Australia's European heritage for cold-weather comfort, but we have to thank Asian-Australian cooks for adding hot-climate soups to our repertoire. Light, fresh and lively with spices, they're magic for a lift on a summer day. Soup-making is easy now that we can buy ready-made stock in the supermarket. While your own home-made stock is always the best and certainly the cheapest, these stocks are perfectly acceptable; just be careful when seasoning the soup, as bought stock is often rather salty.

cream of roasted garlic and potato soup

kumara and coriander soup

lentil and caramelised onion soup

soupe au pistou

cream of roasted garlic and potato soup

preparation time 10 minutes
cooking time 30 minutes
serves 4

2 medium garlic bulbs (140g), unpeeled
2 tablespoons olive oil
2 medium brown onions (300g), chopped coarsely
1 tablespoon fresh thyme leaves
5 medium potatoes (1kg), chopped coarsely
1.25 litres (5 cups) chicken stock
¾ cup (180ml) cream

1 Preheat oven to moderate (180°C/160°C fan-forced).
2 Separate garlic bulbs into cloves; place unpeeled cloves, in single layer, on oven tray. Drizzle with half of the oil. Roast, uncovered, about 15 minutes or until garlic is soft. Remove from oven; when cool enough to handle, squeeze garlic into small bowl, discard skins.
3 Meanwhile, heat remaining oil in large saucepan; cook onion and thyme, stirring, until onion softens. Add potato; cook, stirring, 5 minutes. Add stock; bring to a boil. Reduce heat; simmer, uncovered, about 15 minutes or until potato is just tender. Stir in garlic; simmer, uncovered, 5 minutes.
4 Blend or process soup, in batches, until smooth; return to same cleaned pan. Reheat until hot; stir in cream. Divide soup among serving bowls; sprinkle with extra thyme, if desired.
per serving 31.3g total fat (15.2g saturated fat); 2032kJ (486 cal); 38.6g carbohydrate; 12.7g protein; 10.4g fibre
TIP The amount of time the garlic is cooked makes a big difference to its pungency: the longer it's cooked, the more creamy in texture and subtly nutty in flavour it becomes.

kumara and coriander soup

preparation time 15 minutes
cooking time 20 minutes
serves 4

1 teaspoon peanut oil
2 medium leeks (700g), chopped coarsely
3 cloves garlic, quartered
2 medium kumara (800g), chopped coarsely
1 litre (4 cups) chicken stock
⅔ cup (160ml) light evaporated milk
⅓ cup finely chopped fresh coriander

1 Heat oil in large saucepan; cook leek and garlic, stirring, until leek softens. Add kumara and stock; bring to a boil. Reduce heat; simmer, covered, 15 minutes or until kumara softens.
2 Blend or process soup, in batches, until smooth. Return soup to same cleaned pan; simmer, uncovered, until soup thickens slightly. Add evaporated milk and coriander; stir, without boiling, until heated through.
3 Divide soup among serving bowls; top with fresh coriander leaves, if desired.
per serving 2.9g total fat (0.8g saturated fat); 890kJ (213 cal); 35.3g carbohydrate; 11.8g protein; 6.7g fibre
TIP The smoothest consistency for this soup will be achieved by using a blender, hand-held stick blender or mouli.

lentil and caramelised onion soup

preparation time 10 minutes
cooking time 25 minutes
serves 4

2 cups (400g) red lentils
½ cup (100g) brown rice
1 litre (4 cups) vegetable stock
1 litre (4 cups) water
1 tablespoon ground cumin
40g butter
3 medium brown onions (450g), sliced thinly
2 tablespoons sugar
1 tablespoon balsamic vinegar
pinch cayenne pepper
⅓ cup coarsely chopped fresh coriander
⅓ cup coarsely chopped fresh flat-leaf parsley
1 cup (250ml) vegetable stock, extra

1 Rinse lentils and rice under cold water; drain.
2 Combine stock and the water in large saucepan; bring to a boil. Add lentils, rice and cumin; return to a boil. Reduce heat; simmer, uncovered, stirring occasionally, about 15 minutes or until lentils and rice are just tender.
3 Meanwhile, melt butter in large frying pan; cook onion, stirring, until onion softens. Add sugar and vinegar; cook, stirring, until onion caramelises.
4 Stir pepper, coriander and parsley into lentil mixture; bring to a boil. Stir in caramelised onion and extra stock; cook, stirring, until heated through.

per serving 12.2g total fat (6.5g saturated fat); 2153kJ (515 cal); 72.3g carbohydrate; 31.4g protein; 16.3g fibre

soupe au pistou

preparation time 15 minutes (plus standing time)
cooking time 1 hour 40 minutes
serves 8

1 cup (200g) dried cannellini beans
⅓ cup (80ml) olive oil
2 veal shanks (1.5kg), trimmed
1 large leek (500g), sliced thinly
2 litres (8 cups) water
2 cups (500ml) chicken stock
2 tablespoons toasted pine nuts
1 clove garlic, quartered
¼ cup (20g) finely grated parmesan
½ cup firmly packed fresh basil leaves
2 medium carrots (240g), chopped coarsely
200g green beans, trimmed, chopped coarsely

1 Place cannellini beans in large bowl, cover with cold water; stand, covered, overnight.
2 Heat 1 tablespoon of the oil in large saucepan; cook shanks, uncovered, until browned all over. Remove from pan. Cook leek in same pan, stirring, about 5 minutes or until just softened. Return shanks to pan with the water and stock; bring to a boil. Reduce heat; simmer, covered, 1 hour.
3 Meanwhile, blend or process remaining oil, nuts, garlic and cheese until combined. Add basil; process until pistou mixture forms a paste.
4 Remove shanks from soup. When cool enough to handle, remove meat from bones. Discard bones; chop meat coarsely. Return meat to soup with rinsed and drained cannellini beans; bring to a boil. Reduce heat; simmer, uncovered, 20 minutes. Add carrot; simmer, uncovered, 10 minutes. Add green beans and pistou; simmer, uncovered, 5 minutes.
5 Divide soup among serving bowls. Serve with slices of warm baguette, if desired, for dipping in soup.

per serving 13.5g total fat (2.2g saturated fat); 1129kJ (270 cal); 7.7g carbohydrate; 29.9g protein; 4.7g fibre

white bean, leek and garlic sausage soup

preparation time 30 minutes (plus standing time)
cooking time 1 hour 15 minutes
serves 6

1 cup (200g) dried small white beans
40g butter
2 bacon rashers (140g), rind removed,
  chopped finely
2 cloves garlic, crushed
1 medium leek (350g), sliced thinly
2 trimmed celery stalks (200g), chopped finely
2 medium carrots (240g), chopped finely
1.5 litres (6 cups) chicken stock
1 bay leaf
4 merguez sausages (320g)

PISTOU
2 cups loosely packed fresh basil leaves
1 clove garlic, quartered
¼ cup (20g) coarsely grated parmesan
¼ cup (60ml) extra virgin olive oil

1 Place beans in medium bowl, cover with water, stand overnight; drain. Rinse under cold water; drain.
2 Melt butter in large saucepan; cook bacon, garlic, leek, celery and carrot, stirring, until vegetables soften. Stir in stock, bay leaf and beans; bring to a boil. Reduce heat; simmer, covered, 1 hour or until beans are tender.
3 Meanwhile, blend or process ingredients for pistou until smooth.
4 Heat medium non-stick frying pan; cook sausages until browned. Drain on absorbent paper; chop coarsely.
5 Just before serving, ladle soup into serving bowls; top with sausage and a spoonful of pistou.
per serving 32.2g total fat (13g saturated fat); 1643kJ (393 cal); 11.2g carbohydrate; 16.4g protein; 6.7g fibre

The beans can be soaked overnight or, if time is short, submerged in boiling water in a heatproof bowl and stood, covered, for an hour.

Before processing the pistou, ensure that all of the stems have been removed from the basil because they can impart a bitter taste.

Spicy, firm-textured merguez are a Tunisian sausage which should be drained on absorbent paper before being added to the soup.

chicken laksa

preparation time 30 minutes (plus cooling time)
cooking time 45 minutes
serves 4

1 litre (4 cups) water
12 fresh kaffir lime leaves
2 cloves garlic, quartered
800g chicken thigh fillets
½ cup (150g) laksa paste
3¼ cups (800ml) coconut milk
2 fresh red thai chillies, chopped finely
150g dried rice stick noodles
175g singapore noodles
2 tablespoons grated palm sugar
⅓ cup (80ml) lime juice
2 tablespoons fish sauce
80g fried tofu puffs, halved
1½ cups (120g) bean sprouts
½ cup loosely packed fresh coriander leaves
½ cup loosely packed fresh vietnamese
    mint leaves

1 Place the water in large saucepan; bring to a boil. Add 4 lime leaves, garlic and chicken, reduce heat; simmer, covered, about 15 minutes or until chicken is cooked through. Cool chicken in liquid 15 minutes. Slice chicken thinly; reserve. Strain stock through muslin-lined sieve or colander into large bowl; discard solids. Allow stock to cool; skim fat from surface.
2 Cook paste in large saucepan, stirring, until fragrant. Stir in stock, coconut milk, chilli and remaining torn lime leaves; bring to a boil. Reduce heat; simmer, uncovered, 20 minutes.
3 Meanwhile, place rice stick noodles in large heatproof bowl, cover with boiling water, stand until just tender; drain. Place singapore noodles in separate large heatproof bowl, cover with boiling water, separate with fork; drain. Divide both noodles among serving bowls.
4 Stir sugar, juice, sauce, tofu and chicken into laksa. Ladle laksa over noodles; sprinkle with combined sprouts and herbs.
per serving 59.4g total fat (41.1g saturated fat); 3908kJ (935 cal); 44.5g carbohydrate; 49.4g protein; 6.9g fibre
TIP Commercial laksa pastes vary dramatically in their heat intensity so, while we call for ½ cup here, you might try using less of the laksa paste you've purchased until you can determine how hot it makes the final dish.

mussels in fragrant thai broth

preparation time 20 minutes
cooking time 15 minutes
serves 4

½ cup (100g) jasmine rice
1kg small black mussels
1 tablespoon vegetable oil
2 tablespoons green curry paste
1½ cups (375ml) water
1½ cups (375ml) fish stock
2 teaspoons fish sauce
2 teaspoons brown sugar
1⅔ cups (400ml) coconut milk
¼ cup coarsely chopped fresh coriander
4 green onions, chopped finely
1 tablespoon lime juice

1 Cook rice in large saucepan of boiling water, uncovered, until just tender; drain. Cover to keep warm.
2 Meanwhile, scrub mussels; remove beards.
3 Heat oil in large saucepan; cook paste, stirring, until fragrant. Add the water, stock, sauce and sugar; bring to a boil. Add coconut milk; return to a boil. Reduce heat; simmer, stirring, 1 minute. Add mussels; cook, covered, about 5 minutes or until mussels open (discard any that do not). Remove from heat; stir in coriander, onion and juice.
4 Divide rice among serving bowls; top with mussels and broth.
per serving 30g total fat (19.4g saturated fat); 1777kJ (425 cal); 29.1g carbohydrate; 10.6g protein; 3.5g fibre
TIP Scrub mussels with a stiff brush under cold running water.

bouillabaisse with aïoli and rouille

preparation time 1 hour 15 minutes
cooking time 40 minutes
serves 6

700g uncooked large prawns
2 uncooked medium blue swimmer crabs (650g)
10 small tomatoes (900g)
1 tablespoon olive oil
1 clove garlic, crushed
1 large brown onion (200g), chopped coarsely
1 medium leek (350g), chopped coarsely
1 untrimmed baby fennel (130g), chopped coarsely
1 fresh red thai chilli, seeded, chopped coarsely
1 bay leaf
pinch saffron threads
10cm piece fresh orange peel
1.5 litres (6 cups) water
1 cup (250ml) dry white wine
750g firm white fish fillets, chopped coarsely
500g small black mussels
½ cup coarsely chopped fresh flat-leaf parsley
1 long french bread stick

AIOLI

3 cloves garlic, quartered
2 egg yolks
2 tablespoons lemon juice
½ teaspoon dijon mustard
⅔ cup (160ml) olive oil

ROUILLE

1 medium red capsicum (200g)
1 fresh red thai chilli, seeded, chopped finely
1 clove garlic, quartered
1 cup (70g) stale breadcrumbs
1 tablespoon lemon juice
¼ cup (60ml) olive oil

1 Shell and devein prawns, leaving tails intact. Reserve heads and shells; place prawn meat in medium bowl. Slide knife under top of crab shell at back, lever off; reserve with prawn shells. Discard gills; rinse crabs under cold water. Cut crab bodies into quarters; add to prawn meat.

2 Chop four of the tomatoes coarsely; add to reserved seafood shells.

3 Core then cut shallow cross in base of remaining tomatoes, place in large heatproof bowl; cover with boiling water. Stand 2 minutes; drain then peel, from cross end towards top. Quarter tomatoes; scoop out seeds, add to reserved seafood shells. Chop tomato flesh finely; reserve.

4 Heat oil in large saucepan, add reserved seafood shell mixture, garlic, onion, leek, fennel, chilli, bay leaf, saffron and peel; cook, stirring, about 10 minutes or until shells change in colour and vegetables soften. Add the water and wine, cover; bring to a boil. Reduce heat; simmer, covered, 10 minutes. Remove crab shells.

5 Blend or process seafood mixture (including prawn shells), in batches, until smooth; using wooden spoon, push each batch through large sieve into large saucepan. Discard solids in sieve. Reserve ¼ cup strained seafood mixture for rouille.

6 Make aïoli. Make rouille.

7 Add finely chopped tomatoes to strained seafood mixture; bring to a boil. Add fish and mussels, return to a boil; cook, covered, 5 minutes. Add reserved prawn meat and crab pieces; cook, covered, 5 minutes. Stir parsley into bouillabaisse; serve with sliced toasted bread, aïoli and rouille.

AIOLI
Blend or process garlic, yolks, juice and mustard until smooth. With motor operating, gradually add oil in thin steady stream; process until aïoli thickens.

ROUILLE
Quarter capsicum; discard seeds and membrane. Roast under preheated grill or in very hot oven, skin-side up, until skin blisters and blackens. Cover capsicum with plastic or paper 5 minutes. Peel away skin; chop capsicum coarsely. Blend or process capsicum with chilli, garlic, breadcrumbs, juice and reserved ¼ cup strained seafood mixture liquid until smooth. With motor operating, gradually add oil in thin, steady stream; process until rouille thickens.

per serving 42.6g total fat (6.3g saturated fat); 3306kJ (791 cal); 42.4g carbohydrate; 52.6g protein; 6.9g fibre
TIP Both the aïoli and rouille can be made a day ahead. Cover separately; refrigerate overnight.

thai-style pumpkin soup

preparation time 10 minutes
cooking time 15 minutes
serves 4

¼ cup (75g) red curry paste
2 x 420g cans cream of pumpkin soup
3¼ cups (800ml) light coconut milk
1½ cups (375ml) chicken stock
3 cups (500g) coarsely chopped cooked chicken
4 green onions, sliced thinly
¼ cup coarsely chopped fresh basil

1 Cook curry paste, stirring, in large heated saucepan until fragrant. Add soup, coconut milk and stock; bring to a boil.
2 Add chicken; reduce heat. Simmer, stirring, until soup is heated through. Stir in onion and basil just before serving.
per serving 17.8g total fat (24.4g saturated fat); 2349kJ (562 cal); 18.7g carbohydrate; 32.9g protein; 4.4g fibre
TIPS You can adjust the amount of curry paste to suit your taste. You will need to purchase a barbecued chicken weighing 900g.
SERVING SUGGESTION Herb scones make a great accompaniment to this soup.

thai chicken broth with coriander wontons

preparation time 40 minutes (plus refrigeration time)
cooking time 2 hours 50 minutes
serves 6

4 litres (16 cups) water
2kg chicken bones
2 medium brown onions (300g), chopped coarsely
½ cup coarsely chopped fresh lemon grass
4cm piece fresh ginger (20g), chopped coarsely
2 fresh long red chillies, halved crossways
2 cloves garlic, quartered
1 teaspoon black peppercorns
300g chicken mince
2 teaspoons finely chopped fresh coriander
1 clove garlic, crushed
2cm piece fresh ginger (10g), grated
1 fresh red thai chilli, seeded, chopped finely
¼ cup (60ml) soy sauce
30 wonton wrappers
1 egg white
1 tablespoon lime juice
1 tablespoon mirin
1 cup watercress sprigs
3 green onions, sliced thinly
2 fresh long red chillies, seeded, sliced thinly
⅓ cup loosely packed fresh coriander leaves

1 Combine the water, chicken bones, brown onion, lemon grass, chopped ginger, halved chilli, quartered garlic and peppercorns in large saucepan; bring to a boil. Reduce heat; simmer, uncovered, 2½ hours. Strain broth through muslin-lined sieve or colander into large bowl; discard solids. Allow broth to cool, cover; refrigerate until cold.
2 Combine chicken mince, chopped coriander, crushed garlic, grated ginger, chopped chilli and 1 tablespoon of the soy sauce in medium bowl. Place 1 rounded teaspoon of the chicken mixture in centre of each wrapper; brush around edges with egg white, gather edges around filling, pinch together to seal. Repeat process with remaining filling and wrappers.
3 Skim fat from surface of broth; return broth to large saucepan, bring to a boil. Cook wontons, in two batches, about 4 minutes or until cooked through. Using slotted spoon, transfer wontons from pan to individual serving bowls. Stir remaining soy sauce, juice and mirin into broth; return to a boil. Top wontons with watercress, green onion, sliced chilli and coriander leaves; ladle broth into bowls.
per serving 7.4g total fat (2.7g saturated fat); 1195kJ (286 cal); 30.4g carbohydrate; 23.9g protein; 1.7g fibre
TIPS Broth can be made ahead to the end of step 1; cover, refrigerate overnight. Uncooked wontons can be frozen, covered, for up to 3 months; they can be cooked in the broth straight from the freezer.

pumpkin and eggplant laksa

preparation time 45 minutes
cooking time 20 minutes
serves 6

700g piece butternut pumpkin, diced into
   2cm pieces
5 baby eggplants (300g), sliced thickly
3 cups (750ml) vegetable stock
1⅔ cups (400ml) coconut milk
250g rice stick noodles
500g bok choy, chopped coarsely
2 tablespoons lime juice
1¼ cups (100g) bean sprouts
6 green onions, sliced thinly
½ cup loosely packed fresh coriander leaves
½ cup loosely packed fresh mint leaves

LAKSA PASTE
7 medium dried red chillies
½ cup (125ml) boiling water
1 tablespoon peanut oil
3 cloves garlic, quartered
1 medium brown onion (150g), chopped coarsely
10cm stick (20g) finely chopped fresh lemon grass
4cm piece fresh ginger (20g), grated
1 tablespoon halved macadamias (10g)
roots from 1 bunch coriander, washed,
   chopped coarsely
1 teaspoon ground turmeric
1 teaspoon ground coriander
2 teaspoons salt
¼ cup loosely packed fresh vietnamese
   mint leaves

1 Make laksa paste.
2 Place ½ cup of the laksa paste in large saucepan; cook, stirring, about 1 minute or until fragrant. Add pumpkin and eggplant; cook, stirring, 2 minutes. Add stock and coconut milk; bring to a boil. Reduce heat; simmer laksa mixture, covered, about 10 minutes or until vegetables are just tender.
3 Meanwhile, place noodles in large heatproof bowl, cover with boiling water, stand until just tender; drain.
4 Stir bok choy into laksa; return to a boil. Stir juice into laksa off the heat. Divide noodles among serving bowls; ladle laksa over noodles, sprinkle with combined sprouts, onion and herbs.

LAKSA PASTE
Cover chillies with the boiling water in small heatproof bowl, stand 10 minutes; drain. Blend or process chillies with remaining ingredients until mixture forms a smooth paste. Reserve ½ cup of the paste for this recipe; freeze remaining paste, covered, for future use.
per serving 20.2g total fat (13.4g saturated fat); 1626kJ (389 cal); 41.5g carbohydrate; 10.3g protein; 7.4g fibre

Fry off just ½ cup of the laksa paste now and freeze the rest... you'll be all set the next time you crave a laksa.

Rice stick noodles become pliable after a soak in boiling water; there's no need to actually precook them.

combination noodle soup

preparation time 15 minutes
cooking time 20 minutes
serves 4

2 litres (8 cups) chicken stock
1 tablespoon light soy sauce
500g chicken breast fillets, sliced thinly
125g fresh thin wheat noodles
100g small cooked shelled prawns
200g chinese barbecued pork, sliced thinly
1¼ cups (100g) bean sprouts
4 green onions, sliced thinly

1 Combine stock and sauce in large saucepan, cover; bring to a boil.
2 Add chicken and noodles to same pan; simmer, covered, 10 minutes. Add prawns, pork, sprouts and onion; simmer, uncovered, until heated through.
3 Divide noodles among serving bowls; ladle remaining soup over noodles.
per serving 12.8g total fat (4.9g saturated fat); 1584kJ (379 cal); 13.9g carbohydrate; 52.1g proein; 2.9g fibre

tortilla lime soup

preparation time 20 minutes
cooking time 25 minutes
serves 4

1 medium white onion (150g), chopped coarsely
2 cloves garlic, quartered
1 small fresh red thai chilli, chopped coarsely
4 medium tomatoes (600g), peeled, quartered
1 tablespoon peanut oil
¼ teaspoon ground allspice
1½ cups (375ml) chicken stock
1.25 litres (5 cups) water
2 teaspoons grated lime rind
¼ cup (60ml) lime juice
¼ cup (70g) tomato paste
⅓ cup (80ml) peanut oil, extra
6 corn tortillas, cut into 2cm-wide strips
1 medium avocado (250g), chopped finely
2 green onions, chopped finely
¼ cup coarsely chopped fresh coriander

1 Blend or process white onion, garlic, chilli and tomato until pureed. Heat oil in large saucepan; cook tomato mixture and allspice, stirring, until fragrant.
2 Add stock to pan with the water, rind, juice and paste; bring to a boil. Reduce heat; simmer, uncovered, about 15 minutes or until mixture thickens slightly.
3 Meanwhile, heat extra oil in medium frying pan; cook tortilla strips, in batches, until golden. Drain on absorbent paper.
4 Divide tortilla strips among serving bowls; ladle soup over strips. Top with combined avocado, green onion and coriander.
per serving 35.1g total fat (6.7g saturated fat); 2069kJ (495 cal); 36.4g carbohydrate; 8.6g protein; 7.6g fibre
TIPS The tortilla strips can be fried a day ahead; store in an airtight container. To reduce the fat count, crisp the tortilla strips in a hot oven for about 5 minutes instead of frying them in oil.

tom yum goong

preparation time 30 minutes
cooking time 20 minutes
serves 4

1.5 litres (6 cups) fish stock
1 tablespoon coarsely chopped coriander root
   and stem mixture
10cm stick (20g) thinly sliced fresh lemon grass
8 fresh kaffir lime leaves, torn
8cm piece fresh ginger (40g), sliced thinly
2 fresh small red thai chillies, sliced thinly
1 tablespoon fish sauce
12 uncooked large king prawns (840g)
8 green onions, cut into 2cm lengths
⅓ cup (80ml) lime juice
⅔ cup loosely packed fresh coriander leaves
½ cup loosely packed fresh thai basil leaves, torn

1 Place stock, coriander root and stem mixture, lemon grass, lime leaves, ginger, chilli and sauce in large saucepan; bring to a boil. Reduce heat; simmer, uncovered, 10 minutes.
2 Meanwhile, shell and devein prawns, leaving tails intact.
3 Add prawns to pan with onion and juice; simmer, uncovered, about 4 minutes or until prawns just change in colour. Remove from heat; stir in coriander and basil leaves.
per serving 1.6g total fat (0.5g saturated fat); 606kJ (145 cal); 4.5g carbohydrate; 27.1g protein; 1.3g fibre
TIP After removing the leaves, wash coriander stems and roots really well; chop some of them for this recipe. You can freeze chopped roots and stems, if desired, wrapped tightly in plastic.

vietnamese beef, chicken and tofu soup

preparation time 20 minutes
cooking time 1 hour 5 minutes
serves 4

500g gravy beef
1 star anise
2.5cm piece fresh galangal (45g), halved
¼ cup (60ml) soy sauce
2 tablespoons fish sauce
3 litres (12 cups) water
340g chicken breast fillets
1½ cups (120g) bean sprouts
1 cup loosely packed fresh coriander leaves
4 green onions, sliced thinly
2 small fresh red thai chillies, sliced thinly
⅓ cup (80ml) lime juice
300g firm tofu, diced into 2cm pieces

1 Combine beef, star anise, galangal, sauces and the water in large saucepan; bring to a boil. Reduce heat; simmer, covered, 30 minutes. Remove lid; simmer, uncovered, 20 minutes. Add chicken; simmer, uncovered, further 10 minutes.
2 Combine sprouts, coriander, onion, chilli and juice in medium bowl.
3 Remove beef and chicken from pan; reserve stock. Discard fat and sinew from beef; slice thinly. Slice chicken thinly. Return beef and chicken to pan; reheat soup.
4 Divide tofu among serving bowls; ladle hot soup over tofu, sprinkle with sprout mixture. Serve with lime wedges and extra chilli, if desired.
per serving 12.9g total fat (3.6g saturated fat); 1513kJ (362 cal); 3.9g carbohydrate; 56.6g protein; 3.3g fibre

Sauces,
Salsas and Dressings

Some of these are familiar treasures, some are fairly new to cooks in this country though they come from long traditions elsewhere. All are ready to transform basics into food that sings, and all are friends to the busy cook. They don't call for tricky techniques and you can make any one of them in 15 minutes or less. A good knife, a chopping board, a whisk and a bowl are all the equipment you need, plus a small saucepan for those that require cooking.

250

creamy pancetta, pea and tarragon sauce

hollandaise

mayonnaise

mixed mushroom, red wine and chive sauce

creamy pancetta, pea and tarragon sauce

preparation time 15 minutes
cooking time 15 minutes
makes 1½ cups

1 tablespoon olive oil
2 shallots (50g), chopped finely
1 clove garlic, crushed
100g sliced pancetta, shredded finely
½ cup (125ml) dry white wine
300ml carton pure cream
½ cup (60g) frozen peas, thawed
1 tablespoon coarsely chopped fresh tarragon

1 Heat oil in large frying pan; cook shallots, garlic and pancetta, stirring, over medium heat, until pancetta browns. Add wine; bring to a boil. Reduce heat; simmer, uncovered, about 2 minutes or until reduced by half.
2 Add cream and peas to pan; bring to a boil. Reduce heat; simmer, uncovered, 4 minutes, stirring occasionally. Add tarragon; simmer, uncovered, 2 minutes.
per tablespoon 9.1g total fat (5.2g saturated fat); 397kJ (95 cal); 0.9g carbohydrate; 1.6g protein; 0.2g fibre
SERVING SUGGESTION Goes well drizzled over pan-fried chicken or into cooked pasta.

hollandaise

preparation time 10 minutes (plus cooling time)
cooking time 10 minutes
makes 1 cup

2 tablespoons water
2 tablespoons white vinegar
¼ teaspoon cracked black pepper
2 egg yolks
200g unsalted butter, melted

1 Combine the water, vinegar and pepper in small saucepan; bring to a boil. Reduce heat; simmer, uncovered, until liquid is reduced to 1 tablespoon. Strain over small jug; cool 15 minutes.
2 Combine egg yolks and vinegar mixture in large heatproof bowl set over medium saucepan of simmering water; do not allow water to touch base of bowl. Whisk mixture over heat until thickened.
3 Remove bowl from heat; gradually add melted butter in thin, steady stream, whisking constantly until mixture thickens.
per tablespoon 14.8g total fat (9.4g saturated fat); 560kJ (134 cal); 0.1g carbohydrate; 0.6g protein; 0g fibre
SERVING SUGGESTION Goes well with steamed asparagus, eggs benedict or grilled salmon.

mayonnaise

preparation time 15 minutes
makes 1½ cups

2 egg yolks
½ teaspoon salt
1 teaspoon dijon mustard
½ cup (125ml) extra light olive oil
½ cup (125ml) olive oil
1 tablespoon lemon juice

1 Whisk, process or blend egg yolks with salt and mustard until smooth.
2 While whisking, or with motor operating, add oils in a thin, steady stream until dressing thickens. Add juice and a little hot water for a thinner consistency, if desired.
per tablespoon 16.1g total fat (2.4g saturated fat); 606kJ (145 cal); 0.1g carbohydrate; 0.5g protein; 0g fibre
TIP Add garlic, herbs or mustard for alternative flavours.
SERVING SUGGESTION Goes well with cold poached chicken or seafood, or as the dressing for potato or chicken salad.

mixed mushroom, red wine and chive sauce

preparation time 10 minutes
cooking time 15 minutes
makes 1 cup

40g butter
100g button mushrooms, sliced thinly
100g swiss brown mushrooms, sliced thinly
¾ cup (180ml) dry red wine
2 teaspoons plain flour
1 cup (125ml) beef stock
½ cup finely chopped fresh garlic chives

1 Heat butter in medium frying pan; cook mushrooms, stirring, about 3 minutes or until softened.
2 Add wine to pan; cook, stirring, until mixture reduces by half. Add flour; cook, stirring, until mixture thickens.
3 Gradually stir in stock to pan. Reduce heat; simmer, uncovered, about 5 minutes or until sauce thickens slightly. Add chives; stir until sauce is heated through.
per tablespoon 2.2g total fat (1g saturated fat); 151kJ (36 cal); 0.7g carbohydrate; 0.9g protein; 0.5g fibre
SERVING SUGGESTION Goes well with grilled beef eye-fillet or T-bone steaks, or as an entree served on toasted slices of sourdough bread.

beurre blanc

preparation time 5 minutes (plus cooling time)
cooking time 5 minutes
makes 1 cup

¼ cup (60ml) dry white wine
1 tablespoon lemon juice
¼ cup (60ml) cream
125g cold butter, chopped

1 Combine wine and juice in medium saucepan; bring to a boil. Boil without stirring until reduced by two-thirds.
2 Add cream to pan; return to a boil. Whisk in cold butter, piece by piece, whisking between additions. Pour into medium jug; cover to keep warm.
per tablespoon 32.2g total fat (21.2g saturated fat); 1254kJ (300 cal); 0.8g carbohydrate; 0.5g protein; 0g fibre
TIP Do not let sauce boil once butter is added or sauce will separate.
SERVING SUGGESTION Goes well with poached or grilled ocean trout or salmon.

Boiling the wine and juice until the mixture is reduced by about two-thirds both burns off the alcohol and intensifies the flavours.

The cold butter is whisked into the hot liquid bit by bit so that the temperature of the sauce remains the same and is never cooled down.

spicy tomato salsa

preparation time 10 minutes
cooking time 15 minutes (plus cooling time)
makes 1½ cups

4 medium tomatoes (760g), chopped finely
2 cloves garlic, crushed
1 small brown onion (80g), sliced thinly
1 teaspoon cajun seasoning
2 teaspoons no-added-salt tomato paste

1 Combine tomato with remaining ingredients in
medium saucepan. Cook, stirring, about 15 minutes or
until onion is soft and sauce has thickened; Cool.
per tablespoon 0.3g fat (0g saturated fat); 138kJ
(33 cal); 4.8g carbohydrate; 2.4g protein; 2.9g fibre
TIP Salsa can be made 3 days ahead; cover, refrigerate
until needed.
SERVING SUGGESTION Goes well as an enchilada or
taco sauce, or with grilled pork spareribs.

mango and avocado salsa

preparation time 15 minutes
serves 4

1 medium mango (430g), chopped coarsely
1 large avocado (320g), chopped coarsely
1 small red onion (100g), chopped finely
1 small red capsicum (150g), chopped finely
1 fresh small red thai chilli, chopped finely
2 tablespoons lime juice

1 Place ingredients in medium bowl; toss to combine.
per serving 12.9g total fat (2.7g saturated fat); 744kJ
(178 cal); 12.6g carbohydrate; 2.8g protein; 2.7g fibre
SERVING SUGGESTION Goes well with beef or chicken
fajitas or as a dip with warmed corn tortillas.

salsa verde

preparation time 15 minutes
makes 1½ cups

½ cup finely chopped fresh flat-leaf parsley
¼ cup finely chopped fresh mint
¼ cup finely chopped fresh dill
¼ cup finely chopped fresh chives
1 tablespoon wholegrain mustard
¼ cup (60ml) lemon juice
2 tablespoons drained baby capers,
  rinsed, chopped finely
1 clove garlic, crushed
⅓ cup (80ml) olive oil

1 Combine ingredients in medium bowl.
per serving 3.1g total fat (0.4g saturated fat); 121kJ (29 cal); 0.3g carbohydrate; 0.1g protein; 0.2g fibre
SERVING SUGGESTION Goes well with smashed kipfler potatoes or with grilled chicken fillets.

corn and zucchini salsa

preparation time 10 minutes
cooking time 10 minutes
serves 4

2 corn cobs (800g), trimmed
100g baby zucchini, halved lengthways
2 large avocados (640g), chopped coarsely
200g grape tomatoes, halved
1 medium red onion (170g), halved, sliced thickly
¼ cup coarsely chopped fresh coriander
1 tablespoon sweet chilli sauce
⅓ cup (80ml) lime juice
2 red thai chillies, seeded, sliced thinly

1 Cook corn and zucchini on heated oiled grill plate (or grill or barbecue) until browned lightly and tender. Using a sharp knife, remove corn kernels from cobs.
2 Combine corn and zucchini in large serving bowl with avocado, tomato, onion and coriander.
3 Place remaining ingredients in screw-top jar; shake well. Drizzle over salsa; toss gently to combine.
per serving 27.4g total fat (5.7g saturated fat); 1697kJ (406 cal); 29.6g carbohydrate; 9.7g protein; 10.4g fibre
SERVING SUGGESTION Goes well with crumbed pork or chicken schnitzels, or any Mexican main course.

classic vinaigrette

preparation time 5 minutes
makes ⅔ cup

⅓ cup (80ml) olive oil
2 tablespoons white vinegar
1 teaspoon dijon mustard
1 clove garlic, crushed
¼ teaspoon sugar
½ teaspoon salt

1 Place ingredients in screw-top jar; shake well.
*per tablespoon 12.2g total fat (1.7g saturated fat); 456kJ
(109 cal); 0.3g carbohydrate; 0.1g protein; 0.1g fibre
SERVING SUGGESTION Goes well with mesclun or a
salad of sliced tomatoes and red onions.*

guilt-free dressing

preparation time 5 minutes
makes ⅔ cup

½ cup (125ml) buttermilk
2 tablespoons finely chopped fresh chives
2 tablespoons no-oil french dressing
1 tablespoon wholegrain mustard
1 tablespoon honey

1 Place ingredients in screw-top jar; shake well.
*per tablespoon 0.4g total fat (0.2g saturated fat); 105kJ
(25 cal); 4.7g carbohydrate; 0.8g protein; 0.1g fibre
SERVING SUGGESTION Goes well with a salad of
baby cos leaves, croutons and parmesan flakes.*

hoisin and peanut dipping sauce

preparation time 5 minutes
cooking time 5 minutes
makes ½ cup

2 teaspoons caster sugar
1 tablespoon rice vinegar
¼ cup (60ml) water
¼ cup (60ml) hoisin sauce
1 tablespoon crushed toasted peanuts

1 Combine sugar, vinegar and the water in small saucepan; stir over medium heat until sugar dissolves. Stir in sauce and nuts.
per tablespoon 1.5g total fat (0.2g saturated fat); 163kJ (39 cal); 5.9g carbohydrate; 0.7g protein; 1.3g fibre
SERVING SUGGESTION Goes well with steamed dim sum, deep-fried spring rolls or grilled chicken skewers.

balsamic and garlic dressing

preparation time 5 minutes
makes 1¼ cups

1 tablespoon balsamic vinegar
¼ cup (60ml) lemon juice
1 clove garlic, crushed
¾ cup (180ml) olive oil

1 Place ingredients in a screw-top jar; shake well.
per tablespoon 10.9g total fat (1.5g saturated fat); 410kJ (98 cal); 0.1g carbohydrate; 0g protein; 0g fibre
SERVING SUGGESTION Good with an Italian rocket and fennel salad, steamed vegetables or beef tartare.

mustard and basil cream

preparation time 5 minutes
cooking time 5 minutes
makes 1 cup

2 teaspoons olive oil
1 clove garlic, crushed
¼ cup (60ml) dry white wine
300ml cream
1 tablespoon dijon mustard
¼ cup coarsely chopped fresh basil

1 Heat oil in small frying pan; cook garlic, stirring,
until fragrant. Add wine; bring to a boil. Reduce heat;
simmer, uncovered, until liquid reduces by half.
2 Add cream and mustard to pan; cook, stirring, until
sauce thickens slightly. Remove from heat; stir in basil.
*per tablespoon 11.7g total fat (7.3g saturated fat); 468kJ
(112 cal); 0.8g carbohydrate; 0.6g protein; 0.1g fibre*
*SERVING SUGGESTION Goes well over hot potato
salad, pan-fried fish fillets or grilled lamb cutlets.*

sweet dill dressing

preparation time 15 minutes (plus standing time)
cooking time 10 minutes
makes 1¾ cups

¼ cup (60ml) water
¼ cup (55g) sugar
2 teaspoons dijon mustard
1 egg yolk
¼ cup (60ml) white wine vinegar
1 cup (250ml) extra light olive oil
1 tablespoon coarsely chopped fresh dill

1 Combine the water and sugar in a small saucepan;
stir over medium heat until sugar dissolves. Bring to a
boil; cool.
2 Whisk mustard, egg yolk, vinegar and 1½ tablespoons
of the sugar mixture in medium bowl. Slowly whisk in
oil until combined; stir in dill.
*per tablespoon 11.1g total fat (1.6g saturated fat); 456kJ
(109 cal); 2.6g carbohydrate; 0.2g protein; 0g fibre*
*SERVING SUGGESTION Goes well with a cold mixed
seafood, smoked salmon or ham salad.*

pesto dressing

preparation time 5 minutes
makes 1 cup

2 cloves garlic, crushed
2 tablespoons finely grated parmesan
1 tablespoon toasted pine nuts
1 tablespoon lemon juice
½ cup firmly packed fresh basil leaves
½ cup (125ml) olive oil

1 Blend or process ingredients until smooth.
per tablespoon 10.7g total fat (1.6g saturated fat); 414kJ
(99 cal); 0.2g carbohydrate; 0.7g protein; 0.3g fibre
SERVING SUGGESTION Goes well with barbecued
vegetables, particularly corn and zucchini, and grilled
polenta triangles.

caper dressing

preparation time 5 minutes
makes 1 cup

2 hard-boiled eggs, quartered
1 tablespoon drained capers
2 tablespoons white wine vinegar
2 tablespoons coarsely chopped fresh oregano
1 clove garlic, crushed
⅓ cup (80ml) olive oil

1 Blend or process egg, capers, vinegar, oregano and
garlic until chopped finely.
2 With motor operating, add oil in a thin, steady stream
until dressing thickens.
per tablespoon 7g total fat (1.1g saturated fat); 280kJ
(67 cal); 0.2g carbohydrate; 1.1g protein; 0.1g fibre
SERVING SUGGESTION Goes well with steamed
asparagus, sauteed baby fennel or grilled lamb cutlets.

Salads

Salad classics owe nothing
to fashion and everything to
good cooks in many parts of the
world, working with the best
fresh ingredients they can find.
Each ingredient has been added
for a reason. The results are
salads that live on because their
play of flavours and textures is
so right. Some of those here are
well-loved accompaniments to
meat or seafood. Others have the
substance and goodness that add
up to a main course or nourishing
light meal in their own right.

vietnamese chicken salad

thai beef salad

lamb, spinach and spiced peach salad

prawn, endive and pink grapefruit with lime aïoli

vietnamese chicken salad

preparation time 20 minutes
cooking time 15 minutes
serves 4

500g chicken breast fillets
1 large carrot (180g)
½ cup (125ml) rice wine vinegar
2 teaspoons salt
2 tablespoons caster sugar
1 medium white onion (150g), sliced thinly
1½ cups (120g) bean sprouts
2 cups (160g) finely shredded savoy cabbage
¼ cup firmly packed fresh vietnamese mint leaves
½ cup firmly packed fresh coriander leaves
1 tablespoon crushed toasted peanuts
2 tablespoons fried shallots

VIETNAMESE DRESSING
2 tablespoons fish sauce
¼ cup (60ml) water
2 tablespoons caster sugar
2 tablespoons lime juice
1 clove garlic, crushed

1 Place chicken in medium saucepan of boiling water; return to a boil. Reduce heat; simmer, uncovered, about 10 minutes or until cooked through. Cool chicken in poaching liquid 10 minutes; discard liquid (or reserve for another use). Shred chicken coarsely.
2 Meanwhile, cut carrot into matchstick-sized pieces. Combine carrot in large bowl with vinegar, salt and sugar, cover; stand 5 minutes. Add onion, cover; stand 5 minutes. Add sprouts, cover; stand 3 minutes. Drain pickled vegetables; discard liquid.
3 Place pickled vegetables in large bowl with chicken, cabbage, mint and coriander.
4 Place ingredients for vietnamese dressing in screw-top jar; shake well. Pour dressing over salad in bowl; toss gently to combine. Sprinkle with nuts and shallots.
per serving 5g total fat (1g saturated fat); 11791kJ (282 cal); 25.6g carbohydrate; 32.6g protein; 4.9g fibre

thai beef salad

preparation time 25 minutes (plus refrigeration time)
cooking time 10 minutes
serves 4

¼ cup (60ml) fish sauce
¼ cup (60ml) lime juice
500g beef rump steak
3 lebanese cucumbers (390g), seeded, sliced thinly
4 fresh small red thai chillies, sliced thinly
4 green onions, sliced thinly
250g cherry tomatoes, halved
¼ cup firmly packed fresh vietnamese mint leaves
½ cup firmly packed fresh coriander leaves
½ cup firmly packed fresh thai basil leaves
1 tablespoon grated palm sugar
2 teaspoons soy sauce
1 clove garlic, crushed

1 Combine 2 tablespoons of the fish sauce and 1 tablespoon of the juice in medium bowl; add beef, toss to coat in marinade. Cover; refrigerate 3 hours or overnight.
2 Drain beef; discard marinade. Cook beef on heated oiled grill plate (or grill or barbecue) until cooked as desired. Cover beef, stand 5 minutes; slice thinly.
3 Meanwhile, combine cucumber, chilli, onion, tomato and herbs in large bowl.
4 Place sugar, soy sauce, garlic, remaining fish sauce and remaining juice in screw-top jar; shake well. Add beef and dressing to salad; toss gently to combine.
per serving 8.7g total fat (3.8g saturated fat); 982kJ (235 cal); 7.9g carbohydrate; 30.6g protein; 3.2g fibre

lamb, spinach and spiced peach salad

preparation time 20 minutes
cooking time 15 minutes
serves 4

20g butter
1 teaspoon ground coriander
½ teaspoon ground cardamom
¼ teaspoon ground cinnamon
3 medium peaches (450g), peeled, sliced thickly
2 tablespoons brown sugar
1 tablespoon raspberry vinegar
800g lamb backstrap
1 large red onion (300g), sliced thinly
150g snow peas, trimmed, sliced thinly
150g baby spinach leaves
2 fresh long red chillies, sliced thinly

RASPBERRY DRESSING
120g raspberries
2 tablespoons raspberry vinegar
2 tablespoons olive oil
1 teaspoon sugar
1 teaspoon dijon mustard

1 Melt butter in large frying pan; cook spices, stirring, until fragrant. Add peach; cook, stirring, about 2 minutes or until just tender. Add sugar and vinegar; cook, stirring, until sugar dissolves. Remove peach from pan with slotted spoon; place in large bowl.
2 Add lamb to sugar mixture in pan; cook, uncovered, over low heat until browned both sides and cooked as desired. Cover lamb; stand 10 minutes then slice thickly.
3 Meanwhile, blend or process ingredients for raspberry dressing until smooth.
4 Combine lamb and remaining ingredients in bowl with peach; toss gently. Serve salad drizzled with dressing.
per serving 31.3g total fat (12g saturated fat); 2307kJ (552 cal); 21.4g carbohydrate; 46.1g protein; 5.7g fibre

prawn, endive and pink grapefruit with lime aïoli

preparation time 30 minutes
serves 4

3 small pink grapefruits (1kg)
1kg cooked large prawns
350g curly endive, torn
¼ cup coarsely chopped chives
2 trimmed celery sticks (150g), sliced thinly
1 small red onion (100g), sliced thinly

LIME AIOLI
2 egg yolks
2 teaspoons dijon mustard
½ teaspoon finely grated lime rind
2 tablespoons lime juice
2 cloves garlic, quartered
¾ cup (180ml) light olive oil
1 tablespoon hot water

1 Make lime aïoli.
2 Peel grapefruits; separate the segments. Shell and devein prawns, leaving tails intact.
3 Combine grapefruit and prawns in large serving bowl with remaining ingredients.
4 Serve with lime aïoli.
LIME AIOLI
Blend or process egg yolks, mustard, rind, juice and garlic until combined. With motor operating, gradually add oil in a thin, steady stream until aïoli thickens. With motor operating, add enough of the water (if any) to achieve desired consistency.
per serving 45.2g total fat (6.8g saturated fat); 2395kJ (573 cal); 10.8g carbohydrate; 30.8g protein; 4.3g fibre
TIP The lime aïoli can be prepared a day ahead. Cover; refrigerate.

chicken caesar salad

preparation time 20 minutes
cooking time 35 minutes
serves 4

1 long french bread stick
½ cup (125ml) olive oil
2 cloves garlic, crushed
600g chicken breast fillets
4 bacon rashers (280g), rind removed
1 large cos lettuce, trimmed, torn
6 green onions, sliced thinly
¼ cup coarsely chopped fresh flat-leaf parsley
100g parmesan, shaved

CAESAR DRESSING
1 egg
1 clove garlic, quartered
2 tablespoons lemon juice
1 teaspoon dijon mustard
6 drained anchovy fillets
¾ cup (180ml) olive oil
1 tablespoon hot water, approximately

1 Preheat oven to moderate (180°C/160°C fan-forced).
2 Make caesar dressing.
3 Halve bread lengthways; slice halves on the diagonal into 1cm-thick slices. Combine oil and garlic in large bowl; add bread, toss to coat in oil mixture. Place bread, in single layer, on oven trays; toast, uncovered, about 10 minutes or until croûtes are browned lightly.
4 Meanwhile, cook chicken, in batches, on heated oiled grill plate (or grill or barbecue) until browned both sides and cooked through. Cook bacon on same grill plate until browned and crisp; drain on absorbent paper. Slice chicken thinly; slice bacon thinly.
5 Combine half of the chicken, half of the bacon, half of the croûtes and half of the dressing in large bowl with lettuce, half of the onion, half of the parsley and half of the cheese; toss gently to combine.
6 Divide salad among serving bowls; top with remaining chicken, bacon, croûtes, onion, parsley and cheese, drizzle with remaining dressing.
CAESAR DRESSING
Blend or process egg, garlic, juice, mustard and anchovies until smooth. With motor operating, add oil in thin, steady stream until dressing thickens. If thinner dressing is preferred, with motor operating, add enough of the water (if any) to achieve desired consistency.
per serving 91.2g total fat (18.6g saturated fat); 5187kJ (1241 cal); 43.5g carbohydrate; 63.6g protein; 7.8g fibre
TIP Caesar dressing and croûtes can be prepared a day ahead. Cover, refrigerate dressing; store croûtes in airtight container.

niçoise salad

preparation time 15 minutes
cooking time 10 minutes
serves 4

200g baby green beans, trimmed
3 medium tomatoes (570g), cut into wedges
4 hard-boiled eggs, quartered
425g can tuna in springwater, drained, flaked
½ cup (60g) seeded small black olives
½ cup (80g) drained caperberries, rinsed
¼ cup firmly packed fresh flat-leaf parsley
440g can whole baby potatoes, rinsed,
   drained, halved

DRESSING
2 tablespoons olive oil
1 tablespoon lemon juice
2 tablespoons white wine vinegar

1 Boil, steam or microwave beans until just tender; drain. Rinse under cold water; drain.
2 Meanwhile, combine tomato, egg, tuna, olives, caperberries, parsley and potato in large bowl.
3 Place ingredients for dressing in screw-top jar; shake well.
4 Add beans to salad, drizzle with dressing; toss gently to combine.
per serving 17g total fat (3.7g saturated fat); 1467kJ (351 cal); 18.1g carbohydrate; 30.7g protein; 4.9g fibre
TIP This recipe is best made just before serving.

avocado caprese salad

preparation time 10 minutes
serves 4

4 large vine-ripened tomatoes (480g)
250g cherry bocconcini
1 large avocado (320g), halved
¼ cup loosely packed fresh basil leaves
2 tablespoons olive oil
1 tablespoon balsamic vinegar

1 Slice tomato, cheese and avocado thickly.
2 Place slices of tomato, cheese and avocado on serving platter; top with basil leaves, drizzle with combined oil and vinegar. Sprinkle with freshly ground black pepper, if desired.
per serving 31.4g total fat (10.3g saturated fat); 1434kJ (343 cal); 2.6g carbohydrate; 13.1g protein; 2.4g fibre
TIP We suggest vine-ripened truss tomatoes when you're serving them raw – it takes a simple recipe like this for their brilliant colour, robust flavour and crisp, tangy flesh to stand out at their magnificent best. Use less costly tomatoes for cooking.

panzanella

preparation time 15 minutes
cooking time 10 minutes
serves 4

½ long loaf ciabatta (250g)
1 clove garlic, crushed
¼ cup (60ml) olive oil
500g cherry tomatoes, halved
1 lebanese cucumber (130g), seeded, sliced thinly
1 medium avocado (250g), chopped coarsely
¼ cup (50g) drained capers, rinsed
1 large yellow capsicum (350g), chopped coarsely
2 x 400g cans white beans, rinsed, drained
½ cup coarsely chopped fresh basil

TOMATO VINAIGRETTE
½ cup (125ml) tomato juice
¼ cup (60ml) red wine vinegar
⅓ cup (80ml) olive oil

1 Preheat oven to moderately hot (200°C/180°C fan-forced).
2 Cut bread into 2cm cubes.
3 Combine garlic and oil in large bowl; add bread, toss to coat in oil mixture. Place bread, in single layer, on oven tray; toast, uncovered, about 10 minutes or until browned lightly.
4 Meanwhile, place ingredients for tomato vinaigrette in screw-top jar; shake well.
5 Place bread in same large bowl with remaining ingredients and vinaigrette; toss gently to combine.
per serving 44.7g total fat (7g saturated fat); 2842kJ (680 cal); 54.7g carbohydrate; 15.9g protein; 13g fibre
TIP Ciabatta is available from most supermarkets; any crisp-crusted Italian bread can be used in this recipe.

lentil and goat cheese salad

preparation time 40 minutes
cooking time 30 minutes
serves 4

2 tablespoons extra virgin olive oil
1 medium red capsicum (200g), sliced thickly
½ cup (110g) puy lentils, rinsed, drained
1 medium brown onion (150g), halved
1 bay leaf
16 sprigs fresh thyme
300g piece firm goat cheese
2 tablespoons packaged breadcrumbs
2 teaspoons finely grated lemon rind
1 tablespoon coarsely chopped fresh
    flat-leaf parsley
250g cherry tomatoes, halved
100g mesclun

VINAIGRETTE
1 tablespoon red wine vinegar
2 tablespoons extra virgin olive oil
1 teaspoon dijon mustard
1 teaspoon sugar

1 Preheat oven to hot (220°C/200°C fan-forced).
2 Place half of the oil in large shallow baking dish; add capsicum, toss to coat in oil. Roast, uncovered, about 15 minutes or until capsicum just softens.
3 Meanwhile, combine lentils, onion, bay leaf and thyme in medium saucepan, cover with water; bring to a boil. Reduce heat; simmer, covered, 20 minutes or until lentils are just tender. Drain; discard onion, bay leaf and thyme.
4 Meanwhile, place ingredients for vinaigrette in screw-top jar; shake well.
5 Cut cheese into 16 pieces; coat cheese in breadcrumbs. Heat remaining oil in medium frying pan; cook cheese, uncovered, about 5 minutes or until cheese is browned lightly all over and starting to melt.
6 Meanwhile, combine lentils in medium bowl with rind, parsley, tomato and two-thirds of the vinaigrette. Divide lentils among serving plates; top with capsicum, mesclun then cheese, drizzle with remaining vinaigrette.
per serving 30.5g total fat (10.4g saturated fat); 1534kJ (367 cal); 10.6g carbohydrate; 13.3g protein; 3.3g fibre

baby rocket and parmesan salad

preparation time 25 minutes
cooking time 3 minutes
serves 8

60g parmesan
200g baby rocket leaves
80g semi-dried tomatoes, halved lengthways
¼ cup (40g) pine nuts, toasted
¼ cup (60ml) balsamic vinegar
¼ cup (60ml) extra virgin olive oil

1 Using vegetable peeler, shave cheese into wide, long pieces.
2 Combine rocket, tomato and nuts in large bowl; add cheese, drizzle with combined vinegar and oil, toss gently.
per serve 13.4g total fat (2.8g saturated fat); 665kJ (159 cal); 4.3g carbohydrate; 5.3g protein; 2.1g fibre
TIPS Baby spinach leaves can be substituted for rocket. To keep rocket crisp, rinse under cold water. Place in an airtight plastic bag and refrigerate for several hours or overnight. Nuts of any kind can easily be toasted on top of the stove by stirring them in a dry heavy-base frying pan over medium-to-high heat briefly, until they are just golden-brown.

larb gai (spicy chicken salad)

preparation time 25 minutes
cooking time 20 minutes
serves 4

2 tablespoons long-grain white rice
1 tablespoon peanut oil
1 tablespoon finely chopped fresh lemon grass
2 fresh small red thai chillies, seeded,
    chopped finely
2 cloves garlic, crushed
1 tablespoon finely chopped fresh galangal
750g chicken mince
1 lebanese cucumber (130g), seeded, sliced thinly
1 small red onion (100g), sliced thinly
100g bean sprouts
½ cup loosely packed fresh thai basil leaves
1 cup loosely packed fresh coriander leaves
4 large iceberg lettuce leaves

DRESSING
⅓ cup (80ml) lime juice
2 tablespoons fish sauce
2 tablespoons kecap manis
2 tablespoons peanut oil
2 teaspoons grated palm sugar
½ teaspoon sambal oelek

1 Place ingredients for dressing in screw-top jar; shake well.
2 Heat dry wok; stir-fry rice until lightly browned. Blend or process (or crush using mortar and pestle) rice until it resembles fine breadcrumbs.
3 Heat oil in same wok; stir-fry lemon grass, chilli, garlic and galangal until fragrant. Remove from wok. Stir-fry chicken, in batches, until changed in colour and cooked through.
4 Return chicken and lemon grass mixture to wok with about one-third of the dressing; stir-fry about 5 minutes or until mixture thickens slightly.
5 Place remaining dressing in large bowl with chicken, cucumber, onion, sprouts and herbs; toss gently to combine. Place lettuce leaves on serving plates; divide larb salad among leaves, sprinkle with ground rice.
per serving 29.2g total fat (7g saturated fat); 1977kJ (473 cal); 12.3g carbohydrate; 40.1g protein; 3.2g fibre
TIP Although we used sambal oelek, you can use hot vietnamese chilli paste or, for less heat, a mild sweet thai chilli sauce.

chicken soba salad

preparation time 20 minutes (plus refrigeration time)
cooking time 15 minutes
serves 10

600g chicken breast fillets
300g soba noodles
6 red radishes (210g), trimmed, grated coarsely
2 lebanese cucumbers (260g), seeded,
    sliced thinly
3 green onions, sliced thinly
1 sheet toasted seaweed (yakinori),
    shredded finely

MIRIN DRESSING
⅓ cup (80ml) mirin
¼ cup (60ml) rice vinegar
2 tablespoons soy sauce
1 teaspoon sesame oil
4cm piece fresh ginger (20g), grated

1 Place chicken in medium saucepan of boiling water; return to a boil. Reduce heat; simmer, covered, about 10 minutes or until chicken is cooked through. Cool chicken in poaching liquid 10 minutes. Remove chicken; discard liquid. Shred chicken coarsely.
2 Cook noodles in large saucepan of boiling water, uncovered, until just tender; drain. Rinse under cold water; drain. Cover; refrigerate until cool.
3 Meanwhile, place ingredients for mirin dressing in screw-top jar; shake well.
4 Place noodles, chicken and dressing in large serving bowl; toss gently to combine. Top with radish, cucumber, onion then seaweed. Serve immediately.
per serving 2.2g total fat (0.5g saturated fat); 769kJ (184 cal); 21.7g carbohydrate; 17.5g protein; 1.6g fibre
TIP All ingredients can be prepared ahead of time; cover separately, refrigerate. Use scissors to cut the seaweed into fine shreds.

fruity couscous salad

preparation time 25 minutes
cooking time 5 minutes
serves 10

3 cups (750ml) chicken stock
3 cups (600g) couscous
1 medium red onion (170g), chopped finely
⅔ cup (110g) finely chopped dried apricots
200g red seedless grapes, halved
½ cup (75g) dried currants
½ cup (70g) toasted slivered almonds
⅓ cup coarsely chopped fresh flat-leaf parsley

LEMON DRESSING
⅓ cup (80ml) lemon juice
2 tablespoons olive oil
1 teaspoon dijon mustard

1 Bring stock to a boil in medium saucepan. Remove from heat; stir in couscous. Cover; stand 5 minutes, fluffing with fork occasionally.
2 Place ingredients for lemon dressing in screw-top jar; shake well.
3 Place couscous in large bowl with remaining ingredients and dressing; toss gently to combine.
per serving 8.2g total fat (1.1g saturated fat); 1517kJ (363 cal); 60.7g carbohydrate; 11.1g protein; 3.1g fibre
TIP You can substitute the chicken stock for vegetable stock or water.

greek lamb salad

preparation time 40 minutes (plus refrigeration time)
cooking time 10 minutes
serves 4

2 tablespoons olive oil
2 teaspoons finely grated lemon rind
1 teaspoon finely chopped fresh marjoram
1 clove garlic, crushed
600g lamb fillets, trimmed
1 large green capsicum (350g), sliced thinly
1 telegraph cucumber (400g), diced into 2cm pieces
400g grape tomatoes, halved
2 trimmed celery stalks (200g), sliced thinly
4 green onions, sliced thinly
2 baby cos lettuces, chopped coarsely
1 cup (150g) seeded kalamata olives
200g goat fetta, crumbled

SKORDALIA
2 slices stale white bread
2 cloves garlic, crushed
2 tablespoons olive oil
2 teaspoons white wine vinegar
1 tablespoon lemon juice
⅓ cup (80ml) water

MARJORAM DRESSING
2 tablespoons olive oil
2 tablespoons white wine vinegar
1 tablespoon finely chopped fresh marjoram
pinch cayenne pepper

1 Place oil, rind, marjoram and garlic in large bowl; add lamb, toss to coat in marinade. Cover; refrigerate 1 hour.
2 Meanwhile, make skordalia.
3 Place ingredients for marjoram dressing in screw-top jar; shake well.
4 Heat large non-stick frying pan; cook lamb, in batches, until browned and cooked as desired. Cover; stand 5 minutes. Slice lamb thickly.
5 Place lamb in large bowl with remaining ingredients and dressing; toss gently to combine. Divide salad among serving plates; drizzle with skordalia.
SKORDALIA
Discard crusts from bread, soak in small bowl of cold water; drain. Squeeze out excess water; blend or process bread with remaining ingredients until smooth.
per serving 49.7g total fat (15.2g saturated fat); 2972kJ (711 cal); 23.2g carbohydrate; 43.4g protein; 6.5g fibre

After removing crusts, soak bread in cold water until soft then use your hands to squeeze out excess water.

Process the soaked bread with the remaining skordalia ingredients until the mixture is of a smooth consistency.

duck salad with mandarin and pomegranate

preparation time 25 minutes
cooking time 5 minutes
serves 4

150g sugar snap peas, trimmed
1kg chinese barbecued duck
2 small mandarins (200g), segmented
1 red mignonette lettuce (280g)
⅓ cup (60g) pomegranate pulp
¾ cup (120g) toasted slivered almonds

LEMON DIJON DRESSING
1 clove garlic, crushed
1 teaspoon dijon mustard
2 tablespoons lemon juice
2 tablespoons olive oil

1 Boil, steam or microwave peas until just tender; drain. Rinse under cold water; drain.
2 Remove meat, leaving skin on, from duck; discard bones. Chop meat coarsely; place in large bowl with peas, mandarin, lettuce, pomegranate and nuts.
3 Place ingredients for lemon dijon dressing in screw-top jar; shake well.
4 Pour dressing over salad; toss gently to combine.
per serving 63.2g total fat (13.5g saturated fat); 3123kJ (747 cal); 9.1g carbohydrate; 36.9g protein; 6.8g fibre
TIP You will need one large pomegranate for this recipe.

pork and lychee salad

preparation time 20 minutes (plus standing time)
cooking time 10 minutes
serves 4

1 tablespoon peanut oil
300g pork fillet
565g can lychees, rinsed, drained, halved
1 medium red capsicum (200g), sliced thinly
10cm stick (20g) thinly sliced fresh lemon grass
2 fresh kaffir lime leaves, shredded finely
100g watercress
2 tablespoons coarsely chopped fresh
   vietnamese mint
2 tablespoons drained thinly sliced
   pickled ginger
2 tablespoons fried shallot

PICKLED GARLIC DRESSING
1 tablespoon drained finely chopped
   pickled garlic
2 fresh small red thai chillies, seeded,
   sliced thinly
1 tablespoon rice vinegar
1 tablespoon lime juice
1 tablespoon fish sauce
1 tablespoon grated palm sugar

1 Heat oil in medium frying pan; cook pork, turning, until browned all over and cooked as desired. Cover, stand 10 minutes; slice thinly.
2 Place ingredients for pickled garlic dressing in screw-top jar; shake well.
3 Place dressing in medium bowl; add pork, toss to coat in dressing. Stand 10 minutes.
4 Meanwhile, combine lychees, capsicum, lemon grass, lime leaves, watercress and mint in large bowl.
5 Add pork mixture to lychee mixture; toss gently to combine. Serve sprinkled with pickled ginger and fried shallot.
per serving 7.3g total fat (1.5g saturated fat); 974kJ (233 cal); 22.7g carbohydrate; 19.3g protein; 3.7g fibre

grilled radicchio and roasted tomato salad

preparation time 10 minutes
cooking time 20 minutes
serves 6

⅓ cup (80ml) olive oil
1 clove garlic, crushed
6 medium egg tomatoes (450g), halved
4 small radicchio (600g), quartered
2 tablespoons balsamic vinegar
100g baby rocket leaves
⅔ cup (50g) shaved pecorino cheese

1 Preheat oven to hot (220°/200°C fan-forced).
2 Combine 1 tablespoon of the oil with garlic in small bowl. Place tomato, cut-side up, on oven tray; drizzle with oil mixture. Roast, uncovered, about 20 minutes or until softened.
3 Meanwhile, place 2 tablespoons of the remaining oil in large bowl; add radicchio, toss to coat in oil. Cook radicchio on heated oiled grill plate (or grill or barbecue) until browned all over; cool 5 minutes.
4 Place vinegar and remaining oil in screw-top jar; shake well.
5 Arrange tomato, radicchio and rocket on large serving platter; sprinkle with cheese, drizzle with dressing.
per serving 14.9g total fat (3.2g saturated fat); 694kJ (166 cal); 3.3g carbohydrate; 4.9g protein; 3.5g fibre

green papaya salad

preparation time 25 minutes
cooking time 3 minutes
serves 4

100g snake beans
850g green papaya
250g cherry tomatoes, quartered
3 fresh small green thai chillies, seeded, chopped finely
2 tablespoons finely chopped dried shrimp
¼ cup (60ml) lime juice
1 tablespoon fish sauce
1 tablespoon grated palm sugar
2 cloves garlic, crushed
¼ cup coarsely chopped fresh coriander
2 cups (120g) finely shredded iceberg lettuce
½ cup (50g) coarsely chopped roasted unsalted peanuts

1 Cut beans in 5cm pieces; cut pieces in half lengthways. Boil, steam or microwave beans until just tender; drain. Rinse immediately under cold water; drain.
2 Meanwhile, peel papaya. Quarter lengthways, remove seeds; grate papaya coarsely.
3 Place papaya and beans in large bowl with tomatoes, chilli and shrimp. Add combined juice, sauce, sugar, garlic and half of the coriander; toss gently to combine.
4 Divide lettuce among serving plates; spoon papaya mixture over lettuce, sprinkle with chopped nuts and remaining coriander.
per serving 6.4g total fat (0.7g saturated fat); 640kJ (153 cal); 17.1g carbohydrate; 6.7g protein; 7.1g fibre
TIPS Green (unripe) papayas are readily available in various sizes at many Asian shops and markets. Select one that is very hard and slightly shiny, which indicates that it is freshly picked. It's imperative that it be totally unripe, the flesh so light green it is almost white. Assemble the salad just before serving, otherwise the papaya will lose its crisp texture.

Seafood

Today's seafood classics range
from breezy barbecued feasts to
fine dishes that underline the joys
of fresh fish and shellfish with
a cast of other quality ingredients.
Both work by the same simple
principles. First, cook seafood as
fresh as possible – ideally, the day
you buy it. Second, give it your
undivided attention while it's on the
heat, and take it off the moment it
turns opaque and white (or lighter
pink, for pink fish such as salmon).
For whole fish, push a toothpick
into the thickest part; when it slides
in easily, the fish is done.

beer battered john dory fillets with kumara chips

barbecued seafood and green mango salad

chipotle prawns with grilled pineapple,
red onion and coriander salad

char-grilled lobster tail salad

beer battered john dory fillets with kumara chips

preparation time 30 minutes
cooking time 20 minutes
serves 4

4 x 240g john dory fillets, skinned
½ cup (75g) sesame seeds
¼ cup (35g) plain flour
¼ cup (60ml) vegetable oil
vegetable oil, extra, for deep-frying
1 large kumara (500g), cut into 5mm slices
1 lime, cut into wedges

BEER BATTER
1 cup (150g) plain flour
1 teaspoon sweet paprika
1¼ cups (310ml) beer

1 Place ingredients for beer batter in medium bowl; whisk until smooth.
2 Cut each fish fillet into three pieces. Combine seeds and flour in shallow medium bowl; coat fish in mixture.
3 Heat oil in large deep frying pan; cook fish, in batches, until browned both sides and cooked through. Cover to keep warm.
4 Meanwhile, heat extra oil in wok or large frying pan. Dip kumara slices in batter, draining away excess. Deep-fry kumara, in batches, until crisp and tender; drain on absorbent paper.
5 Serve kumara topped with fish and lime wedges.
per serving 38.7g total fat (5.3g saturated fat); 3189kJ (763 cal); 50.5g carbohydrate; 48g protein; 5.9g fibre

barbecued seafood and green mango salad

preparation time 40 minutes (plus refrigeration time)
cooking time 15 minutes
serves 4

250g squid hoods
500g uncooked medium king prawns
500g cleaned baby octopus, halved lengthways
1 large green mango (600g)
200g mizuna
250g cherry tomatoes, halved
100g snow pea sprouts
1 cup loosely packed fresh vietnamese mint leaves

LEMON GRASS DRESSING
2 fresh small red thai chillies, seeded, chopped finely
2 tablespoons fish sauce
1 tablespoon grated palm sugar
⅓ cup (80ml) peanut oil
¼ cup finely chopped fresh lemon grass
¼ cup (60ml) lime juice

1 Place ingredients for lemon grass dressing in screw-top jar; shake well.
2 Cut squid down centre to open out, score inside in diagonal pattern; cut into 5cm squares. Shell and devein prawns, leaving tails intact.
3 Place half of the dressing in large bowl; add squid, prawns and octopus, toss to combine in dressing. Cover; refrigerate 2 hours.
4 Meanwhile, slice mango thinly; cut slices into matchstick-sized pieces.
5 Cook seafood, in batches, on heated oiled grill plate (or grill or barbecue) until browned and cooked as desired.
6 Combine seafood and mango in large bowl with remaining dressing and remaining ingredients; toss gently to combine.
per serving 22.2g total fat (4.2g saturated fat); 2266kJ (542 cal); 22.8g carbohydrate; 58.2g protein; 5.9g fibre

chipotle prawns with grilled pineapple, red onion and coriander salad

preparation time 10 minutes (plus cooling time)
cooking time 25 minutes
serves 4

1kg uncooked medium king prawns
2 medium red onions (340g), cut into wedges
1 small pineapple (800g), chopped coarsely
½ cup firmly packed fresh coriander leaves

CHIPOTLE PASTE
3 chipotle chillies
2 tablespoons apple cider vinegar
2 tablespoons water
1 small brown onion (80g), chopped coarsely
2 cloves garlic, quartered
2 teaspoons ground cumin

1 Make chipotle paste.
2 Shell and devein prawns, leaving tails intact. Combine prawns in medium bowl with half of the chipotle paste.
3 Cook onion and pineapple on heated oiled flat plate, uncovered, about 10 minutes or until just tender.
4 Cook prawns on heated oiled flat plate, uncovered, until changed in colour.
5 Combine onion and pineapple in medium bowl with coriander; serve with prawns and remaining chipotle paste.
CHIPOTLE PASTE
Soak chillies in vinegar in small bowl for 10 minutes. Blend or process chilli mixture with remaining ingredients until smooth. Place chipotle paste in small saucepan; bring to a boil. Reduce heat; simmer, uncovered, about 10 minutes or until paste thickens. Cool 15 minutes.
per serving 1g total fat (0.1 saturated fat); 765kJ (183 cal); 14.2g carbohydrate; 28.5g protein; 4.1g fibre

char-grilled lobster tail salad

preparation time 15 minutes
cooking time 20 minutes
serves 4

4 uncooked small lobster tails in shell (800g)
2 radicchio (400g), trimmed, leaves separated
1 medium avocado (250g), chopped coarsely
4 radishes (140g), trimmed, sliced thinly
⅓ cup (50g) toasted pine nuts
4 green onions, sliced thinly
150g semi-dried tomatoes, drained,
    chopped coarsely

ROSEMARY VINAIGRETTE
⅓ cup (80ml) vegetable oil
¼ cup (60ml) red wine vinegar
1 tablespoon coarsely chopped fresh rosemary
1 tablespoon dijon mustard

1 Place ingredients for rosemary vinaigrette in screw-top jar; shake well.
2 Using kitchen scissors, discard soft shell from underneath lobster tails to expose meat; cook, in batches, on heated oiled grill plate (or grill or barbecue) until browned and cooked through, brushing with one-third of the vinaigrette. Cut lobster tails in half lengthways.
3 Meanwhile, place remaining salad ingredients in large bowl with remaining vinaigrette; toss gently to combine. Serve lobster on salad.
per serving 40.7g total fat (5.5g saturated fat); 2550kJ (610 cal); 16.5g carbohydrate; 44.2g protein; 9.6g fibre

seared tuna with kipfler smash and salsa verde

preparation time 25 minutes
cooking time 20 minutes
serves 4

1kg kipfler potatoes, peeled, halved
30g butter
1 tablespoon extra virgin olive oil
4 x 175g tuna steaks
80g baby rocket leaves

SALSA VERDE
½ cup firmly packed fresh flat-leaf parsley
¼ cup loosely packed fresh mint leaves
⅔ cup (160ml) extra virgin olive oil
¼ cup (50g) drained capers, rinsed
2 teaspoons dijon mustard
2 tablespoons lemon juice
8 anchovy fillets, drained
1 clove garlic, quartered

1 Boil, steam or microwave potatoes until tender; drain. Using potato masher, crush potato roughly in large bowl with butter and oil. Cover to keep warm.
2 Meanwhile, blend or process ingredients for salsa verde until just combined; transfer to medium jug.
3 Cook fish, in batches, on heated oiled grill plate (or grill or barbecue) until browned both sides and cooked as desired.
4 Divide rocket and potato among serving plates; top with fish. Whisk salsa verde; drizzle over fish.
per serving 58.3g total fat (14g saturated fat); 3578kJ (856 cal); 30.8g carbohydrate; 52.2g protein; 4.7g fibre

salt-crusted ocean trout with thai-flavours hollandaise

preparation time 20 minutes
cooking time 1 hour
serves 8

2kg cooking salt
3 egg whites
2.4kg whole ocean trout

THAI-FLAVOURS HOLLANDAISE
10cm stick (20g) fresh lemon grass
2 tablespoons water
½ cup (125ml) white wine vinegar
1 tablespoon lemon juice
1 teaspoon black peppercorns
1 tablespoon finely chopped fresh lemon grass
6 egg yolks
250g butter, melted
2 tablespoons lime juice
4 fresh kaffir lime leaves, shredded finely

1 Preheat oven to moderately hot (200°C/180°C fan-forced).
2 Combine salt with egg whites in medium bowl (mixture will resemble wet sand). Spread about half of the salt mixture evenly over base of shallow 30cm x 40cm baking dish; place fish on salt mixture then cover completely (except for tail) with remaining salt mixture. Bake, uncovered, 1 hour.
3 Meanwhile, make thai-flavours hollandaise.
4 Remove fish from oven; break salt crust with heavy knife, taking care not to cut into fish. Discard salt crust; transfer fish to large serving platter.
5 Carefully remove skin from fish; flake fish into large pieces. Serve with hollandaise.

THAI-FLAVOURS HOLLANDAISE
Bruise lemon grass stick with side of heavy knife. Place lemon grass stick in small saucepan, add the water, vinegar, juice and peppercorns; bring to a boil. Reduce heat; simmer, uncovered, until reduced to 2 tablespoons. Strain over small jug; stir in chopped lemon grass. Cool 10 minutes. Combine vinegar mixture with egg yolks in medium heatproof bowl over medium saucepan of simmering water; whisk mixture constantly about 5 minutes or until thickened. Gradually add butter in thin, steady stream, whisking constantly until mixture thickens. Whisk in juice and lime leaves.
per serving 35.9g total fat (19.6g saturated fat); 1944kJ (465 cal); 0.7g carbohydrate; 34.9g protein; 0.2g fibre

steamed scallops with asian flavours

preparation time 15 minutes
cooking time 15 minutes
serves 4

1½ cups (300g) jasmine rice
3cm piece fresh ginger (15g)
20 scallops (800g), in half shell, roe removed
2 tablespoons thinly sliced fresh lemon grass
4 green onions, sliced thinly
1 tablespoon sesame oil
¼ cup (60ml) kecap manis
¼ cup (60ml) soy sauce

1 Cook rice in large saucepan of boiling water, uncovered, until just tender; drain.
2 Meanwhile, slice ginger thinly; cut slices into thin strips. Place scallops, in batches, in single layer in large bamboo steamer, top with ginger, lemon grass and onion; steam, covered, about 5 minutes or until scallops tender and cooked as desired.
3 Divide scallops among serving plates; top scallops with combined remaining ingredients. Serve with rice.
per serving 5.6g total fat (0.9g saturated fat); 1513kJ (362 cal); 61.3g carbohydrate; 15.7g protein; 0.9g fibre
TIP You can also use scallops with the roe attached, if you prefer.

tuna, kingfish and salmon carpaccio

preparation time 50 minutes
  (plus freezing and refrigeration times)
serves 6

350g piece sashimi tuna
350g piece sashimi kingfish
350g piece sashimi salmon
⅓ cup (80ml) lime juice
⅔ cup (160ml) lemon juice
4cm piece fresh ginger (20g), grated finely
¼ cup (60ml) soy sauce
1 baby fennel (130g)
⅓ cup (80ml) extra virgin olive oil
1 tablespoon drained baby capers, rinsed
½ small red onion (50g), sliced thinly
1 teaspoon finely chopped fresh dill

1 Tightly wrap each piece of fish, separately, in plastic wrap; freeze about 1 hour or until slightly firm.
2 Unwrap each piece of fish, slice as thinly as possible; arrange slices on separate serving platters. Drizzle tuna with lime juice; drizzle kingfish and salmon with lemon juice. Cover; refrigerate 1 hour.
3 Meanwhile, combine ginger and sauce in small jug; stand while fish is under refrigeration. Finely chop enough fennel leaves to make 1 level tablespoon; discard remaining leaves. Finely chop fennel bulb.
4 Drain excess juice from platters. To serve, divide fish among serving plates: drizzle tuna with strained sauce mixture; sprinkle kingfish with chopped fennel, leaves and half of the oil; sprinkle salmon with capers, onion, dill and remaining oil. Serve with crusty bread, if desired.
per serving 21.1g total fat (4.5g saturated fat); 1505kJ (360 cal); 2.4g carbohydrate; 39.2g protein; 0.6g fibre

Wrapping each piece of fish separately and freezing it until it's just slightly firm will make slicing it thinly an easy job.

Squeezing fresh citrus juice over the fish and then resting it an hour or so adds flavour and slightly 'cooks' the fish.

steamed belgian mussels

preparation time 30 minutes
cooking time 10 minutes
serves 4

1.3kg black mussels
2 teaspoons olive oil
2 cloves garlic, crushed
3 shallots (75g), sliced thinly
2 trimmed celery stalks (200g), sliced thinly
2 large egg tomatoes (180g), chopped finely
½ cup (125ml) dry white wine
200g curly endive
½ cup loosely packed fresh flat-leaf parsley leaves
¼ cup coarsely chopped fresh chives
¼ cup (60ml) lemon juice

1 Scrub mussels; remove beards.
2 Heat oil in wok; stir-fry garlic, shallot and celery until shallot softens. Add tomato; stir-fry 30 seconds. Add wine; bring to a boil. Reduce heat; simmer, uncovered, until liquid reduces by half.
3 Add mussels; simmer, covered, about 5 minutes or until mussels open (discard any that do not).
4 Add remaining ingredients to wok; toss gently to combine. Serve mussels with broth in large serving bowls.

per serving 3.8g total fat (0.7g saturated fat); 514kJ (123 cal); 6.7g carbohydrate; 9.9g protein; 3.4g fibre SERVING SUGGESTION Serve with garlic bread.

smoky octopus stew with red wine and olives

preparation time 20 minutes
cooking time 1 hour 10 minutes
serves 4

1kg cleaned baby octopus
2 bay leaves
2 tablespoons olive oil
2 cloves garlic, crushed
1 large brown onion (200g), sliced thinly
1½ teaspoons bittersweet smoked paprika
5 medium tomatoes (750g), peeled, chopped coarsely
2 tablespoons tomato paste
¾ cup (180ml) dry red wine
⅓ cup (50g) drained sun-dried tomatoes, chopped coarsely
¼ cup (60ml) water
1¼ cups (200g) seeded kalamata olives
2 tablespoons coarsely chopped fresh flat-leaf parsley

1 Cut heads from octopus; cut tentacles in two pieces.
2 Place octopus and bay leaves in large saucepan of water; bring to a boil. Reduce heat; simmer, covered, about 30 minutes or until octopus is just tender, drain. Discard bay leaves.
3 Heat oil in same cleaned pan; cook garlic and onion, stirring, until onion softens. Add paprika, fresh tomato, tomato paste, wine, sun-dried tomato, the water and octopus; bring to a boil. Reduce heat; simmer, covered, 30 minutes. Stir in olives.
4 Sprinkle stew with parsley; serve with a loaf of warmed sourdough bread, if desired.

per serving 15g total fat (2.5g saturated fat); 2257kJ (540 cal); 24.5g carbohydrate; 68.2g protein; 5.9g fibre

asian-spiced salmon with nashi, mint and coriander salad

preparation time 20 minutes
cooking time 20 minutes
serves 4

cooking-oil spray
2 teaspoons sichuan peppercorns, crushed
2 star anise
1 tablespoon soy sauce
2 tablespoons honey
4 x 200g salmon fillets
2 medium nashi (400g), sliced thinly
1 fresh long red chilli, sliced thinly
1 medium red onion (170g), sliced thinly
2 green onions, sliced thinly
¾ cup loosely packed fresh mint leaves
¾ cup loosely packed fresh coriander leaves

SESAME SOY DRESSING
2 tablespoons soy sauce
¼ cup (60ml) mirin
2 teaspoons caster sugar
¼ teaspoon sesame oil

1 Preheat oven to moderate (180°C/160°C fan-forced). Line large shallow baking dish with aluminium foil, extending foil 5cm above long sides of dish; coat lightly with cooking-oil spray.
2 Dry-fry spices in small frying pan until fragrant. Add sauce and honey; bring to a boil. Reduce heat; simmer, uncovered, 2 minutes.
3 Place fish in prepared baking dish; brush both sides with spice mixture. Bake, uncovered, about 15 minutes or until cooked as desired.
4 Meanwhile, place ingredients for sesame soy dressing in screw-top jar; shake well.
5 Place remaining ingredients in large bowl, add dressing; toss gently to combine. Serve salad with fish.
per serving 15.3g total fat (3.3g saturated fat); 1764kJ (422 cal); 27.8g carbohydrate; 41.8g protein; 4g fibre

malaysian swordfish curry

preparation time 25 minutes
cooking time 35 minutes
serves 4

6 fresh red thai chillies, chopped coarsely
2 cloves garlic, quartered
10 shallots (250g), chopped coarsely
½ cup coarsely chopped fresh lemon grass
5cm piece galangal (25g), quartered
1 teaspoon curry powder
1 teaspoon ground coriander
¼ teaspoon ground turmeric
2 tablespoons vegetable oil
1 tablespoon fish sauce
1⅔ cups (400ml) coconut milk
1⅔ cups (400ml) coconut cream
2 cups (400g) jasmine rice
4 x 220g swordfish steaks, skinned
¼ cup (10g) flaked coconut, toasted
4 kaffir lime leaves, shredded finely

1 Blend or process chilli, garlic, shallot, lemon grass, galangal, curry powder, coriander, turmeric and half of the oil until mixture forms a paste.
2 Heat remaining oil in large frying pan; cook paste, stirring, over medium heat about 3 minutes or until fragrant. Add sauce, coconut milk and cream; bring to a boil. Reduce heat; simmer, uncovered, about 15 minutes or until mixture thickens slightly.
3 Meanwhile, cook rice in large saucepan of boiling water, uncovered, until tender; drain. Cover to keep warm.
4 Cook swordfish on heated oiled grill plate (or grill or barbecue), in batches, until browned both sides and cooked as desired.
5 Divide fish among serving bowls; top with sauce, sprinkle with toasted coconut and lime leaves. Serve rice separately.
per serving 57.8g total fat (40.6g saturated fat); 4602kJ (1101 cal); 89.4g carbohydrate; 56.8g protein; 5.8g fibre
TIP If you can't find shallots, substitute a medium brown onion and a small clove of crushed garlic.

tuna tartare

preparation time 45 minutes
cooking time 5 minutes
serves 4

200g green beans, halved
600g piece sashimi tuna
3 cups (240g) finely shredded chinese cabbage
4 green onions, sliced thinly
½ cup firmly packed fresh coriander leaves
2 cups (160g) bean sprouts

GINGER DRESSING
7cm piece fresh ginger (35g)
⅓ cup (80ml) lime juice
¼ cup (60ml) olive oil
1 tablespoon soy sauce
2 teaspoons finely chopped coriander root
2 cloves garlic, crushed
2 teaspoons sesame oil
2 teaspoons sugar

1 Boil, steam or microwave beans until just tender; drain. Rinse under cold water; drain.
2 Make ginger dressing.
3 Cut tuna into 5mm pieces. Place in medium bowl with one-third of the dressing; toss gently to combine.
4 Place beans in large bowl with cabbage, onion, coriander, sprouts and remaining dressing; toss gently to combine.
5 Divide undrained tuna among serving plates, shaping into mound; serve with cabbage salad.
GINGER DRESSING
Cut ginger into thin slices; cut slices into thin strips. Combine ginger with remaining ingredients in small bowl.
per serving 24.8g total fat (5.7g saturated fat); 1735kJ (415 cal); 6.1g carbohydrate; 41.6g protein; 4.3g fibre
TIP Sashimi salmon can be used in place of the tuna.

hot and sour fish
steamed in banana leaves

preparation time 25 minutes (plus marinating time)
cooking time 20 minutes
serves 4

4 medium whole bream (1.8kg)
1 large banana leaf
4 fresh small red thai chillies, seeded, sliced thinly
2 fresh kaffir lime leaves, shredded finely
2 green onions, sliced thinly
¼ cup loosely packed fresh coriander leaves
¼ cup loosely packed fresh thai basil leaves
2 sticks fresh lemon grass
cotton string

LIME AND SWEET CHILLI DRESSING
¼ cup (60ml) sweet chilli sauce
2 tablespoons fish sauce
2 tablespoons lime juice
2 tablespoons peanut oil
1 clove garlic, crushed
1 teaspoon grated fresh ginger

1 Place ingredients for lime and sweet chilli dressing in screw-top jar; shake well.

2 Score fish both sides through thickest part of flesh; place on large tray, drizzle with half of the lime and sweet chilli dressing. Cover; refrigerate 1 hour.

3 Meanwhile, trim banana leaf into four 30cm squares. Using tongs, dip one square at a time into large saucepan of boiling water; remove immediately. Rinse under cold water; pat dry with absorbent paper.

4 Place leaves on work surface. Combine chilli, lime leaves, onion, coriander and basil in medium bowl. Halve lemon grass sticks lengthways, then halve crossways; you will have eight pieces.

5 Place two pieces cut lemon grass on each leaf; place one fish on each. Top fish with equal amounts of herb mixture, fold opposite corners of the leaf to enclose centre part of fish; secure each parcel with cotton string.

6 Place parcels, in single layer, in large bamboo steamer; steam, covered, in two batches, over wok or large frying pan of simmering water about 15 minutes or until fish is cooked through. Serve fish still in parcel, sprinkled with remaining dressing.

per serving 21.8g total fat (6g saturated fat); 1697kJ; (406 cal); 4.2g carbohydrate; 48g protein; 1.4g fibre
TIPS If bream is unavailable, use any of your favourite whole firm-fleshed fish for this recipe. Cooking times will vary depending on the fish you select.
Banana leaves are sold in bundles, trimmed, in the vegetable section of most supermarkets. If you can't find them, use trimmed coconut palm leaves or even line your steamer and cover the fish with corn cob husks. Foil can be used if it's pierced in a few places to allow the steam to permeate the fish.
Fish parcels can also be cooked on a barbecue or grill plate about 15 minutes or until fish is cooked as desired.

Scoring the fish helps the lime and chilli dressing to permeate the flesh and infuse it with flavour.

Banana leaves must be softened in boiling water to become pliable enough to wrap fish without tearing.

red snapper parcels with caper anchovy salsa

preparation time 30 minutes
cooking time 15 minutes
serves 4

1 baby fennel bulb (130g), sliced thinly
2 cloves garlic, crushed
4 x 200g red snapper fillets
4 large fresh basil leaves
⅓ cup (80ml) dry white wine
¼ cup coarsely chopped fresh chives
⅓ cup loosely packed fresh tarragon leaves
⅓ cup loosely packed fresh basil leaves
½ cup loosely packed fresh chervil leaves
30g watercress, trimmed
1 tablespoon lemon juice
1 teaspoon olive oil

CAPER ANCHOVY SALSA
1 small red capsicum (150g), chopped finely
2 tablespoons finely chopped seeded
   kalamata olives
1 tablespoon drained baby capers, rinsed
8 drained anchovy fillets, chopped finely
¼ cup finely chopped fresh basil
1 tablespoon balsamic vinegar

1 Preheat oven to hot (220°C/200°C fan-forced).
2 Combine fennel and garlic in small bowl.
3 Place each fillet, skin-side down, on a square of lightly oiled foil large enough to completely enclose fish. Divide fennel mixture among fillets, top each with 1 basil leaf and drizzle with 1 tablespoon of the wine. Gather corners of foil together above each fish; twist to enclose securely.
4 Place parcels on oven tray; bake 15 minutes or until fish is cooked as desired.
5 Meanwhile, combine ingredients for caper anchovy salsa in small bowl.
6 Place herbs, watercress, juice and oil in medium bowl; toss gently to combine.
7 Unwrap parcels just before serving; divide fish, fennel-side up, among serving plates. Top with salsa; accompany with salad.
per serving 5.4g total fat (1.5g saturated fat); 1078kJ (258 cal); 4.3g carbohydrate; 44g protein; 2g fibre
SERVING SUGGESTION Serve with sliced steamed pontiac potatoes.

singapore chilli crab

preparation time 45 minutes (plus standing time)
cooking time 35 minutes
serves 4

2 whole uncooked mud crabs (1.5kg)
2 tablespoons peanut oil
1 fresh long red chilli, chopped finely
2 cloves garlic, crushed
2cm piece fresh ginger (10g), grated
⅓ cup (80ml) chinese cooking wine
400g can crushed tomatoes
1 cup (250ml) water
1 tablespoon brown sugar
2 lebanese cucumbers (260g), halved lengthways,
   sliced thinly
10cm piece fresh ginger (50g), sliced thinly
3 green onions, sliced thinly
¼ cup loosely packed fresh coriander leaves
2 fresh long red chillies, seeded, sliced thinly

1 Place crabs in large container filled with ice and water; stand about 1 hour. Prepare crabs, leaving flesh in claws and legs. Using cleaver or heavy knife, chop each body into sixths.
2 Heat oil in wok; stir-fry chopped chilli, garlic and grated ginger until fragrant. Add wine; cook until liquid has reduced by half. Add undrained tomatoes, the water and sugar; bring to a boil. Reserve half of the sauce in small bowl.
3 Add half of the crab to wok, reduce heat; simmer, covered, about 15 minutes or until crab has changed in colour. Stir in half of the cucumber. Transfer to large serving bowl; cover to keep warm. Repeat with reserved sauce, remaining crab and cucumber.
4 Cut sliced ginger into thin strips. Combine with onion, coriander and sliced chilli; sprinkle over crab. Serve with steamed jasmine rice, if desired.
per serving 10.6g total fat (1.8g saturated fat); 1070kJ (256 cal); 11.7g carbohydrate; 23.8g protein; 3g fibre
TIP Provide finger bowls filled with warm water and lemon slices – and plenty of napkins – with this dish.

tuna skewers with soba

preparation time 20 minutes
cooking time 10 minutes
serves 4

2 tablespoons olive oil
3 teaspoons wasabi paste
1 teaspoon ground coriander
800g tuna steaks, diced into 2cm pieces
⅓ cup finely chopped fresh coriander
300g dried soba noodles
1 medium carrot (120g), cut into matchsticks
4 green onions, sliced thickly
¼ cup firmly packed fresh coriander leaves

MIRIN DRESSING
¼ cup (60ml) mirin
2 tablespoons soy sauce
1cm piece fresh ginger (5g), grated
1 teaspoon sesame oil
1 teaspoon fish sauce
1 teaspoon sugar

1 Combine oil, wasabi and ground coriander in large bowl; add tuna, toss to coat in marinade. Thread tuna onto eight skewers; sprinkle with chopped coriander.
2 Cook soba in large saucepan of boiling water, uncovered, until just tender; drain. Rinse under cold water; drain.
3 Meanwhile, place ingredients for mirin dressing in screw-top jar; shake well.
4 Combine soba in large bowl with carrot, onion, coriander leaves and half of the dressing.
5 Cook skewers on heated oiled grill plate (or grill or barbecue), uncovered, until cooked as desired. Serve skewers on noodles, drizzled with remaining dressing.
per serving 22.5g total fat (6.2g saturated fat); 2817kJ (674 cal); 55g carbohydrate; 59.8g protein; 3.7g fibre
TIP If using bamboo skewers, soak them in cold water for 1 hour before use to prevent them from splintering or scorching.

balmain bugs and citrus salad

preparation time 20 minutes
cooking time 15 minutes
serves 4

2kg uncooked balmain bugs
1 tablespoon olive oil
2 tablespoons orange juice
2 teaspoons finely grated orange rind
1 tablespoon wholegrain mustard

CITRUS SALAD
1 medium grapefruit (425g)
1 large orange (300g)
1 lemon (140g)
150g curly endive, chopped coarsely
1 large fennel bulb (550g), trimmed, sliced thinly
1 tablespoon wholegrain mustard
1 tablespoon olive oil

1 Make citrus salad.
2 Place balmain bugs upside down on chopping board; cut tail from body, discard body. Halve tail lengthways; discard back vein. Cook bugs on heated oiled grill plate (or grill or barbecue), uncovered, until cooked through.
3 Place bugs in large bowl with combined oil, juice, rind and mustard; toss bugs to coat in mixture. Serve with citrus salad.
CITRUS SALAD
Cut unpeeled grapefruit, orange and lemon into equal size wedges; cook on heated oiled grill plate, uncovered, until browned. Place fruit in large bowl with endive, fennel and combined mustard and oil; toss gently to combine.
per serving 11g total fat (1.6g saturated fat); 1233kJ (295 cal); 11.8g carbohydrate; 36g protein; 5.3g fibre

Casseroles
and Curries

Every mother (or cooking father)
of a family knows that casseroles
and curries have two lovable
characteristics: you can make them
today and serve them tomorrow,
and they are better made with cheap
than with expensive cuts of meat.
Cooking ahead gives the flavours
time to deepen and blend, while
cheap cuts are better because their
high content of connective tissue,
which makes them tough if grilled,
softens to gelatinous richness with
long, slow cooking. Best of all, these
are among the world's great dishes,
as splendidly right for a dinner party
as for the family.

beef massaman curry

lamb and lentil curry

maple syrup-glazed lamb shanks

chicken panang curry

beef massaman curry

preparation time 20 minutes
cooking time 2 hours
serves 4

1kg beef skirt steak, cut into 3cm pieces
2 x 400ml cans coconut milk
1½ cups (375ml) beef stock
¼ teaspoon ground clove
2 star anise
5 cardamom pods, bruised
1 tablespoon grated palm sugar
2 tablespoons fish sauce
1 tablespoon tamarind concentrate
2 tablespoons massaman curry paste
2 teaspoons tamarind concentrate, extra
½ cup (125ml) beef stock, extra
8 baby brown onions (300g), halved
1 medium kumara (400g), chopped coarsely
¼ cup (35g) coarsely chopped unsalted
    roasted peanuts
2 green onions, sliced thinly

1 Place beef, half of the coconut milk, stock, clove, star anise, cardamom, sugar, sauce and tamarind in large saucepan; bring to a boil. Reduce heat; simmer, uncovered, about 1 hour 30 minutes or until beef is almost tender.
2 Strain beef over large bowl; reserve spicy beef sauce, discard star anise and cardamom.
3 Place curry paste in same cleaned pan; stir over heat until fragrant. Add remaining coconut milk, extra tamarind and extra stock; bring to a boil, stir about 1 minute or until mixture is smooth. Add beef, brown onion, kumara and 1 cup of reserved spicy beef sauce; cook, uncovered, about 30 minutes or until vegetables and beef are tender.
4 Place curry in serving bowl; sprinkle with peanuts and green onion.
per serving 55.6g total fat (39.8g saturated fat); 3699kJ (885 cals); 30g carbohydrate; 68g protein; 8.3g fibre

lamb and lentil curry

preparation time 15 minutes
cooking time 55 minutes
serves 4

1 cup (200g) yellow split peas
1 tablespoon olive oil
600g lamb fillets, diced into 4cm pieces
2 large brown onions (400g), sliced thinly
5cm piece fresh ginger (25g), chopped finely
2 cloves garlic, crushed
2 tablespoons ground coriander
1 tablespoon sweet paprika
½ teaspoon cayenne pepper
200g yogurt
2 medium tomatoes (300g), chopped coarsely
1¾ cups (430ml) chicken stock
⅔ cup (160ml) light coconut cream
150g baby spinach leaves
⅓ cup coarsely chopped fresh coriander

1 Cook split peas in medium saucepan of boiling water, uncovered, until just tender; drain.
2 Meanwhile, heat half of the oil in large saucepan; cook lamb, in batches, stirring, until cooked as desired. Drain on absorbent paper.
3 Heat remaining oil in same pan; cook onion, stirring, about 15 minutes or until caramelised. Add ginger, garlic, ground coriander, paprika and cayenne; cook, stirring, until fragrant. Add yogurt; cook 5 minutes, without boiling, stirring occasionally.
4 Add tomato, stock and coconut cream; bring to a boil. Reduce heat; simmer, uncovered, about 15 minutes or until sauce thickens slightly.
5 Return lamb to pan with split peas and spinach; cook, stirring, until heated through. Remove from heat; stir in fresh coriander.
per serving 19.3g total fat (9.8g saturated fat); 2153kJ (515 cal); 33.5g carbohydrate; 51.7g protein; 8.9g fibre

maple syrup-glazed lamb shanks

preparation time 10 minutes
cooking time 2 hours
serves 4

⅓ cup (80ml) pure maple syrup
1 cup (250ml) chicken stock
1 tablespoon dijon mustard
1½ cups (375ml) orange juice
8 french-trimmed lamb shanks (2kg)

ROAST POTATOES
6 medium potatoes (1.2kg), halved
2 tablespoons olive oil

1 Combine syrup, stock, mustard and juice in large deep flameproof casserole dish; add lamb, toss to coat in syrup mixture. Bring to a boil then cover tightly. Reduce heat; cook lamb, turning every 20 minutes, about 2 hours or until lamb is tender.
2 Meanwhile, make roast potatoes.
3 Serve lamb with roast potatoes and, if desired, just-wilted baby spinach leaves.
ROAST POTATOES
Preheat oven to hot (220°C/200°C fan-forced). Lightly oil oven tray. Boil, steam or microwave potatoes 5 minutes; drain. Pat dry with absorbent paper; cool 10 minutes. Gently rake rounded sides of potatoes with tines of fork; place potato in single layer, cut-side down, on prepared oven tray. Brush with oil; roast, uncovered, about 50 minutes or until potatoes are browned lightly and crisp.
per serving (incl. potatoes) 14.6g total fat (3.7g saturated fat); 2805kJ (671 cals); 65.3g carbohydrate; 68.3g protein; 5.1g fibre

chicken panang curry

preparation time 15 minutes
cooking time 20 minutes
serves 4

2 x 400ml cans coconut milk
3 tablespoons panang curry paste
2 tablespoons grated palm sugar
2 tablespoons fish sauce
2 fresh kaffir lime leaves, torn
2 tablespoons peanut oil
1kg chicken thigh fillets, quartered
100g snake beans, chopped coarsely
½ cup firmly packed fresh thai basil leaves
½ cup (75g) coarsely chopped roasted
  unsalted peanuts
2 fresh long red thai chillies, sliced thinly

1 Place coconut milk, paste, sugar, sauce and lime leaves in wok; bring to a boil. Reduce heat; simmer, stirring, about 15 minutes or until sauce mixture reduces by about one-third.
2 Meanwhile, heat oil in large frying pan; cook chicken, in batches, until browned lightly. Drain on absorbent paper.
3 Add beans, chicken and half of the basil leaves to wok; cook, uncovered, stirring occasionally, about 5 minutes or until beans are just tender and chicken is cooked through.
4 Place curry in serving bowl; sprinkle with peanuts, chilli and remaining basil.
per serving 82.9g total fat (45g saturated fat); 4326kJ (1035 cal); 17.9g carbohydrate; 57.6g protein; 7.9g fibre
TIP If panang curry paste is hard to find, use any thai curry paste of your choice.

braised lamb shanks with white bean puree

preparation time 40 minutes
cooking time 2 hours 10 minutes
serves 4

1 tablespoon olive oil
8 french-trimmed lamb shanks (2kg)
1 large red onion (300g), chopped coarsely
2 cloves garlic, crushed
1 cup (250ml) chicken stock
2 cups (500ml) water
400g can diced tomatoes
1 tablespoon fresh rosemary leaves
4 anchovy fillets, drained, chopped coarsely
2 large red capsicums (700g)
2 large green capsicums (700g)

WHITE BEAN PUREE
20g butter
1 small brown onion (80g), chopped finely
1 clove garlic, crushed
¼ cup (60ml) dry white wine
¾ cup (180ml) chicken stock
2 x 400g cans white beans, rinsed, drained
2 tablespoons cream

1 Heat oil in large deep saucepan; cook lamb, in batches, until browned all over.
2 Cook onion and garlic in same pan, stirring, until onion softens. Add stock, the water, undrained tomatoes, rosemary and anchovy; bring to a boil. Return lamb to pan, reduce heat; simmer, covered, 1 hour, stirring occasionally. Uncover; simmer about 45 minutes or until lamb is tender.
3 Meanwhile, quarter capsicums; discard seeds and membranes. Roast under hot grill or in very hot oven, skin-side up, until skin blisters and blackens. Cover capsicum with plastic wrap or paper for 5 minutes; peel away skin, slice thickly.
4 Meanwhile, make white bean puree.
5 Add capsicum to lamb; cook, uncovered, 5 minutes. Serve lamb on white bean puree.
WHITE BEAN PUREE
Melt butter in medium frying pan; cook onion and garlic, stirring, until onion softens. Add wine; cook, stirring, until liquid is reduced by half. Add stock and beans; bring to a boil. Reduce heat; simmer, uncovered, about 10 minutes or until liquid is almost evaporated. Blend or process bean mixture and cream until smooth.
per serving 18.8g total fat (8.4g saturated fat); 2312kJ (553 cals); 21g carbohydrate; 72.1g protein; 8.6 fibre

Rest the browned lamb shanks on a tray to catch any of their juices; return both shanks and juices to saucepan with the rest of the braising ingredients.

Wrapping the hot charred capsicum in paper creates steam which assists in loosening and lifting the skin, making peeling an easy task once capsicums cool.

chicken tagine with olives and preserved lemon

preparation time 15 minutes
cooking time 45 minutes
serves 4

1 tablespoon olive oil
10g butter
8 chicken thigh cutlets (1.3kg), skinned
1 large red onion (300g), chopped finely
½ teaspoon saffron threads, toasted, crushed
1 teaspoon ground cinnamon
1 teaspoon ground ginger
1½ cups (375ml) chicken stock
16 seeded large green olives (120g)
2 tablespoons finely chopped preserved lemon

1 Heat oil and butter in large heavy-based saucepan with tight-fitting lid; cook chicken, in batches, until browned all over.
2 Place onion and spices in same pan; cook, stirring, until onion softens. Return chicken to pan with stock; bring to a boil. Reduce heat; simmer, covered, about 30 minutes or until chicken is cooked through.
3 Remove chicken from pan; cover to keep warm. Skim and discard fat from top of sauce; bring to a boil. Reduce heat; cook, stirring, until sauce reduces by half.
4 Return chicken to pan with olives and lemon; stir over medium heat until heated through.
per serving 25.6g total fat (8.5g saturated fat); 1889kJ (452 cal); 11.5g carbohydrate; 44.6g protein; 1.3g fibre

pork vindaloo

preparation time 20 minutes (plus standing time)
cooking time 1 hour 30 minutes
serves 4

1 tablespoon vegetable oil
1kg pork neck, cut into 3cm pieces
2 large brown onions (400g), sliced thinly
1 cup (250ml) vegetable stock

VINDALOO PASTE
2 teaspoons ground cumin
1 teaspoon chilli powder
2 teaspoons black mustard seeds
1½ teaspoons ground cinnamon
⅓ cup (80ml) white wine vinegar
1 teaspoon salt
1 teaspoon sugar
1 teaspoon ground cardamom
2 teaspoons ground turmeric
½ teaspoon ground cloves
1 teaspoon cracked black pepper
3 cloves garlic, crushed
1½ teaspoons ground ginger

MANGO SAMBAL
1 medium mango (430g), chopped finely
1 fresh red thai chilli, chopped finely
1 tablespoon lemon juice
1 tablespoon finely chopped fresh mint

1 Combine ingredients for vindaloo paste in small bowl; stand 30 minutes before using.
2 Heat oil in large saucepan; cook pork, in batches, until browned all over.
3 Cook onion in same pan, stirring, until soft. Add vindaloo paste; cook, stirring, until fragrant. Add stock; return pork to pan. Bring to a boil. Reduce heat to low; simmer, covered, stirring occasionally, about 1 hour or until pork is tender.
4 Meanwhile, combine ingredients for mango sambal in small bowl. Cover, refrigerate at least 1 hour.
5 Serve vindaloo with mango sambal.
per serving 25.2g total fat (7.5g saturated fat); 2157kJ (516 cal); 15.4g carbohydrate; 56.1g protein; 3g fibre
TIP Pork vindaloo can be made a day ahead and refrigerated, covered, or frozen for up to 3 months.

braised sweet ginger duck

preparation time 20 minutes
cooking time 1 hour 50 minutes
serves 4

2kg duck
3 cups (750ml) water
½ cup (125ml) chinese cooking wine
⅓ cup (80ml) soy sauce
¼ cup (55g) firmly packed brown sugar
1 whole star anise
3 green onions, halved
3 cloves garlic, quartered
10cm piece fresh ginger (50g), unpeeled,
   chopped coarsely
2 teaspoons sea salt
1 teaspoon five-spice powder
800g baby bok choy, halved

1 Preheat oven to moderate (180°C/160°C fan-forced).
2 Discard neck from duck, wash duck; pat dry with absorbent paper. Score duck in thickest parts of skin; cut duck in half through breastbone and along both sides of backbone, discard backbone. Tuck wings under duck.
3 Place duck, skin-side down, in medium shallow baking dish; add combined water, wine, sauce, sugar, star anise, onion, garlic and ginger. Roast, covered, about 1 hour or until duck is cooked as desired.
4 Increase oven temperature to hot (220°C/200°C fan-forced). Remove duck from braising liquid; strain liquid through muslin-lined sieve into large saucepan. Place duck, skin-side up, on wire rack in same dish. Rub combined salt and five-spice all over duck; roast duck, uncovered, about 30 minutes or until skin is crisp.
5 Skim fat from surface of braising liquid; bring to a boil. Reduce heat; simmer, uncovered, 10 minutes. Add bok choy; simmer, covered, about 5 minutes or until bok choy is just tender.
6 Cut duck halves into two pieces; divide bok choy, braising liquid and duck among plates. Serve with steamed jasmine rice, if desired.
per serving 105.7g total fat (31.7g saturated fat); 4974kJ (1190 cals); 7.9g carbohydrate; 40.8g protein; 3.5g fibre

braised oxtail with orange gremolata

preparation time 20 minutes
cooking time 3 hours 15 minutes
serves 4

1.5kg oxtails, cut into 5cm pieces
2 tablespoons plain flour
2 tablespoons olive oil
1 medium brown onion (150g), chopped
2 cloves garlic, crushed
½ cup (125ml) sweet sherry
400g can crushed tomatoes
1 cup (250ml) beef stock
1 cup (250ml) water
4 sprigs fresh thyme
2 bay leaves
10cm strip orange rind
4 medium tomatoes (600g), chopped

ORANGE GREMOLATA
¼ cup finely chopped fresh flat-leaf parsley
1 tablespoon finely grated orange rind
1 clove garlic, crushed

1 Preheat oven to moderately slow (170°C/150°C fan-forced).
2 Coat oxtail in flour; shake off excess. Heat half of the oil in large flameproof casserole dish; cook oxtail pieces, in batches, until browned all over.
3 Heat remaining oil in same dish; cook onion and garlic, stirring, until onion softens. Return oxtails to dish with sherry, undrained tomatoes, stock, the water, herbs and rind, cover; bake, uncovered, about 3 hours or until oxtail is tender. Stir in chopped tomato.
4 Meanwhile, combine ingredients for orange gremolata in small bowl.
5 Serve oxtail sprinkled with gremolata on mashed potato, if desired.
per serving 110.2g total fat (40g saturated fat); 5656 kJ (1353 cals); 15.8g carbohydrate; 69.5g protein; 4.1g fibre

braised beef cheeks in red wine

preparation time 20 minutes
cooking time 3 hours 10 minutes
serves 4

2 tablespoons olive oil
1.6kg beef cheeks, trimmed
1 medium brown onion (150g), chopped coarsely
1 medium carrot (120g), chopped coarsely
3 cups (750ml) dry red wine
¼ cup (60ml) red wine vinegar
2 x 400g cans whole tomatoes
¼ cup (55g) firmly packed brown sugar
2 sprigs fresh rosemary
6 black peppercorns
2 tablespoons fresh oregano leaves
1 large fennel bulb (550g), cut into thin wedges
400g spring onions, trimmed, halved
200g swiss brown mushrooms

CHEESY POLENTA
2⅓ (580ml) cups water
2⅓ (580ml) cups milk
1 cup (170g) polenta
½ cup (40g) finely grated parmesan
30g butter

1 Preheat oven to moderately slow (170°C/150°C fan-forced).
2 Heat half of the oil in large flameproof casserole dish; cook beef, in batches, until browned all over.
3 Heat remaining oil in same dish; cook brown onion and carrot, stirring, until onion softens. Return beef to dish with wine, vinegar, undrained tomatoes, sugar, rosemary, peppercorns, oregano and fennel; bring to a boil. Cover; bake 2 hours.
4 Stir in spring onion and mushrooms; cook, uncovered, about 45 minutes or until beef is tender.
5 Meanwhile, make cheesy polenta; serve with beef.
CHEESY POLENTA
Combine water and milk in large saucepan; bring to a boil. Gradually add polenta to liquid, stirring constantly. Reduce heat; simmer, stirring, about 10 minutes or until polenta thickens. Stir in cheese and butter.
per serving (incl. polenta) 39.8g total fat (16.2g saturated fat); 4828kJ (1155 cals); 67.1g carbohydrate; 100.8g protein; 10.3g fibre

cassoulet

preparation time 40 minutes (plus standing time)
cooking time 2 hours 10 minutes
serves 6

1½ cups (300g) dried white beans
300g boned pork belly, rind removed, sliced thinly
150g piece streaky bacon, rind removed,
   diced into 1cm pieces
800g piece boned lamb shoulder,
   diced into 3cm pieces
1 large brown onion (200g), chopped finely
1 small leek (200g), sliced thinly
2 cloves garlic, crushed
3 sprigs fresh thyme
400g can crushed tomatoes
2 bay leaves
1 cup (250ml) water
1 cup (250ml) chicken stock
2 cups (140g) stale breadcrumbs
⅓ coarsely chopped fresh flat-leaf parsley

1 Place beans in medium bowl, cover with water; soak overnight, drain. Rinse under cold water; drain. Place beans in medium saucepan of boiling water; bring to a boil. Reduce heat; simmer, covered, about 15 minutes or until beans are just tender. Drain.
2 Preheat oven to moderately slow (170°C/150°C fan-forced).
3 Cook pork in large flameproof casserole dish over heat, pressing down with back of spoon on pork until browned all over; remove from dish. Cook bacon in same pan, stirring, until crisp; remove from dish. Cook lamb, in batches, in same pan, until browned all over.
4 Cook onion, leek and garlic in same dish, stirring, until onion softens. Add thyme, undrained tomatoes, bay leaves, the water, stock, beans and meat; bring to a boil. Cover; cook in oven 45 minutes. Remove from oven; sprinkle with combined breadcrumbs and parsley. Return to oven; cook, uncovered, about 45 minutes or until liquid is nearly absorbed and beans are tender.
per serving 27.6g total fat (10.8g saturated fat); 2324kJ (556 cal); 25.7g carbohydrate; 51.7g protein; 5.7g fibre

chicken green curry

preparation time 20 minutes
cooking time 20 minutes
serves 4

¼ cup (75g) green curry paste
2 x 400ml cans coconut milk
2 fresh kaffir lime leaves, torn
1kg chicken thigh fillets
2 tablespoons peanut oil
2 tablespoons fish sauce
2 tablespoons lime juice
1 tablespoon grated palm sugar
150g pea eggplants, quartered
1 small zucchini (150g), cut into 5cm pieces
½ cup loosely packed fresh thai basil leaves
¼ cup coarsely chopped fresh coriander
1 tablespoon fresh coriander leaves
1 long green thai chilli, sliced thinly
2 green onions, sliced thinly

1 Place curry paste in large saucepan; stir over heat until fragrant. Add coconut milk and lime leaves; bring to a boil. Reduce heat; simmer, stirring, 5 minutes.
2 Meanwhile, quarter chicken pieces. Heat oil in large frying pan; cook chicken, in batches, until just browned. Drain on absorbent paper.
3 Add chicken to curry mixture with sauce, juice, sugar and eggplants; simmer, covered, about 5 minutes or until eggplants are tender and chicken is cooked through. Add zucchini, basil and chopped coriander; cook, stirring, until zucchini is just tender.
4 Place curry in serving bowl; sprinkle with coriander leaves, sliced chilli and onion.
per serving 74.7g total fat (44.1g saturated fat); 3900kJ (933 cal); 14.6g carbohydrate; 53.3g protein; 7.4g fibre

Curry pastes have oil included as part of their content so there's no need to add any extra to the pan when you fry off the paste.

Quartering the chicken pieces before browning them ensures they'll cook through faster when mixed with the other ingredients.

Looking like a cluster of green grapes, only smaller, pea eggplants have to be pulled from their stems and then quartered before use.

braised spatchcock with peas and lettuce

preparation time 30 minutes
cooking time 1 hour
serves 6

3 x 500g spatchcocks
1 medium leek (350g)
2 bay leaves
1 sprig fresh thyme
1 sprig fresh rosemary
4 fresh flat-leaf parsley stalks
50g unsalted butter
2 cloves garlic, crushed
1 large brown onion (200g), chopped finely
8 bacon rashers (560g), rinds removed,
 chopped coarsely
¼ cup (35g) plain flour
1½ cups (375ml) dry white wine
3 cups (750ml) chicken stock
1.5kg potatoes, chopped coarsely
¾ cup (180ml) milk
50g unsalted butter
500g frozen peas
1 large butter lettuce, shredded finely
½ cup coarsely chopped fresh mint

1 Cut along both sides of spatchcocks' backbones; discard backbones. Cut in half between breasts. Rinse spatchcock halves under cold water; pat dry.
2 Cut leek in half crossways; chop white bottom half finely, reserve. Using kitchen string, tie green top half of leek, bay leaves, thyme, rosemary and parsley stalks into a bundle.
3 Heat butter in large saucepan; cook spatchcock, in batches, until browned lightly both sides. Cook reserved chopped leek, garlic, onion and bacon in same pan, stirring, about 10 minutes or until onion softens. Add flour; cook, stirring, 2 minutes. Gradually add wine and stock; bring to a boil, stirring constantly until mixture boils and thickens. Return spatchcock to pan with herb bundle, reduce heat; simmer, covered, 30 minutes.
4 Meanwhile, boil, steam or microwave potato until tender; drain. Mash potato with warmed milk and butter in large bowl until smooth. Cover to keep warm.
5 Discard herb bundle. Add peas, lettuce and mint to pan; simmer, uncovered, about 5 minutes or until peas are just tender. Divide mashed potato among serving plates; top with spatchcock mixture.
per serving 42.5g total fat (18.5g saturated fat); 3377kJ (808 cal); 45.7g carbohydrate; 49.9g protein; 12.6g fibre
TIPS Chicken pieces, quails or pigeons can be used rather than spatchcocks, if desired.
Spatchcock can be made ahead up to the end of step 3; cover, refrigerate overnight.

veal shin on mushroom ragoût

preparation time 15 minutes
cooking time 2 hours 25 minutes
serves 4

40g butter
4 pieces veal shin (osso buco) (1kg)
2 cloves garlic, crushed
1 tablespoon fresh rosemary leaves
½ cup (125ml) port
1 cup (250ml) beef stock

MUSHROOM RAGOUT
40g butter
2 cloves garlic, crushed
1 large flat mushroom (100g), sliced thickly
200g swiss brown mushrooms, trimmed
200g shiitake mushrooms, sliced thickly
1 medium red capsicum (200g), sliced thickly
1 medium green capsicum (200g), sliced thickly
½ cup (125ml) beef stock
2 tablespoons port

1 Preheat oven to moderately slow (170°C/150°C fan-forced).
2 Melt butter in medium flameproof casserole dish; cook veal, uncovered, until browned both sides. Add garlic, rosemary, port and stock; cover, bake 2¼ hours.
3 Meanwhile, make mushroom ragoût.
4 Divide veal and ragoût among serving dishes; serve with soft polenta, if desired.
MUSHROOM RAGOUT
Heat butter in large frying pan; cook garlic, mushrooms and capsicums, stirring, until vegetables are browned lightly and tender. Stir in stock and port; cook, covered, 30 minutes.
per serving 17.8g total fat (11.1g saturated fat); 1785kJ (427 cal); 16.2g carbohydrate; 41.1g protein; 4.3g fibre

beef and prune tagine with spinach couscous

preparation time 20 minutes
cooking time 2 hours 30 minutes
serves 4

2 large red onions (600g), chopped finely
2 tablespoons olive oil
1 teaspoon cracked black pepper
pinch saffron threads
1 teaspoon ground cinnamon
¼ teaspoon ground ginger
1kg beef blade steak, diced into 4cm pieces
50g butter, chopped
425g can diced tomatoes
1 cup (250ml) water
2 tablespoons white sugar
¾ cup (100g) toasted slivered almonds
1½ cups (250g) seeded prunes
1 teaspoon finely grated lemon rind
¼ teaspoon ground cinnamon, extra

SPINACH COUSCOUS
1½ cups (300g) couscous
1½ cups (375ml) boiling water
80g baby spinach leaves, shredded finely

1 Combine onion, oil, pepper, saffron, cinnamon and ginger in large bowl; add beef, toss to coat in mixture.
2 Place beef in large deep saucepan with butter, undrained tomatoes, the water, half of the sugar and ½ cup of the nuts; bring to a boil. Reduce heat; simmer, covered, 1½ hours. Remove 1 cup cooking liquid; reserve. Simmer tagine, uncovered, 30 minutes.
3 Meanwhile, place prunes in small bowl, cover with boiling water; stand 20 minutes, drain.
4 Place prunes in small saucepan with rind, extra cinnamon, remaining sugar and reserved cooking liquid; bring to a boil. Reduce heat; simmer, uncovered, about 15 minutes or until prunes soften. Stir into tagine.
5 Make spinach couscous.
6 Divide couscous and tagine among serving plates; sprinkle tagine with remaining nuts.

SPINACH COUSCOUS
Combine couscous with boiling water in large heatproof bowl, cover; stand for about 5 minutes or until water is absorbed, fluffing with fork occasionally. Stir in spinach.

per serving (incl. couscous) 50.5g total fat (16g saturated fat); 4780 kJ (1165 cal); 106g carbohydrate; 72.1g protein; 11.7g fibre

lamb and quince tagine with pistachio couscous

preparation time 20 minutes
cooking time 2 hours
serves 4

40g butter
600g diced lamb
1 medium red onion (170g), chopped coarsely
2 cloves garlic, crushed
1 cinnamon stick
2 teaspoons ground coriander
1 teaspoon ground cumin
1 teaspoon ground ginger
1 teaspoon dried chilli flakes
1½ cups (375ml) water
425g can crushed tomatoes
2 medium quinces (600g), quartered
1 large green zucchini (150g), chopped coarsely
2 tablespoons coarsely chopped fresh coriander

PISTACHIO COUSCOUS

1½ cups (300g) couscous
1 cup (250ml) boiling water
20g butter, softened
½ cup finely chopped fresh coriander
¼ cup (35g) toasted shelled pistachios,
   chopped coarsely

1 Melt butter in large saucepan; cook lamb, in batches, until browned. Add onion to same pan; cook, stirring, until softened. Add garlic, cinnamon, ground coriander, cumin, ginger and chilli; cook, stirring, until mixture is fragrant.
2 Return lamb to pan. Stir in the water, undrained tomatoes and quince; bring to a boil. Reduce heat; simmer, covered, 30 minutes. Uncover; simmer, stirring occasionally, about 1 hour or until quince is tender and sauce has thickened.
3 Add zucchini; cook, stirring, about 10 minutes or until zucchini is just tender.
4 Meanwhile, make pistachio couscous.
5 Serve tagine with couscous; sprinkle with coriander.
PISTACHIO COUSCOUS
Combine couscous with the water and butter in large heatproof bowl, cover; stand about 5 minutes or until water is absorbed, fluffing with fork occasionally. Stir in coriander and nuts.

per serving 31g total fat (14.7g saturated fat); 3214kJ (769 cal); 76.7g carbohydrate; 45.4g protein; 12.3g fibre

osso buco with caper gremolata

preparation time 25 minutes
cooking time 2 hours 45 minutes
serves 4

8 pieces veal shin (osso buco) (2kg)
2 tablespoons plain flour
¼ cup (60ml) olive oil
1 medium brown onion (150g), chopped coarsely
2 cloves garlic, crushed
3 trimmed celery stalks (300g), chopped coarsely
2 large carrots (360g), chopped coarsely
2 x 400g cans crushed tomatoes
2 tablespoons tomato paste
1 cup (250ml) dry white wine
1 cup (250ml) beef stock
3 sprigs fresh thyme

CAPER GREMOLATA

1 tablespoon finely grated lemon rind
⅓ cup finely chopped fresh flat-leaf parsley
2 cloves garlic, chopped finely
1 tablespoon drained capers, rinsed, chopped finely

1 Toss veal in flour; shake away excess. Heat 2 tablespoons of the oil in large flameproof casserole dish; cook veal, in batches, until browned all over.
2 Heat remaining oil in same dish; cook onion, garlic, celery and carrot, stirring, until vegetables soften. Stir in undrained tomatoes, tomato paste, wine, stock and thyme.
3 Return veal to dish, fitting pieces upright and tightly together in single layer; bring to a boil. Reduce heat; simmer, covered, 2 hours. Uncover; cook further 30 minutes or until veal is almost falling off the bone.
4 Combine ingredients for caper gremolata in small bowl.
5 Divide veal among serving plates; top with sauce, sprinkle with caper gremolata. Serve with soft polenta, if desired.

per serving 15.9g total fat (2.3g saturated fat); 2378kJ (569 cal); 20.1g carbohydrate; 74.9g protein; 8.1g fibre

Roasts

Ask 10 people to name their favourite meal and it's good odds that at least seven will say a roast. This is the chapter to turn to when you want to delight diners from grandparents to the very young. It's also the chapter to remember when you don't have a lot of time: once in the oven, a roast will largely look after itself while you get on with other things. And after you take it out, it not only can but should be left to rest unattended for at least another 15 minutes, to allow the juices to settle.

lamb shanks in five-spice, tamarind and ginger

slow-roasted greek lamb

asian mini lamb roasts

veal rack with rosemary and rocket pesto

lamb shanks in five-spice, tamarind and ginger

preparation time 20 minutes
cooking time 2 hours 10 minutes
serves 4

2 teaspoons five-spice powder
1 teaspoon dried chilli flakes
1 cinnamon stick
2 star anise
¼ cup (60ml) soy sauce
½ cup (125ml) chinese rice wine
2 tablespoons tamarind concentrate
2 tablespoons brown sugar
8cm piece fresh ginger (40g), grated
2 cloves garlic, chopped coarsely
1¼ cups (310ml) water
8 french-trimmed lamb shanks (1.6kg)
500g choy sum, chopped into 10cm lengths
350g gai larn, trimmed

1 Preheat oven to moderate (180°C/160°C fan-forced).
2 Dry-fry five-spice, chilli, cinnamon and star anise in small heated frying pan, stirring, until fragrant.
3 Combine spices with sauce, wine, tamarind, sugar, ginger, garlic and the water in medium jug.
4 Place lamb, in single layer, in large shallow baking dish; drizzle with spice mixture. Bake, covered, turning occasionally, about 2 hours or until meat is almost falling off the bone. Remove lamb from dish; cover to keep warm. Skim away excess fat; strain sauce into small saucepan.
5 Boil, steam or microwave choy sum and gai larn, separately, until tender; drain.
6 Bring sauce to a boil; boil, uncovered, 2 minutes. Divide vegetables among serving plates; serve with lamb, drizzle with sauce.

per serving 20g total fat (9g saturated fat); 1906kJ (456 cal); 12g carbohydrate; 49.3 protein; 5.6g fibre

slow-roasted greek lamb

preparation time 30 minutes
cooking time 3 hours 45 minutes
serves 4

2kg leg of lamb
3 cloves garlic, quartered
¼ cup loosely packed fresh oregano
½ cup (125ml) dry white wine
1 cup (250ml) chicken stock
⅓ cup (80ml) lemon juice
1kg tiny new potatoes, quartered lengthways
2 medium lemons (280g), quartered
⅔ cup (80g) black olives, seeded
1 tablespoon olive oil
2 tablespoons plain flour
1 cup (250ml) water

1 Preheat oven to hot (220°C/200°C fan-forced). Using sharp knife, pierce 12 cuts into lamb; press garlic and oregano into cuts.
2 Place lamb in large flameproof baking dish; pour wine, stock and juice over lamb. Roast, covered tightly, 30 minutes. Reduce oven temperature to moderately slow (160°C/140°C fan-forced); roast lamb, covered tightly, brushing occasionally with pan juices, further 3 hours or until lamb is extremely tender.
3 Meanwhile, place potato, lemon and olives in separate large baking dish; drizzle with oil. When lamb has about 1 hour left to roast, place baking dish with potato mixture in oven; roast, uncovered, until browned and tender.
4 Transfer lamb to serving dish; cover to keep warm.
5 Heat 1 tablespoon of the reserved lamb juices in same flameproof baking dish; stir in flour. Cook, stirring, until mixture is well browned. Gradually stir in remaining lamb juices and the water; stir until gravy boils and thickens.
6 Slice lamb; serve with potato mixture and gravy.

per serving 32.5g total fat (12.8g saturated fat); 3946kJ (944 cal); 38.2g carbohydrate; 117.5g protein; 5.3g fibre

asian mini lamb roasts

preparation time 15 minutes (plus standing time)
cooking time 30 minutes
serves 4

2 lamb mini roasts (700g)
2 tablespoons kecap manis
1 tablespoon sesame seeds
2 cloves garlic, crushed
2 teaspoons sesame oil
1 teaspoon grated fresh ginger
1 small red capsicum (150g), sliced thinly
600g gai larn, chopped coarsely
⅓ cup (80ml) oyster sauce
2 tablespoons water
1 tablespoon lime juice

1 Preheat oven to moderately hot (200°C/180°C fan-forced).
2 Cook lamb, uncovered, in heated, lightly oiled wok or large frying pan about 5 minutes or until browned. Place lamb on oiled wire rack in baking dish; brush with combined kecap manis, sesame seeds and half of the garlic. Roast lamb, uncovered, about 25 minutes or until cooked as desired. Cover; stand 5 minutes, slice thickly.
3 Meanwhile, heat oil in same wok; stir-fry ginger and remaining garlic until fragrant. Add remaining ingredients; stir-fry until gai larn is just wilted.
4 Serve lamb on gai larn mixture; drizzle with sauce from wok.

per serving 21.4g total fat (7.7g saturated fat); 1668kJ (399 cal); 8.1g carbohydrate; 43.3g protein; 6.8g fibre

veal rack with rosemary and rocket pesto

preparation time 15 minutes
cooking time 1 hour 5 minutes (plus standing time)
serves 4

1kg tiny new potatoes
1 clove garlic, quartered
50g baby rocket leaves
¼ cup (60ml) extra virgin olive oil
¼ cup coarsely chopped fresh rosemary
1kg veal rack (8 cutlets)
½ cup (40g) finely grated parmesan
1 tablespoon plain flour
¾ cup (180ml) beef stock
¼ cup (60ml) dry white wine
1 tablespoon redcurrant jelly
500g asparagus, trimmed

1 Preheat oven to moderately hot (200°C/180°C fan-forced). Lightly oil shallow medium baking dish.
2 Place potatoes in prepared baking dish; roast, uncovered, about 50 minutes or until tender.
3 Meanwhile, blend or process garlic, rocket, oil and 2 tablespoons of the rosemary until mixture forms a paste. Stir remaining rosemary into pesto.
4 Place veal rack on wire rack over large shallow flameproof baking dish; coat veal with pesto. Roast, uncovered, about 40 minutes or until veal is browned and cooked as desired. Remove veal from dish; cover to keep warm.
5 When potatoes are tender, sprinkle with cheese; roast, uncovered, about 5 minutes or until cheese melts.
6 Place flameproof baking dish holding veal juices over heat, add flour; cook, stirring, until mixture thickens and bubbles. Gradually add stock, wine and jelly, stirring, until sauce boils and thickens slightly.
7 Meanwhile, boil, steam or microwave asparagus until just tender; drain.
8 Serve veal, sliced into cutlets, with potatoes, asparagus and sauce.

per serving 21.2g total fat (5.2g saturated fat); 2374kJ (568 cal); 40.5g carbohydrate; 50.3g protein; 6.6g fibre

roasted pork belly with plum sauce

preparation time 20 minutes
cooking time 1 hour 55 minutes
serves 4

800g boned pork belly, rind-on
2 teaspoons salt
1 teaspoon olive oil
1 cup (250ml) water
1½ cups (375ml) chicken stock
2 tablespoons soy sauce
¼ cup (60ml) chinese cooking wine
¼ cup (55g) firmly packed brown sugar
2 cloves garlic, sliced thinly
3cm piece fresh ginger (15g), sliced thinly
1 cinnamon stick, crushed
1 teaspoon dried chilli flakes
⅓ cup (80ml) orange juice
6 whole cloves
1 teaspoon fennel seeds
4 plums (450g), cut into eight wedges

CUCUMBER SALAD
1 lebanese cucumber (130g)
1 long green chilli, sliced thinly
⅔ cup coarsely chopped fresh mint
1 tablespoon olive oil
1 tablespoon lemon juice
1 teaspoon caster sugar

1 Preheat oven to moderate (180°C/160°C fan-forced).
2 Place pork on board, rind-side up. Using sharp knife, score rind by making shallow cuts diagonally in both directions at 3cm intervals; rub combined salt and oil into cuts.
3 Combine the water, stock, sauce, wine, sugar, garlic, ginger, cinnamon, chilli, juice, cloves and fennel in large shallow baking dish. Place pork in dish, rind-side up; roast, uncovered, 1 hour 20 minutes. Increase oven temperature to very hot (240°C/220°C fan-forced). Roast pork, uncovered, further 15 minutes or until crackling is crisp.
4 Remove pork from dish; cover to keep warm. Strain liquid in baking dish into medium saucepan, skim away surface fat; bring to a boil. Add plum, reduce heat; simmer, uncovered, about 15 minutes or until plum sauce thickens.
5 Meanwhile, make cucumber salad.
6 Serve thickly sliced pork with plum sauce and salad.
CUCUMBER SALAD
Using vegetable peeler, cut cucumber lengthways into ribbons. Place cucumber in large bowl with remaining ingredients; toss gently to combine.
per serving 51g total fat (16.2g saturated fat); 3010kJ (720 cal); 25.6g carbohydrate; 39.1g protein; 3.4g fibre

Scoring the pork breaks up the fat up so that the salt and oil rubbed into the cuts permeate deep into the meat and give it flavour.

The pork should be cooked with the scored side facing up to guarantee that the crackling emerges from the oven brown and crisp.

slow-roasted duck with sour cherry, apple and walnut salad

preparation time 40 minutes
cooking time 2 hours
serves 4

680g jar morello cherries
½ cup (125ml) chicken stock
½ cup (125ml) port
1 cinnamon stick
3 whole cloves
1 clove garlic, crushed
4 duck marylands (1.2kg), excess fat removed
2 small green apples (260g)
1 cup (100g) toasted walnuts, chopped coarsely
3 green onions, sliced thinly
1 cup firmly packed fresh flat-leaf parsley leaves
2 tablespoons olive oil
1 tablespoon lemon juice

1 Preheat oven to moderately slow (170°C/150°C fan-forced).
2 Strain cherries over small bowl. Combine cherry juice with stock, port, cinnamon, cloves and garlic in large baking dish. Place duck on metal rack over baking dish; cover tightly with oiled foil. Roast, covered, about 2 hours or until duck meat is tender. Strain pan liquid into large jug; skim away fat.
3 Cut apples into thin slices; cut slices into matchstick-sized pieces. Place apple and seeded cherries in large bowl with nuts, onion, parsley, oil and juice; toss gently to combine. Serve duck with salad and cherry sauce.
per serving 30.5g total fat (3.6g saturated fat); 1935kJ (463 cal); 26.1g carbohydrate; 15g protein; 5g fibre
TIP Do not slice apples until you're ready to assemble the salad or they will discolour.

roasted eye fillet with red wine risotto

preparation time 15 minutes
cooking time 40 minutes (plus standing time)
serves 4

500g piece eye fillet
1 tablespoon olive oil
1 teaspoon ground black pepper
¼ cup (60ml) dry red wine
½ cup (125ml) beef stock

RED WINE RISOTTO
3 cups (750ml) vegetable stock
40g butter
1 medium brown onion (150g), chopped finely
1 cup (200g) arborio rice
1 cup (250ml) dry red wine
¼ cup (20g) finely grated parmesan
3 green onions, sliced thinly

1 Preheat oven to moderately hot (200°C/180°C fan-forced).
2 Trim excess fat from fillet; tie fillet with kitchen string at 3cm intervals. Place fillet in lightly oiled shallow flameproof baking dish; brush all over with oil, sprinkle with pepper. Roast, uncovered, about 20 minutes or until cooked as desired.
3 Meanwhile, start making red wine risotto.
4 Remove fillet from dish, cover; stand 10 minutes. Place baking dish over low heat, add wine; simmer, stirring, about 2 minutes or until mixture reduces by half. Add stock; stir until sauce comes to a boil. Strain sauce into small jug. Serve sliced fillet with red wine risotto, drizzled with sauce.
RED WINE RISOTTO
Place stock in medium saucepan; bring to a boil. Reduce heat; simmer, covered. Heat half of the butter in large saucepan; cook brown onion, stirring, until softened. Add rice; stir to coat rice in onion mixture. Add wine; bring to a boil. Reduce heat; simmer, stirring, 2 minutes. Stir in ½ cup of the simmering stock; cook, stirring, over low heat, until liquid is absorbed. Continue adding stock mixture, in ½-cup batches, stirring until absorbed after each addition. Total cooking time should be 35 minutes or until rice is just tender. Add cheese, remaining butter and green onion, stirring until butter melts.
per serving 23g total fat (10.7g saturated fat); 2383kJ (570 cal); 43g carbohydrate; 34.9g protein; 1.2g fibre

raan with lemon pilau

preparation time 25 minutes (plus refrigeration time)
cooking time 2 hours 35 minutes
serves 6

2 teaspoons coriander seeds
1 teaspoon cumin seeds
5 cardamom pods, bruised
1 teaspoon chilli powder
1 teaspoon ground turmeric
1 cinnamon stick
2 cloves
2 star anise
1 medium brown onion (150g), chopped coarsely
4 cloves garlic, peeled
2cm piece fresh ginger (10g), grated finely
¼ cup (40g) blanched almonds
½ cup (140g) yogurt
2 tablespoons lemon juice
2kg leg of lamb, trimmed

LEMON PILAU
1 tablespoon vegetable oil
5 cardamom pods, bruised
4 cloves
1 cinnamon stick
¼ teaspoon saffron threads
2 cups (400g) white long-grain rice
3 cups (750ml) boiling water
⅓ cup (80ml) lemon juice
1 tablespoon sugar
20g butter
2 teaspoons finely grated lemon rind
2 tablespoons slivered toasted almonds

1 Dry-fry seeds, cardamom, chilli, turmeric, cinnamon, cloves and star anise in heated small frying pan, stirring, about 2 minutes or until fragrant. Blend or process spices with onion, garlic, ginger, nuts, yogurt and juice until mixture forms a paste.
2 Pierce lamb all over with sharp knife; place on wire rack in large shallow baking dish. Spread paste over lamb, pressing firmly into cuts. Cover; refrigerate overnight.
3 Preheat oven to moderately hot (200°C/180°C fan-forced). Remove lamb from refrigerator; pour enough water into baking dish to completely cover base. Cover dish with foil; roast 30 minutes. Reduce oven temperature to slow (150°C/130°C fan-forced); roast lamb, covered with foil, further 1½ hours. Remove foil; roast further 30 minutes or until lamb is cooked as desired.
4 Meanwhile, make lemon pilau.
5 Cover lamb; stand 10 minutes before slicing. Serve with pilau and, if desired, yogurt with coarsely chopped fresh coriander stirred through it.

LEMON PILAU
Heat oil in large saucepan; cook spices, stirring, about 1 minute or until fragrant. Add rice; stir until rice is coated in spice mixture. Add the water, juice and sugar; bring to a boil. Reduce heat; simmer rice, partially covered, about 10 minutes or until steam holes appear on surface. Reduce heat to as low as possible, cover tightly; steam 10 minutes (do not remove lid). Remove from heat; stand, covered, 10 minutes. Fluff with fork; stir in butter, rind and nuts before serving.
per serving 30.9g total fat (11.1g saturated fat); 3532kJ (845 cal); 58.8g carbohydrate; 82g protein; 2.2g fibre
TIP Lamb can be prepared to the end of step 2, up to two days ahead; cover, refrigerate or freeze if desired.

baked mustard pork with caramelised apple

preparation time 10 minutes
cooking time 25 minutes
serves 4

1 medium red onion (170g), cut into thin wedges
1 tablespoon olive oil
750g pork fillets, trimmed
½ cup (140g) honey dijon wholegrain mustard
½ cup (125ml) apple juice
⅓ cup (80ml) vegetable stock
¼ cup coarsely chopped fresh flat-leaf parsley
60g butter
4 large apples (800g), peeled, cored, sliced thinly
2 tablespoons brown sugar

1 Preheat oven to very hot (240°C/220°C fan-forced).
2 Combine onion and oil in large flameproof baking dish. Brush pork all over with mustard; place on onion in baking dish. Bake, uncovered, about 20 minutes or until cooked as desired. Remove pork from dish, cover; rest 5 minutes.
3 Place dish over heat; add juice and stock, bring to a boil. Reduce heat; simmer, uncovered, about 3 minutes or until sauce thickens slightly. Stir in parsley.
4 Meanwhile, melt butter in large frying pan. Add apple and sugar; cook, stirring occasionally, about 10 minutes or until almost caramelised. Cover to keep warm.
5 Slice pork thickly; serve with onion sauce and apple.
per serving 22.5g total fat (10.3g saturated fat); 2077kJ (497 cal); 30.5g carbohydrate; 44.5g protein; 4.8g fibre
SERVING SUGGESTION Accompany with a watercress salad, if desired.

spatchcocks with prosciutto and herb butter

preparation time 20 minutes
cooking time 50 minutes
serves 4

50g butter, softened
2 cloves garlic, crushed
2 tablespoons finely chopped fresh flat-leaf parsley
2 tablespoons finely chopped fresh basil
4 x 500g spatchcocks
12 sprigs fresh thyme
4 slices prosciutto (60g)
2 tablespoons olive oil
2 tablespoons lemon juice

1 Preheat oven to hot (220°C/200°C fan-forced).
2 Combine butter, garlic and herbs in small bowl.
3 Wash spatchcocks under cold water; pat dry with absorbent paper. Loosen skin of spatchcock by sliding fingers between skin and meat at neck joint; push an eighth of the herb butter under skin on spatchcock breast and spread evenly. Place one thyme sprig inside cavity; tie legs together with kitchen string. Wrap prosciutto around spatchcock; secure with toothpick. Repeat with remaining spatchcocks.
4 Place spatchcocks in large deep baking dish; drizzle with combined oil and juice. Roast, uncovered, 30 minutes. Brush spatchcocks with pan juices; top with remaining thyme sprigs. Roast, uncovered, about 20 minutes or until spatchcocks are browned and cooked through.
5 Serve spatchcocks topped with remaining herb butter.
per serving 59.8g total fat (20.7g saturated fat); 3106kJ (743 cal); 0.6g carbohydrate; 52g protein; 0.4g fibre

asian-style baked ham

preparation time 15 minutes (plus refrigeration time)
cooking time 1 hour 30 minutes
serves 12

7kg cooked leg of ham
1 cup (250ml) soy sauce
¾ cup (180ml) dry sherry
⅓ cup (75g) firmly packed brown sugar
⅓ cup (120g) honey
2 teaspoons red food colouring
4 cloves garlic, crushed
2 teaspoons five-spice powder
60 cloves (approximately)

1 Cut through rind about 10cm from shank end of leg in decorative pattern; run thumb around edge of rind just under skin to remove rind. Start pulling rind from shank end to widest edge of ham; discard rind.
2 Using sharp knife, make shallow cuts in one direction diagonally across fat at 3cm intervals, then shallow-cut in opposite direction, forming diamonds. Do not cut through top fat or fat will spread apart during cooking.
3 Combine soy sauce, sherry, sugar, honey, colouring, garlic and five-spice in small bowl. Place ham on wire rack in large baking dish; brush ham with soy mixture. Centre a clove in each diamond shape, cover; refrigerate overnight.
4 Preheat oven to moderate (180°C/160°C fan-forced).
5 Place ham on wire rack in large baking dish; pour marinade into small jug. Cover ham with greased foil; bake 1 hour. Uncover; bake about 30 minutes or until ham is lightly caramelised, brushing frequently with marinade during cooking.
per serve 32.8g total fat (11.2g saturated fat); 2859kJ (684 cal); 15.1g carbohydrate; 78.5g protein; 0.2g fibre

slow-roasted portuguese chicken

preparation time 15 minutes
cooking time 2 hours
serves 4

1.6kg chicken
1 fresh red thai chilli, seeded, chopped finely
1 tablespoon sweet paprika
3 cloves garlic, crushed
2 teaspoons salt
½ cup (125ml) lemon juice
2 tablespoons olive oil
1 tablespoon coarsely chopped fresh oregano

1 Preheat oven to moderately slow (170°C/150°C fan-forced).
2 Wash chicken under cold running water; pat dry with absorbent paper. Using kitchen scissors, cut along both sides of backbone; discard backbone. Place chicken, skin-side up, on board; using heel of hand, press down on breastbone to flatten chicken. Insert metal skewer through thigh and opposite wing of chicken to keep chicken flat. Repeat with other thigh and wing.
3 Combine remaining ingredients in small bowl.
4 Place chicken in large baking dish; pour chilli mixture over chicken. Roast, uncovered, brushing occasionally with pan juices, about 2 hours or until chicken is browned and cooked through.
per serving 41.4g total fat (11.3g saturated fat); 2245kJ (537 cal); 1.1g carbohydrate; 40.3g protein; 0.4g fibre

roasted chicken with 40 cloves of garlic

preparation time 20 minutes
cooking time 1 hour 20 minutes
* (plus standing time)*
serves 4

3 bulbs garlic, unpeeled
60g butter, softened
1.5kg chicken
2 teaspoons salt
2 teaspoons cracked black pepper
1 cup (250ml) water

ROASTED POTATOES
1kg tiny new potatoes
cooking-oil spray

1 Preheat oven to moderately hot (200°C/180°C fan-forced).
2 Separate cloves from garlic bulb, leaving unpeeled. Rub butter over outside of chicken and inside cavity; press combined salt and pepper onto skin and inside cavity. Place half of the garlic cloves inside cavity; tie legs together with kitchen string.
3 Place remaining garlic cloves, in single layer, in medium baking dish; place chicken on garlic. Pour the water carefully into dish; roast chicken, uncovered, brushing occasionally with pan juices, about 1 hour 20 minutes or until browned and cooked through.
4 Meanwhile, make roasted potatoes.
5 Stand chicken on platter, covered with foil, 15 minutes before serving with roasted garlic and potatoes.
ROASTED POTATOES
Boil steam or microwave potatoes 5 minutes; drain. Pat dry with absorbent paper; cool 10 minutes. Place potatoes, in single layer, in large oiled baking dish; spray with cooking-oil spray. Roast, uncovered, for the last 30 minutes of chicken cooking time or until potatoes are tender.
per serving 45g total fat (17.9g saturated fat); 3131kJ (749 cal); 38.9g carbohydrate; 46.9g protein; 13.4g fibre

pork loin with spinach and pancetta stuffing

preparation time 30 minutes
cooking time 1 hour 30 minutes
serves 8 to 12

4 slices white bread (120g)
2 tablespoons olive oil
1 clove garlic, crushed
1 medium brown onion (150g), chopped coarsely
6 slices pancetta (90g), chopped coarsely
100g baby spinach leaves
¼ cup (35g) toasted macadamias, chopped coarsely
½ cup (125ml) chicken stock
2kg boned pork loin

PLUM AND RED WINE SAUCE
1½ cups (480g) plum jam
2 tablespoons dry red wine
⅔ cup (160ml) chicken stock

1 Preheat oven to moderately hot (200°C/180°C fan-forced).
2 Discard bread crusts; cut bread into 1cm cubes. Heat half of the oil in large frying pan; cook bread, stirring, until browned and crisp. Drain croutons on absorbent paper.
3 Heat remaining oil in same pan; cook garlic, onion and pancetta until onion browns lightly. Stir in spinach; remove from heat. Gently stir in croutons, nuts and stock.
4 Place pork on board, fat-side down; slice through thickest part of pork horizontally, without cutting through other side. Open out pork to form one large piece; press stuffing mixture against loin along width of pork. Roll pork to enclose stuffing, securing with kitchen string at 2cm intervals.
5 Place rolled pork on rack in large shallow baking dish. Roast, uncovered, 1¼ hours or until cooked through.
6 Meanwhile, make plum and red wine sauce. Serve sliced pork with sauce.
PLUM AND RED WINE SAUCE
Combine ingredients in small saucepan; bring to a boil. Reduce heat; simmer, uncovered, about 10 minutes or until sauce thickens slightly.
per serving 13.1g total fat (4.7g saturated fat); 953kJ (228 cal); 11.8g carbohydrate; 16.1g protein; 0.5g fibre
TIP When you order the pork loin, ask your butcher to leave a flap measuring about 20cm in length to help make rolling the stuffed loin easier.

Slice through thickest part of pork horizontally, without cutting through, so it opens out into one large piece.

Press the spinach and pancetta stuffing mixture hard up against the loin, along entire width of pork.

Roll pork loin carefully to enclose all of the stuffing then secure it with kitchen string at 2cm intervals.

pomegranate-glazed turkey with cornbread seasoning

preparation time 1 hour 30 minutes
cooking time 3 hours 30 minutes
  (plus cooling and standing time)
serves 10

4kg turkey
20g butter
6 shallots (150g)
1 large apple (200g), cut into 6 wedges
1 tablespoon fresh sage leaves
20 black peppercorns
2 cups (500ml) water
1 cup (250ml) chicken stock
½ cup (125ml) brandy
50g butter, melted
½ cup (125ml) pomegranate molasses
2 tablespoons plain flour

MACERATED FRUIT
¼ cup (35g) coarsely chopped dried apricots
¼ cup (35g) dried currants
⅓ cup (80ml) brandy

CORNBREAD SEASONING
350g chorizo, chopped finely
1 medium brown onion (150g), chopped coarsely
2 shallots (50g), chopped coarsely
1 large apple (200g), chopped coarsely
1 tablespoon fresh sage leaves, torn
2 cups (500ml) apple juice
3½ cups (340g) coarsely chopped
  stale cornbread

1 Two days before, make macerated fruit.
2 On the day you want to roast the turkey, preheat oven to moderate (180°C/160°C fan-forced). Discard neck from turkey. Rinse turkey under cold water; pat dry inside and out with absorbent paper.
3 Heat butter in large saucepan; cook whole shallots and apple, stirring, until browned lightly. Cool 10 minutes; stir in sage and peppercorns. Tuck wings under turkey, fill large cavity loosely with stuffing; tie legs together with kitchen string.
4 Place turkey on oiled wire rack in large shallow flameproof baking dish; pour the water, stock and brandy into dish. Brush turkey all over with melted butter; cover dish tightly with two layers of greased foil. Roast 2 hours 10 minutes.
5 Meanwhile, make cornbread seasoning.
6 Uncover turkey; brush with half of the molasses. Roast, uncovered, about 20 minutes or until browned all over and cooked through, brushing frequently with remaining molasses. Remove turkey from dish, cover turkey; stand 20 minutes.
7 Pour juice from dish into large jug; skim 1 tablespoon of the fat from juice, return to same dish. Skim and discard remaining fat from juice. Add flour to dish; cook, stirring, until mixture bubbles and is well browned. Gradually stir in juice; bring to a boil, stirring, until gravy boils and thickens. Strain gravy into same jug; serve turkey with cornbread seasoning and gravy.
MACERATED FRUIT
Combine ingredients in small glass jar, cover; stand at room temperature for two days.
CORNBREAD SEASONING
Line 7cm x 21cm loaf pan with baking paper, extending paper 5cm over long sides. Cook chorizo in large frying pan, stirring, until browned lightly. Add onion and shallot; cook, stirring, until onion softens. Add apple; cook, stirring, until browned lightly. Remove from heat; stir in sage, juice, cornbread and ⅔ cup (180g) macerated fruit. Place seasoning in prepared pan in oven alongside turkey; cook, uncovered, during last 30 minutes of turkey roasting time.
per serve 45.5g total fat (16.3g saturated fat); 3461kJ (828 cal); 42.9g carbohydrate; 53g protein; 2.3g fibre
TIP To test if turkey is cooked, insert a skewer sideways into the thickest part of the thigh then remove and press flesh to release the juices. If the juice runs clear, the turkey is cooked. Alternatively, insert a meat thermometer into the thickest part of the thigh, without touching bone; it should reach 90°C.

Grills and
Barbecues

With the advent of the ridged grill pan that goes on a cooktop burner, you don't have to fire up the barbecue every time you want to char-grill. But both methods have their place. The barbecue is wonderful for adding good smoky flavours to the food, and is certainly the way to go when you're grilling for a crowd, while the grill pan gives you char-grilling as an easy, everyday technique. Whichever way you're grilling, always give the cooking surface time to get to the right heat, and oil the food, rather than the cooking surface, before you add it.

italian blt

asian chicken burger with pickled
cucumber and wasabi mayonnaise

tamarind-glazed riblets with rice noodle stir-fry

harissa lamb cutlets with grilled corn and garlic

italian blt

preparation time 15 minutes
cooking time 15 minutes
serves 4

1 tablespoon balsamic vinegar
1 tablespoon finely chopped fresh basil
¼ cup (60ml) olive oil
4 medium egg tomatoes (300g), quartered
8 slices pancetta (120g)
1 loaf ciabatta (350g)
1 clove garlic, crushed
100g bocconcini, sliced thickly
25g baby rocket leaves

1 Place vinegar, basil and 1 tablespoon of the oil in medium bowl; add tomato, toss to coat in mixture.
2 Cook tomato and pancetta on heated oiled flat plate, uncovered, until tomato is browned and pancetta crisp.
3 Cut bread into quarters, split quarters in half horizontally; brush cut sides with combined garlic and remaining oil. Toast bread, cut-side down, on heated flat plate.
4 Sandwich tomato, pancetta, bocconcini and rocket between bread pieces.
per serving 25g total fat (6.4g saturated fat); 2069kJ (495 cal); 48.4g carbohydrate; 18.9g protein; 4.5g fibre

asian chicken burger with pickled cucumber and wasabi mayonnaise

preparation time 15 minutes (plus refrigeration time)
cooking time 15 minutes
serves 4

500g chicken mince
1 tablespoon soy sauce
1 egg
1 cup (70g) stale breadcrumbs
1 teaspoon sesame oil
2 green onions, chopped finely
4 hamburger buns
50g mizuna

PICKLED CUCUMBER
1 lebanese cucumber (130g)
¼ cup (70g) drained pickled pink ginger
½ cup (125ml) rice vinegar
1 teaspoon salt
1 tablespoon sugar

WASABI MAYONNAISE
¼ cup (75g) mayonnaise
2 teaspoons wasabi paste

1 Make pickled cucumber.
2 Combine ingredients for wasabi mayonnaise in small bowl.
3 Meanwhile, using hand, combine mince, sauce, egg, breadcrumbs, oil and onion in large bowl; shape mixture into four burgers.
4 Cook burgers on heated oiled flat plate, uncovered, about 15 minutes or until cooked through.
5 Meanwhile, split buns in half horizontally; toast, cut-side up. Spread wasabi mayonnaise on bun bases; sandwich mizuna, burgers and drained pickled cucumber between bun halves.
PICKLED CUCUMBER
Using sharp knife, mandoline or v-slicer, slice cucumber thinly. Combine cucumber in small bowl with remaining ingredients. Cover; refrigerate 30 minutes.
per serving 22g total fat (4.8g saturated fat); 2399kJ (574 cal); 57.6g carbohydrate; 35.2g protein; 4.2g fibre

tamarind-glazed riblets with rice noodle stir-fry

preparation time 15 minutes (plus refrigeration time)
cooking time 15 minutes
serves 4

2 cloves garlic, crushed
2cm piece fresh ginger (10g), grated
⅓ cup (80ml) chinese rice wine
¼ cup (55g) firmly packed brown sugar
2 tablespoons kecap manis
1 tablespoon tamarind concentrate
1 teaspoon sichuan peppercorns, crushed
1kg lamb riblets
1 large carrot (180g)
2 large zucchini (300g)
500g fresh rice noodles
1 teaspoon sesame oil
6 green onions, cut into 8cm lengths

1 Combine garlic, ginger, wine, sugar, kecap manis, tamarind and pepper in large bowl; add lamb, toss to coat in marinade. Cover; refrigerate overnight.
2 Drain lamb; reserve marinade. Cook lamb on heated oiled grill plate (or grill or barbecue), covered, over low heat about 15 minutes or until cooked as desired.
3 Meanwhile, using vegetable peeler, slice carrot and zucchini into ribbons. Place noodles in large heatproof bowl, cover with boiling water, separate with fork; drain.
4 Heat oil in wok; stir-fry carrot, zucchini and onion 1 minute. Add reserved marinade; bring to a boil. Add noodles; stir-fry until heated through. Serve lamb with noodle stir-fry.
per serving 18.6g total fat (7.6g saturated fat); 2387kJ (571 cal); 70.1g carbohydrate; 26g protein; 4.3g fibre

harissa lamb cutlets with grilled corn and garlic

preparation time 15 minutes (plus refrigeration time)
cooking time 15 minutes
serves 4

¼ cup (75g) harissa
2 tablespoons olive oil
12 lamb cutlets (900g)
4 fresh corn cobs (1.5kg), husks on
4 bulbs garlic

HARISSA BUTTER
3 teaspoons harissa
80g butter, softened

1 Combine harissa and oil in large bowl; add lamb, toss to coat in marinade. Cover; refrigerate overnight.
2 Carefully pull husk down corn cob, leaving it attached at base. Remove as much silk as possible then bring husk back over cob to cover kernels. Tie each cob with kitchen string to hold husk in place; soak corn overnight in large bowl of water.
3 Combine ingredients for harissa butter in small bowl. Spread 2 teaspoons of the harissa butter over each garlic bulb; wrap garlic bulbs individually in foil.
4 Drain corn. Cook corn and garlic parcels on heated oiled grill plate (or grill or barbecue), uncovered, about 15 minutes or until corn is cooked as desired and garlic is tender.
5 Meanwhile, cook lamb on heated oiled grill plate, uncovered, until cooked as desired.
6 Spread corn with remaining harissa butter; serve with lamb and garlic.
per serving 50g total fat (21.7g saturated fat); 3398kJ (813 cal); 52.4g carbohydrate; 38.7g protein; 24.5g fibre

lamb kofta with tabbouleh

preparation time 35 minutes
cooking time 15 minutes
serves 4

1kg lamb mince
1 medium brown onion (150g), chopped finely
1 egg white
2 tablespoons finely chopped fresh flat-leaf parsley
2 tablespoons finely chopped fresh mint
1 tablespoon finely grated lemon rind
3 teaspoons ground cumin
2 cloves garlic, crushed
¼ teaspoon chilli powder
½ cup (80g) burghul
2 cups loosely packed, coarsely chopped
   fresh flat-leaf parsley, extra
¼ cup loosely packed, coarsely chopped
   fresh mint, extra
2 medium tomatoes (380g), seeded,
   chopped finely
1 small red onion (100g), chopped finely
2 green onions, sliced thinly
1 lebanese cucumber (130g), seeded,
   chopped finely
¼ cup (60ml) olive oil
¼ cup (60ml) lemon juice
1 clove garlic, crushed, extra
4 large pitta breads, quartered

MINTED YOGURT
200g plain yogurt
1 tablespoon coarsely chopped fresh mint
2 tablespoons lemon juice

1 Using your hand, combine mince in large bowl with brown onion, egg white, parsley, mint, rind, cumin, garlic and chilli powder. Roll tablespoons of kofta mixture into balls (you will have 32 in total); place on tray. Cover; refrigerate 30 minutes.
2 Meanwhile, cover burghul with cold water in small bowl; stand 15 minutes. Drain; squeeze burghul with hand to remove as much water as possible.
3 Place burghul in large bowl with extra parsley, extra mint, tomato, red and green onions, cucumber, oil, juice and extra garlic; toss to combine. Cover; refrigerate.
4 Cook kofta, in batches, on heated oiled grill plate (or grill or barbecue) until browned all over and cooked through.
5 Combine ingredients for minted yogurt in small bowl.
6 To serve, sandwich two kofta in each pitta quarter; spoon in tabbouleh. Drizzle with minted yogurt.
per serving 46g total fat (14g saturated fat); 4310kJ (1031 cal); 81.6g carbohydrate; 72.9g protein; 9.4g fibre

cajun chicken with pineapple salsa

preparation time 15 minutes
cooking time 15 minutes
serves 4

1 tablespoon sweet paprika
1 teaspoon cayenne pepper
2 teaspoons garlic powder
2 teaspoons dried oregano
1 tablespoon olive oil
8 chicken thigh fillets (880g)

PINEAPPLE SALSA
4 bacon rashers (280g), rind removed
1 small pineapple (800g), chopped finely
1 small red thai chilli, chopped finely
¼ cup coarsely chopped fresh flat-leaf parsley
1 medium red capsicum (200g), chopped coarsely
¼ cup (60ml) lime juice
1 teaspoon olive oil

1 Combine spices, oregano and oil in large bowl; add chicken, toss to coat in mixture.
2 Make pineapple salsa.
3 Meanwhile, cook chicken on heated oiled flat plate, uncovered, until cooked through.
4 Serve chicken with pineapple salsa and lemon wedges, if desired.
PINEAPPLE SALSA
Cook bacon on heated oiled flat plate, uncovered, until crisp; drain, then chop coarsely. Place bacon in medium bowl with remaining ingredients; toss gently to combine.
per serving 26.7g total fat (7.5g saturated fat); 2011kJ (481 cal); 10.4g carbohydrate; 50g protein; 2.9g fibre

grilled sausages, ratatouille and polenta triangles

preparation time 25 minutes (plus refrigeration time)
cooking time 25 minutes
serves 4

1 litre (4 cups) water
1 cup (170g) polenta
½ cup (40g) finely grated parmesan
1 tablespoon coarsely chopped fresh basil
50g butter
1 tablespoon olive oil
1 small red onion (100g), chopped coarsely
1 medium red capsicum (200g), chopped coarsely
2 medium green zucchini (240g), chopped coarsely
2 baby eggplant (120g), chopped coarsely
2 medium tomatoes (380g), chopped coarsely
2 teaspoons sambal oelek
2 tablespoons tomato paste
½ cup (125ml) beef stock
1 tablespoon coarsely chopped fresh chives
8 veal and mushroom sausages (640g)

1 Place the water in large saucepan; bring to a boil. Add polenta in slow, steady stream, stirring constantly. Reduce heat; simmer, stirring constantly, 20 minutes or until polenta thickens. Stir in cheese, basil and butter. Spread polenta evenly in lightly oiled 19cm x 29cm slice pan. When cool, cover; refrigerate 2 hours or overnight.
2 Meanwhile, heat oil in medium saucepan; cook onion and capsicum, stirring, until onion softens. Add zucchini and eggplant; cook, stirring, 3 minutes. Stir in tomato, sambal, paste and stock; bring to a boil. Reduce heat; simmer, uncovered, about 8 minutes or until mixture thickens. Stir in chives.
3 Turn polenta onto board; trim edges. Cut polenta into quarters; cut each quarter in half diagonally to form two triangles. Cook polenta triangles on heated oiled grill plate (or grill or barbecue) until browned both sides and heated through; cover to keep warm. Cook sausages on same heated oiled grill plate (or grill or barbecue) until cooked through.
4 Serve sausages on ratatouille with polenta triangles.
per serving 60.1g total fat (29.1g saturated fat); 3428kJ (820 cal); 41.3g carbohydrate; 29.7g protein; 9.5g fibre

butterflied spatchcock with nam jim

preparation time 15 minutes
cooking time 25 minutes
serves 4

4 spatchcocks (2kg)
⅓ cup (90g) grated palm sugar
2 teaspoons ground cumin
1 teaspoon salt
2 lebanese cucumbers (260g), seeded, sliced thinly
½ cup firmly packed fresh mint leaves
1 cup firmly packed fresh thai basil leaves
1 cup firmly packed fresh coriander leaves

NAM JIM
2 cloves garlic, chopped coarsely
3 long green chillies, seeded, chopped coarsely
2 teaspoons finely chopped coriander root
1 tablespoon fish sauce
1 tablespoon grated palm sugar
2 shallots (50g), chopped coarsely
¼ cup (60ml) lime juice

1 Rinse spatchcocks under cold water; pat dry with absorbent paper. Using kitchen scissors, cut along each side of each spatchcock's backbone; discard backbones. Turn each spatchcock skin-side up; use heel of hand to press flat. Using fork, prick skin several times. Rub each spatchcock with combined sugar, cumin and salt; stand 5 minutes.
2 Meanwhile, blend or process ingredients for nam jim until smooth.
3 Cook spatchcocks on heated oiled grill plate (or grill or barbecue), covered, over low heat about 20 minutes or until cooked through.
4 Meanwhile, place remaining ingredients in large bowl with 2 tablespoons nam jim; toss gently to combine.
5 Serve spatchcocks with salad and remaining nam jim.
per serving 23.1g total fat (7.3g saturated fat); 2261kJ (541 cal); 28.3g carbohydrate; 56g protein; 3.1g fibre

Use kitchen scissors to cut along both sides of the backbone of each spatchcock; discard bone.

With spatchcock positioned skin-side up on board, press down hard with the heels of your hands to flatten it.

Remove seeds from chillies by scraping out with a small spoon; if you want more heat, don't seed them at all.

texas ribs

preparation time 20 minutes (plus refrigeration time)
cooking time 2 hours
serves 8

2 tablespoons sweet paprika
1 tablespoon ground cumin
1 teaspoon cayenne pepper
3kg american-style pork ribs
2 x 800ml bottles beer
1 cup (250ml) barbecue sauce
¼ cup (60ml) water
¼ cup (60ml) maple syrup
¼ cup (60ml) apple cider vinegar

1 Combine spices in small bowl; rub spice mixture onto ribs. Cover; refrigerate 3 hours or overnight.
2 Preheat oven to moderate (180°C/160°C fan-forced).
3 Bring beer to a boil in medium saucepan. Reduce heat; simmer, uncovered, 20 minutes. Divide beer and ribs between two large baking dishes; cook, covered, 1½ hours. Remove from oven; discard beer.
4 Meanwhile, combine sauce, the water, syrup and vinegar in small saucepan; bring to a boil. Reduce heat; simmer, uncovered, 5 minutes.
5 Cook ribs, in batches, on heated oiled grill plate (or grill or barbecue), brushing with sauce mixture, until browned all over.

per serving 20g total fat (7.8g saturated fat); 2211kJ (529 cal); 25.4g carbohydrate; 49.1g protein; 0.4g fibre

lemon-pepper lamb with minted broad bean risoni

preparation time 35 minutes (plus refrigeration time)
cooking time 20 minutes
serves 4

1 tablespoon finely grated lemon rind
2 teaspoons sea salt
1 tablespoon cracked black pepper
1 clove garlic, sliced thinly
2 tablespoons olive oil
4 lamb backstraps (800g)
500g frozen broad beans
¾ cup (165g) risoni
4 green onions, sliced thinly
⅔ cup coarsely chopped fresh flat-leaf parsley
½ cup coarsely chopped fresh mint
2 tablespoons lemon juice

1 Combine rind, salt, pepper, garlic and half of the oil in large bowl; add lamb, toss to coat in lemon-pepper mixture. Cover; refrigerate 1 hour.
2 Meanwhile, place broad beans in large heatproof bowl, cover with boiling water; stand 10 minutes. Drain. When cool enough to handle, peel grey outer shell from beans, discard shells; reserve beans.
3 Cook risoni in large saucepan of boiling water until just tender; drain. Rinse under cold water; drain.
4 Meanwhile, heat remaining oil in large non-stick frying pan; cook lamb, uncovered, until cooked as desired. Cover lamb, stand 5 minutes; slice lamb thickly.
5 Cook onion, stirring, in same pan until just softened. Add risoni and beans; cook, stirring, until heated through. Remove from heat; stir in herbs and juice.
6 Serve broad bean risoni with lamb.

per serving 17.2g total fat (4.6g saturated fat); 2190kJ (524 cal); 37.4g carbohydrate; 53.6g protein; 10.4g fibre

fajitas with salsa cruda and avocado mash

preparation time 25 minutes (plus refrigeration time)
cooking time 15 minutes
serves 4

2 tablespoons vegetable oil
⅓ cup (80ml) lime juice
¼ cup coarsely chopped fresh oregano
2 cloves garlic, crushed
¼ cup coarsely chopped fresh coriander
2 teaspoons ground cumin
800g beef skirt steak
1 medium red capsicum (200g), sliced thickly
1 medium green capsicum (200g), sliced thickly
1 medium yellow capsicum (200g), sliced thickly
1 large red onion (300g), sliced thickly
20 small flour tortillas

SALSA CRUDA

2 cloves garlic, crushed
3 medium tomatoes (450g), seeded, chopped finely
1 small white onion (80g), chopped finely
2 trimmed red radishes (30g), chopped finely
1 lebanese cucumber (130g), chopped finely
2 tablespoons coarsely chopped fresh coriander
1 fresh long red chilli, chopped finely
2 tablespoons lime juice

AVOCADO MASH

2 small avocados (400g)
2 tablespoons lime juice

1 Combine oil, juice, oregano, garlic, coriander and cumin in large bowl; add beef, toss to coat in marinade. Cover; refrigerate overnight.
2 Cook beef, capsicums and onion on heated oiled flat plate, uncovered, until beef is cooked as desired and vegetables are just tender. Cover to keep warm.
3 Meanwhile, combine ingredients for salsa cruda in small bowl.
4 Mash ingredients for avocado mash in small bowl.
5 Make four foil parcels of five tortillas each; heat parcels both sides on heated flat plate until tortillas are warm and just softened.
6 Cut beef into 1cm slices; combine with cooked vegetables in large bowl. Serve with salsa cruda, avocado mash and tortillas.

per serving 46.7g total fat (9.1g saturated fat); 5229kJ (1251 cal); 134g carbohydrate; 71.6g protein; 13.2g fibre

caramelised barbecued pork neck

preparation time 15 minutes
cooking time 1 hour 30 minutes (plus standing time)
serves 8

1.2kg piece pork neck
1 clove garlic, sliced thinly
4cm piece fresh ginger (20g), sliced thinly
2 star anise, quartered
2 tablespoons sea salt

HOT AND SWEET GLAZE
1¾ cups (400g) grated palm sugar
1¼ cups (310ml) water
3 fresh long red chillies, sliced thinly
2 fresh small red thai chillies, sliced thinly
1 star anise
⅓ cup (80ml) soy sauce
½ cup (125ml) lime juice

1 Make hot and sweet glaze.
2 Using sharp knife, make eight small cuts in pork. Press garlic, ginger and star anise pieces into cuts; rub pork with salt. Brush ¼ cup of the glaze over pork.
3 Place pork on heated barbecue; cook, covered, over low heat 30 minutes. Turn pork; cook, covered, further 30 minutes. Uncover; cook pork 10 minutes, brushing with remaining glaze constantly. Increase heat to high; cook 5 minutes, turning and brushing with glaze constantly. Remove pork from heat; stand 15 minutes before slicing.
HOT AND SWEET GLAZE
Combine sugar and the water in medium saucepan; bring to a boil. Reduce heat; simmer, uncovered, about 10 minutes or until glaze thickens slightly. Remove from heat; stir in chillies, star anise, sauce and juice.
per serving 2.5g total fat (0.8g saturated fat); 1476kJ (353 cal); 49.1g carbohydrate; 34.8g protein; 0.2g fibre

t-bones with blue-cheese butter and pear salad

preparation time 15 minutes
cooking time 10 minutes
serves 4

4 beef t-bone steaks (1.6kg)
2 tablespoons olive oil
100g mesclun
1 pear (300g), sliced thinly
½ cup (60g) toasted pecans

BLUE-CHEESE BUTTER
50g soft blue cheese
50g butter, softened
2 green onions, chopped finely

MUSTARD DRESSING
1 tablespoon wholegrain mustard
1 teaspoon honey
¼ cup (60ml) olive oil
1 tablespoon red wine vinegar

1 Brush beef with oil; cook on heated oiled grill plate (or grill or barbecue) until browned both sides and cooked as desired.
2 Meanwhile, combine ingredients for blue-cheese butter in small bowl.
3 Place ingredients for mustard dressing in screw-top jar; shake well.
4 Place mesclun, pear and mustard dressing in medium bowl; toss gently to combine. Sprinkle with nuts.
5 Spread blue-cheese butter on hot beef; serve with pear salad.
per serving 64.7g total fat (20.4g saturated fat); 3574kJ (855 cal); 11.6g carbohydrate; 58.5g protein; 3.1g fibre

lamb patties with beetroot and tzatziki

preparation time 20 minutes
cooking time 10 minutes
serves 4

500g lamb mince
1 small brown onion (80g), chopped finely
1 medium carrot (120g), grated coarsely
1 egg
2 tablespoons finely chopped fresh flat-leaf parsley
½ teaspoon dried oregano leaves
1 teaspoon finely grated lemon rind
1 clove garlic, crushed
1 loaf turkish bread (430g)
1 cup (60g) coarsely shredded cos lettuce
225g can sliced beetroot, drained
1 lemon (140g), cut into wedges

TZATZIKI
½ cup (140g) plain yogurt
1 lebanese cucumber (130g), seeded,
  chopped finely
1 tablespoon finely chopped fresh mint

1 Using hand, combine lamb, onion, carrot, egg, parsley, oregano, rind and garlic in medium bowl; shape lamb mixture into four patties.
2 Cook patties on heated oiled grill plate (or grill or barbecue) until cooked as desired.
3 Meanwhile, combine ingredients for tzatziki in small bowl.
4 Cut bread into four pieces; split each piece in half horizontally. Toast bread cut-side up.
5 Sandwich lettuce, patties, tzatziki and beetroot between bread pieces. Serve with lemon wedges.
per serving 22.6g total fat (7.6g saturated fat); 2834kJ (678 cal); 72.5g carbohydrate; 45.3g protein; 7.6g fibre

steak sandwich revisited

preparation time 20 minutes
cooking time 1 hour 20 minutes
serves 4

4 scotch fillet steaks (800g)
8 thick slices crusty white bread (320g)
2 tablespoons olive oil
60g rocket, trimmed

CHILLI TOMATO JAM
1 tablespoon olive oil
2 cloves garlic, crushed
4 medium tomatoes (760g), chopped coarsely
1 tablespoon worcestershire sauce
½ cup (125ml) sweet chilli sauce
⅓ cup (75g) firmly packed brown sugar
1 tablespoon coarsely chopped fresh coriander

CARAMELISED LEEK
30g butter
1 medium leek (350g), sliced thinly
2 tablespoons brown sugar
2 tablespoons dry white wine

1 Make chilli tomato jam.
2 Meanwhile, make caramelised leek.
3 Cook steaks on heated oiled grill plate (or grill or barbecue) until browned both sides and cooked as desired.
4 Meanwhile, brush both sides of bread slices with oil; toast, both sides, under hot grill.
5 Sandwich rocket, steaks, chilli tomato jam and caramelised leek between bread slices.
CHILLI TOMATO JAM
Heat oil in medium saucepan; cook garlic, stirring, until browned lightly. Add tomato, sauces and sugar; bring to a boil. Reduce heat; simmer, uncovered, about 45 minutes or until mixture thickens. Stand 10 minutes; stir in coriander.
CARAMELISED LEEK
Melt butter in medium frying pan; cook leek, stirring, until softened. Add sugar and wine; cook, stirring occasionally, about 20 minutes or until leek caramelises.
per serving 36.1g total fat (11.6g saturated fat); 3607kJ (863 cal); 80.5g carbohydrate; 53.6g protein; 8.9g fibre

chermoulla chicken with chickpea salad

preparation time 25 minutes (plus standing time)
cooking time 20 minutes
serves 4

1 cup (200g) dried chickpeas
4 single chicken breast fillets (680g)
1 medium red capsicum (150g), chopped finely
1 medium green capsicum (150g), chopped finely
2 large egg tomatoes (180g), chopped finely
1 small white onion (80g), chopped finely
2 tablespoons lemon juice

CHERMOULLA
½ cup finely chopped fresh coriander
½ cup finely chopped fresh flat-leaf parsley
3 cloves garlic, crushed
2 tablespoons white wine vinegar
2 tablespoons lemon juice
1 teaspoon sweet paprika
½ teaspoon ground cumin
2 tablespoons olive oil

1 Place chickpeas in large bowl of cold water; stand overnight, drain. Rinse under cold water; drain.
2 Cook chickpeas in medium saucepan of boiling water, uncovered, until just tender; drain. Rinse under cold water; drain.
3 Meanwhile, combine ingredients for chermoulla in large bowl; reserve half for chickpea salad.
4 Place chicken in large bowl with remaining half of the chermoulla; turn chicken to coat in chermoulla. Cook chicken, in batches, on heated oiled grill plate (or grill or barbecue) until cooked through. Cover to keep warm.
5 Place chickpeas in large bowl with capsicums, tomato, onion and reserved chermoulla; toss gently to combine. Serve chickpea salad with sliced chicken; drizzle with juice.
per serving 21.6g total fat (4.6g saturated fat); 1994kJ (477 cal); 22.5g carbohydrate; 47.2g protein; 9g fibre

veal with salsa verde and potato rösti

preparation time 20 minutes
cooking time 15 minutes
serves 4

800g piece veal tenderloin, halved lengthways
4 medium potatoes (800g)
1 egg
SALSA VERDE
⅔ cup finely chopped fresh flat-leaf parsley
⅓ cup finely chopped fresh mint
⅓ cup finely chopped fresh dill
⅓ cup finely chopped fresh chives
1 tablespoon wholegrain mustard
¼ cup (60ml) lemon juice
¼ cup (50g) drained baby capers, rinsed
2 cloves garlic, crushed
½ cup (125ml) olive oil

1 Combine ingredients for salsa verde in medium bowl.
2 Rub veal with half of the salsa verde; cook veal on heated oiled flat plate, uncovered, until cooked as desired. Cover veal, stand 5 minutes; slice thickly.
3 Meanwhile, grate potatoes coarsely. Using hands, squeeze excess moisture from potato.
4 Combine potato and egg in medium bowl; divide into eight portions. Cook rösti portions on heated oiled flat plate, flattening with spatula, until browned both sides. Drain on absorbent paper.
5 To serve, divide veal and potato rösti among serving plates; top veal with remaining salsa verde.
per serving 33.3g total fat (5.2g saturated fat); 2554kJ (611 cal); 25.4g carbohydrate; 51.6g protein; 4.9g fibre

char-grilled veal and vegetables with tomato and caper salsa

preparation time 15 minutes
cooking time 20 minutes
serves 6

6 baby eggplant (360g), halved lengthways
6 small zucchini (540g), halved lengthways
¼ cup (60ml) olive oil
12 veal cutlets (2kg)
1 tablespoon cracked black pepper
2 medium tomatoes (300g), seeded, chopped finely
1 small red onion (100g), chopped finely
1 clove garlic, crushed
2 tablespoons baby capers, drained, rinsed
1 tablespoon balsamic vinegar
1 tablespoon fresh baby basil leaves

1 Cook eggplant and zucchini, in batches, on heated oiled grill plate (or grill or barbecue) until browned and tender, brushing with 2 tablespoons of the oil. Cover to keep warm.
2 Sprinkle veal with pepper; cook on same heated grill plate until cooked as desired.
3 Meanwhile, combine tomato, onion, garlic, capers, vinegar and remaining oil in small bowl.
4 Divide eggplant, zucchini, veal and salsa among serving plates; sprinkle with basil.
per serving 15.7g total fat (3.2g saturated fat); 1722kJ (412 cal); 4.5g carbohydrate; 62.3g protein; 3.4g fibre
TIP Antipasto eggplant and zucchini may be used instead of fresh for a quicker alternative.

pork chops with cranberry sauce and kumara craisin salad

preparation time 15 minutes
cooking time 30 minutes
serves 4

1 tablespoon ground ginger
1 tablespoon ground coriander
1 teaspoon sweet paprika
½ cup (160g) cranberry sauce
2 tablespoons orange juice
2 tablespoons lemon juice
1 tablespoon dijon mustard
4 pork loin chops (1.2kg)

KUMARA CRAISIN SALAD
3 large kumara (1.5kg), diced into 2cm pieces
2 tablespoons olive oil
½ cup (80g) toasted pine nuts
⅓ cup (50g) craisins
1 cup coarsely chopped fresh coriander
¼ cup (60ml) white wine vinegar
2 teaspoons olive oil, extra

1 Combine ginger, coriander, paprika, sauce, juices and mustard in large bowl; add pork, toss to coat in mixture.
2 Make kumara craisin salad.
3 Cook pork on heated oiled grill plate (or grill or barbecue), uncovered, until cooked as desired.
4 Divide pork among serving plates; serve with salad.
KUMARA CRAISIN SALAD
Boil, steam or microwave kumara until just tender; drain. Combine kumara with oil in large bowl; cook kumara on heated oiled flat plate, uncovered, until browned lightly. Return kumara to same bowl with remaining ingredients; toss gently to combine.
per serving 48.1g total fat (10g saturated fat); 3833kJ (917 cal); 73.3g carbohydrate; 49.3g protein; 8g fibre

Stir-fries
and Pan-fries

For all frying, have everything
ready before you start – prepared
ingredients and seasonings
at hand, plates or bowls hot,
accompaniments ready.
For stir-frying, heat the empty
wok until it smokes, then add
the oil – it will start to smoke
immediately, so start putting the
food in, keeping the heat high.
For pan-frying, heat pan and oil
together on medium-high heat until
the oil starts to give off a haze,
add the food and let the underside
brown before turning. Cook the
second side as briefly as you like
(for example, to keep meat pink)
and serve browned-side up.

tamarind duck stir-fry

chicken and thai basil stir-fry

sweet soy fried noodles

twice-fried sichuan beef

tamarind duck stir-fry

preparation time 20 minutes (plus standing time)
cooking time 10 minutes
serves 4

25g tamarind pulp
½ cup (125ml) boiling water
30g piece fresh ginger, peeled
1 tablespoon peanut oil
2 cloves garlic, crushed
2 fresh long red thai chillies, chopped finely
1 large whole barbecued duck (1kg),
    cut into 12 pieces
1 medium red capsicum (200g), sliced thinly
¼ cup (60ml) chicken stock
2 tablespoons oyster sauce
1 tablespoon fish sauce
2 tablespoons grated palm sugar
200g baby bok choy, chopped coarsely
100g snow peas, sliced thinly
8 green onions, cut into 5cm lengths
⅓ cup firmly packed fresh coriander leaves

1 Soak tamarind pulp in the water for 30 minutes. Pour tamarind into a fine strainer over a small bowl; push as much pulp through the strainer as possible, scraping underside of strainer occasionally. Discard any tamarind solids left in strainer; reserve pulp liquid in bowl.
2 Slice ginger thinly; stack slices, then slice again into thin slivers.
3 Heat oil in wok; stir-fry ginger, garlic and chilli until fragrant. Add duck and capsicum; stir-fry until capsicum is tender and duck is heated through.
4 Add stock to wok with sauces, sugar and reserved pulp liquid, bring to a boil; boil, 1 minute. Add bok choy; stir-fry until just wilted. Add snow peas and onion; stir-fry until both are just tender. Remove wok from heat; toss coriander leaves through stir-fry.
per serving 28.4g total fat (7.9g saturated fat); 1655kJ (396 cal); 14.7g carbohydrate; 21.2g protein; 2.9g fibre

chicken and thai basil stir-fry

preparation time 20 minutes
cooking time 15 minutes
serves 4

2 tablespoons peanut oil
600g chicken breast fillets, sliced thinly
2 cloves garlic, crushed
2 cm piece fresh ginger (10g), grated
4 fresh small red thai chillies, sliced thinly
4 kaffir lime leaves, shredded
1 medium brown onion (150g), sliced thinly
100g mushrooms, quartered
1 large carrot (180g), sliced thinly
¼ cup (60ml) oyster sauce
1 tablespoon soy sauce
1 tablespoon fish sauce
⅓ cup (80ml) chicken stock
1 cup (80g) bean sprouts
¾ cup loosely packed fresh thai basil leaves

1 Heat half of the oil in wok; stir-fry chicken, in batches, until browned all over and cooked through.
2 Heat remaining oil in wok; stir-fry garlic, ginger, chilli, lime leaves and onion until onion softens and mixture is fragrant.
3 Add mushroom and carrot to wok; stir-fry until carrot is just tender.
4 Return chicken to wok with sauces and stock; stir-fry until sauce thickens slightly. Remove wok from heat; toss bean sprouts and basil leaves through stir-fry.
per serving 13.1g total fat (2.6g saturated fat); 1275kJ (305 cal); 8.6g carbohydrate; 37.9g protein; 3.6g fibre

sweet soy fried noodles

preparation time 15 minutes
cooking time 15 minutes
serves 4

1kg fresh wide rice noodles
2 teaspoons sesame oil
2 cloves garlic, crushed
2 fresh small red thai chillies, sliced thinly
600g chicken thigh fillets, chopped coarsely
250g baby bok choy, quartered lengthways
4 green onions, sliced thinly
2 tablespoons kecap manis
1 tablespoon oyster sauce
1 tablespoon fish sauce
1 tablespoon grated palm sugar
¼ cup coarsely chopped fresh coriander
1 tablespoon fried onion

1 Place noodles in large heatproof bowl, cover with boiling water; separate with fork. Drain.
2 Heat oil in large wok; stir-fry garlic and chilli until fragrant. Add chicken; stir-fry until browned lightly. Add bok choy and green onion; stir-fry until green onion softens and chicken is cooked through.
3 Add noodles to wok with kecap manis, sauces and sugar; stir-fry, tossing gently to combine.
4 Remove wok from heat; add coriander, tossing gently to combine. Sprinkle with fried onion.
per serving 14.4g total fat (3.6g saturated fat); 2140kJ (512 cal); 59.7g carbohydrate; 35g protein; 2.7g fibre

twice-fried sichuan beef

preparation time 20 minutes (plus standing time)
cooking time 25 minutes
serves 4

2 tablespoons dry sherry
2 tablespoons salt-reduced soy sauce
1 teaspoon brown sugar
600g piece eye fillet, sliced thinly
½ cup (75g) cornflour
1½ cups (300g) jasmine rice
vegetable oil, for deep-frying
2 teaspoons sesame oil
1 clove garlic, crushed
1 fresh red thai chilli, chopped finely
1 medium brown onion (150g), sliced thickly
1 medium carrot (120g), halved, sliced thinly
1 small red capsicum (150g), sliced thinly
500g gai larn, chopped coarsely
1 tablespoon cracked sichuan peppercorns
2 tablespoons oyster sauce
¼ cup (60ml) salt-reduced soy sauce, extra
½ cup (125ml) beef stock
2 teaspoons brown sugar, extra

1 Combine sherry, sauce and sugar in medium bowl; add beef, toss to coat in marinade. Stand 10 minutes; drain. Toss beef in cornflour; shake off excess.
2 Meanwhile, cook rice in large saucepan of boiling water, uncovered, until just tender; drain. Cover to keep warm.
3 Heat vegetable oil in wok; deep-fry beef, in batches, until crisp. Drain on absorbent paper. Reserve oil for another use.
4 Heat sesame oil in same cleaned wok; stir-fry garlic, chilli and onion until onion softens. Add carrot and capsicum; stir-fry until just tender. Add gai larn; stir-fry until just wilted.
5 Add beef to wok with peppercorns, oyster sauce, extra soy sauce, stock and extra sugar; stir-fry until heated through. Serve beef and vegetables with rice.
per serving 20.5g total fat (5.2g saturated fat); 3010kJ (720 cal); 87.5g carbohydrate; 43g protein; 7g fibre
TIP It is easier to slice beef thinly if it is partially frozen.

mee krob (crisp fried noodles)

preparation time 35 minutes
cooking time 20 minutes
serves 4

150g fresh silken firm tofu
vegetable oil, for deep-frying
125g rice vermicelli
2 tablespoons peanut oil
2 eggs, beaten lightly
1 tablespoon water
2 cloves garlic, crushed
2 fresh small red thai chillies, chopped finely
1 small green thai chilli, chopped finely
2 tablespoons grated palm sugar
2 tablespoons fish sauce
2 tablespoons tomato sauce
1 tablespoon rice wine vinegar
200g pork mince
200g small shelled cooked prawns,
   chopped coarsely
6 green onions, sliced thinly
¼ cup firmly packed fresh coriander leaves

1 Pat tofu all over with absorbent paper; cut into slices, then cut each slice into 1cm-wide matchsticks. Spread tofu on tray lined with absorbent paper; cover tofu with more absorbent paper, stand at least 10 minutes.
2 Meanwhile, heat vegetable oil in wok; deep-fry vermicelli quickly, in batches, until puffed. Drain on absorbent paper.
3 Using same heated oil, deep-fry drained tofu, in batches, until browned lightly. Drain on absorbent paper. Cool oil; remove from wok and reserve for another use.
4 Heat 2 teaspoons of the peanut oil in same cleaned wok; add half of the combined egg and water, swirl wok to make thin omelette. Cook, uncovered, until egg is just set. Remove from wok; roll omelette, cut into thin strips. Heat 2 more teaspoons of the peanut oil in same wok; repeat process with remaining egg mixture.
5 Combine garlic, chillies, sugar, sauces and vinegar in small bowl; reserve half of the chilli mixture in small jug.
6 Combine pork in bowl with remaining half of the chilli mixture. Heat remaining peanut oil in same wok; stir-fry pork mixture about 5 minutes or until pork is cooked through. Add prawns; stir-fry 1 minute. Add tofu; stir-fry, tossing gently to combine.
7 Remove wok from heat; add reserved chilli mixture and half of the onion, toss to combine. Add vermicelli; toss gently to combine. Remove wok from heat; sprinkle with remaining onion, omelette strips and coriander.
per serving 22.3g total fat (4.7g saturated fat); 1877kJ (449 cal); 31g carbohydrate; 31.2g protein; 2.2g fibre

hokkien noodle and pork stir-fry

preparation time 20 minutes
cooking time 10 minutes
serves 4

600g hokkien noodles
1 tablespoon cornflour
½ cup (125ml) water
¼ cup (60ml) kecap manis
¼ cup (60ml) hoisin sauce
2 tablespoons rice vinegar
2 tablespoons peanut oil
600g pork fillet, sliced thinly
1 medium brown onion (150g), sliced thickly
2 cloves garlic, crushed
2 cm piece fresh ginger (10g), grated
150g sugar snap peas, trimmed
1 medium red capsicum (200g), sliced thinly
1 medium yellow capsicum (200g), sliced thinly
200g baby bok choy, quartered

1 Place noodles in large heatproof bowl, cover with boiling water, separate with fork; drain.
2 Blend cornflour with the water in small bowl; stir in sauces and vinegar.
3 Heat half of the oil in wok; stir-fry pork, in batches, until browned all over. Remove from wok.
4 Heat remaining oil in same wok; stir-fry onion, garlic and ginger until onion softens. Add peas, capsicums and bok choy; stir-fry until vegetables are just tender.
5 Return pork to wok with noodles and sauce mixture; stir-fry until sauce thickens slightly.
per serving 14.3g total fat (3g saturated fat); 2165kJ (518 cal); 52.7g carbohydrate; 43.7g protein; 7.6g fibre

stir-fried beef and mixed mushrooms

preparation time 15 minutes
cooking time 15 minutes
serves 4

¼ cup (60ml) peanut oil
800g beef rump steak, sliced thinly
1 medium brown onion (150g), sliced thickly
2 cloves garlic, crushed
2cm piece fresh ginger (10g), grated
2 fresh long red chillies, sliced thinly
150g oyster mushrooms, halved
100g fresh shiitake mushrooms, halved
100g enoki mushrooms
450g hokkien noodles
6 green onions, sliced thickly
1 tablespoon kecap manis
¼ cup (60ml) oyster sauce
1 teaspoon sesame oil

1 Heat half of the peanut oil in wok; stir-fry beef, in batches, until browned.
2 Heat remaining peanut oil in same wok; stir-fry brown onion until soft. Add garlic, ginger, chilli and mushrooms; stir-fry until mushrooms are just tender.
3 Meanwhile, place noodles in large heatproof bowl, cover with boiling water, separate with fork; drain.
4 Return beef to wok with noodles, green onion, kecap manis, sauce and sesame oil; stir-fry until mixture boils and thickens slightly.
per serving 29.9g total fat (8.9g saturated fat); 3298kJ (789 cal); 70.1g carbohydrate; 59.2g protein; 6.6g fibre

pad thai (thai fried rice stick noodles)

preparation time 20 minutes (plus standing time)
cooking time 10 minutes
serves 4

40g tamarind pulp
½ cup (125ml) boiling water
2 tablespoons grated palm sugar
⅓ cup (80ml) thai sweet chilli sauce
⅓ cup (80ml) fish sauce
375g rice stick noodles
12 medium uncooked prawns (500g)
2 cloves garlic, crushed
2 tablespoons finely chopped preserved turnip
2 tablespoons dried shrimp
4 cm piece fresh ginger (20g), grated
2 fresh small red thai chillies, seeded,
    chopped coarsely
1 tablespoon peanut oil
250g pork mince
3 eggs, beaten lightly
2 cups (160g) bean sprouts
4 green onions, sliced thinly
⅓ cup coarsely chopped fresh coriander
¼ cup (35g) coarsely chopped roasted
    unsalted peanuts
1 lime, quartered

1 Soak tamarind pulp in the water for 30 minutes. Pour tamarind into fine strainer over small bowl; push as much tamarind pulp through strainer as possible, scraping underside of strainer occasionally. Discard any tamarind solids left in strainer; reserve pulp liquid in bowl. Add sugar and sauces to reserved pulp liquid; stir to combine. Reserve.

2 Meanwhile, place noodles in large heatproof bowl, cover with boiling water, stand until just softened; drain.

3 Shell and devein prawns, leaving tails intact.

4 Blend or process (or crush using mortar and pestle) garlic, turnip, dried shrimp, ginger and chilli until mixture forms a paste.

5 Heat oil in wok; stir-fry spice paste until fragrant. Add pork; stir-fry until just cooked through. Add prawns; stir-fry 1 minute. Add egg; stir-fry until egg just sets. Add noodles, reserved tamarind mixture, sprouts and half of the green onion; stir-fry, tossing gently until combined. Remove from heat; gently toss remaining green onion, coriander and nuts through pad thai.

6 Divide among serving plates; serve with lime wedges.
per serving 19.8g total fat (4.5g saturated fat); 2750kJ (658 cal); 76.3g carbohydrate; 42.6g protein; 5.8g fibre

Press the tamarind with the back of a spoon to extract as much of the pulp liquid as possible. Discard the solids left in the the sieve.

Chop the preserved turnip into as small a dice as possible so that the fibrous material breaks down when pounded in the mortar.

Using a mortar and pestle, pound the dried shrimp with the preserved turnip, garlic, ginger and chilli until mixture forms a coarse paste.

prawn, asparagus and sesame stir-fry

preparation time 30 minutes
cooking time 15 minutes
serves 4

1kg uncooked large king prawns
1 tablespoon peanut oil
5cm piece fresh ginger (25g), grated
2 cloves garlic, crushed
1 medium brown onion (150g), sliced thinly
300g asparagus, trimmed, chopped coarsely
1 fresh long red chilli, sliced thinly
2 tablespoons rice wine
¼ cup (60ml) soy sauce
2 teaspoons sesame oil
2 teaspoons brown sugar
2 teaspoons toasted sesame seeds

1 Shell and devein prawns, leaving tails intact.
2 Heat half of the peanut oil in wok; stir-fry ginger, garlic and onion until fragrant. Add asparagus; stir-fry until tender. Remove from wok.
3 Heat remaining peanut oil in same wok; cook prawns, in batches, until cooked through.
4 Return prawns to wok with asparagus mixture, chilli and combined wine, sauce, sesame oil and sugar; stir-fry until mixture is heated through. Serve stir-fry sprinkled with seeds.
per serving 8.5g total fat (1.4g saturated fat); 907kJ (217 cal); 4.7g carbohydrate; 28.7g protein; 1.8g fibre

twice-cooked chicken with asian greens

preparation time 45 minutes
  (plus standing and refrigeration time)
cooking time 1 hour
serves 4

2.5 litres (10 cups) water
1 litre (4 cups) chicken stock
2 cups (500ml) chinese cooking wine
8 cloves garlic, crushed
10cm piece fresh ginger (50g), sliced thinly
1 teaspoon sesame oil
1.6kg chicken
peanut oil, for deep-frying
1 tablespoon peanut oil
150g snow peas, trimmed
500g choy sum, chopped coarsely
350g gai larn, chopped coarsely
2 green onions, sliced thinly

CHAR SIU DRESSING
2 cloves garlic, crushed
5cm piece fresh ginger (25g), grated finely
¼ cup (60ml) char siu sauce
2 tablespoons soy sauce
1 teaspoon white sugar
1 tablespoon rice vinegar

1 Combine the water, stock, wine, garlic, ginger and sesame oil in large saucepan; bring to a boil. Boil, uncovered, 10 minutes. Add chicken, reduce heat; simmer, uncovered, 15 minutes. Remove pan from heat, cover; stand chicken in stock 3 hours. Remove chicken; pat dry with absorbent paper. Reserve stock for another use.
2 Using sharp knife, halve chicken lengthways; cut halves crossways through centre. Cut breasts from wings, and thighs from legs to give you eight chicken pieces in total. Cut wings in half; cut breast and thighs into thirds. Place chicken pieces on tray; refrigerate, uncovered, 3 hours or overnight.
3 Make char siu dressing.
4 Heat peanut oil for deep-frying in wok; deep-fry chicken pieces, in batches, until browned. Drain.
5 Heat the 1 tablespoon of peanut oil in same cleaned wok; stir-fry snow peas, choy sum and gai larn until just tender. Add 2 tablespoons of the char siu dressing; stir-fry to combine.
6 Divide asian green mixture among serving plates; top with chicken pieces, drizzle with remaining dressing, sprinkle with green onion.
CHAR SIU DRESSING
Stir garlic, ginger, sauces and sugar over heat in small saucepan until mixture comes to a boil. Remove from heat; stir in vinegar.
per serving 47.4g total fat (12.5g saturated fat); 3081kJ (737 cal); 17.8g carbohydrate; 43.8g protein; 8.9g fibre

layered grapevine leaves, eggplant and lamb

preparation time 20 minutes
cooking time 20 minutes
serves 4

2 large red capsicums (700g)
1 medium eggplant (300g), cut crossways
    into 12 slices
1 medium brown onion (150g), chopped finely
1 clove garlic, crushed
500g lamb mince
2 teaspoons baharat
1 tablespoon brandy
1 tablespoon tomato paste
½ cup (125ml) beef stock
1 tablespoon lime juice
1 tablespoon toasted pine nuts
1 cup coarsely chopped fresh flat-leaf parsley
8 fresh grapevine leaves

1 Quarter capsicums; remove seeds and membrane. Roast capsicum, skin-side up, and eggplant on lightly oiled oven tray under grill or in very hot oven until capsicum skin blisters and blackens. Cover capsicum with plastic wrap or paper for 5 minutes; peel away skin, then slice thinly.

2 Meanwhile, cook onion and garlic in heated lightly oiled large frying pan, stirring, until onion just softens. Add lamb and baharat; cook, stirring, until mince changes colour. Stir in combined brandy, paste and stock; bring to a boil. Reduce heat; simmer, uncovered, stirring, about 2 minutes or until liquid reduces by half. Remove from heat; stir in juice, nuts and parsley. Cover to keep warm.

3 Place vine leaves in large saucepan of boiling water, uncovered, about 30 seconds or just until pliable; drain, in single layer, on absorbent paper.

4 Place one leaf on each plate; layer each leaf with one slice of eggplant, a few capsicum slices, ¼ cup mince mixture and another vine leaf. Repeat layering with remaining eggplant, capsicum and mince.

per serving 15.5g total fat (5.9g saturated fat); 1321kJ (316 cal); 10.4g carbohydrate; 31.1g protein; 5.6g fibre

TIPS Baharat is an aromatic all-purpose spice blend; if hard to find, make your own by combining 2 teaspoons paprika, 1 tablespoon ground cumin, 1 tablespoon ground coriander, 1 crushed clove and ½ teaspoon ground nutmeg.

If fresh vine leaves are unavailable, buy those preserved in brine and sold in cryovac packages; rinse thoroughly under cold water, then follow step 3 above, reducing time in boiling water to 10 seconds.

orange-glazed pork cutlets with spinach and pecan salad

preparation time 20 minutes
cooking time 20 minutes
serves 4

½ cup (125ml) orange juice
¼ cup (55g) white sugar
2 cloves garlic, crushed
4 pork cutlets (950g), trimmed

SPINACH AND PECAN SALAD
150g baby spinach leaves
¼ cup (35g) toasted pecans, chopped coarsely
150g snow peas, trimmed, halved
4 medium oranges (960g), peeled

CITRUS DRESSING
2 tablespoons orange juice
1 tablespoon lemon juice
½ teaspoon dijon mustard
½ teaspoon white sugar
2 teaspoons olive oil

1 Combine juice, sugar and garlic in small saucepan, bring to a boil. Reduce heat; simmer, without stirring, 10 minutes or until glaze reduces to about ⅓ cup.
2 Brush cutlets both sides with glaze; cook, uncovered, in heated lightly oiled large frying pan about 10 minutes or until cooked as desired, brushing frequently with remaining glaze. Cover to keep warm.
3 Meanwhile, make spinach and pecan salad.
4 Place ingredients for citrus dressing in screw-top jar; shake well. Pour dressing over salad; toss gently to combine. Serve salad with cutlets.
SPINACH AND PECAN SALAD
Combine spinach, nuts and snow peas in large bowl. Segment oranges over salad to catch juice, add segments to salad; toss gently to combine.
per serving 17g total fat (3.8g saturated fat); 1935kJ (463 cal); 33.2g carbohydrate; 44.1g protein; 6.4g fibre

stir-fried chicken and gai larn

preparation time 10 minutes
cooking time 15 minutes
serves 4

2 tablespoons sesame oil
500g chicken thigh fillets, sliced thinly
2 teaspoons sambal oelek
190g can sliced water chestnuts, drained
227g can bamboo shoot strips, drained
1 large red capsicum (350g), sliced thinly
⅓ cup (80ml) kecap manis
500g gai larn, chopped coarsely
2 cups (160g) bean sprouts

1 Heat half of the oil in wok; stir-fry chicken, in batches, until browned lightly.
2 Heat remaining oil in same wok; stir-fry sambal, water chestnuts, bamboo shoots and capsicum for 2 minutes.
3 Return chicken to wok with kecap manis and gai larn; stir-fry until gai larn is just wilted and chicken is cooked through. Remove wok from heat; stir in sprouts.
per serving 18.8g total fat (4.1g saturated fat); 1359kJ (325 cal); 9g carbohydrate; 30.3g protein; 8.1g fibre

crisp-skinned soy chicken with spiced salt

preparation time 20 minutes
   (plus standing and refrigeration time)
cooking time 30 minutes
serves 4

4 litres (16 cups) water
1 cup (250ml) light soy sauce
5cm piece ginger (25g), peeled, sliced thickly
2 cloves garlic, crushed
2 teaspoons five-spice powder
1.5kg chicken
vegetable oil, for deep-frying

SOY MARINADE
1 tablespoon honey
1 tablespoon light soy sauce
1 tablespoon dry sherry
½ teaspoon five-spice powder
½ teaspoon sesame oil

SPICED SALT
¼ cup (60g) sea salt
½ teaspoon cracked black pepper
1 teaspoon five-spice powder

1 Combine the water, sauce, ginger, garlic and five-spice in large saucepan; bring to a boil. Boil, uncovered, 2 minutes. Add chicken; return to a boil. Reduce heat; simmer, uncovered, about 10 minutes, turning once during cooking. Remove pan from heat, cover; stand 30 minutes. Remove chicken from stock; pat dry with absorbent paper.
2 Combine ingredients for soy marinade in small bowl.
3 Using kitchen scissors, cut chicken in half through breastbone and along side of backbone; cut legs and wings from chicken halves. Place chicken pieces on oven tray; coat skin in soy marinade. Cover; refrigerate 2 hours.
4 Make spiced salt.
5 Heat oil in wok; deep-fry chicken, in batches, until browned all over. Drain on absorbent paper.
6 Cut chicken into serving-sized pieces; serve with spiced salt.
SPICED SALT
Heat small non-stick frying pan; cook salt and pepper, stirring, 2 minutes. Add five-spice; cook, stirring, about 1 minute or until fragrant.
per serving 42.5g total fat (11g saturated fat); 2441kJ (584 cal); 8g carbohydrate; 41.3g protein; 0.5g fibre
TIPS When deep-frying the chicken, have the pan no more than one-third filled with oil.
The stock can be used as a base for an asian soup; refrigerate until cold, then discard the fat from the top before using.

Gently poach the chicken uncovered, turning it once, so the flavours of the Asian spices are absorbed deep into the meat of the bird.

After the chicken has cooled in the cooking liquid, use ktichen scissors to cut it into pieces then coat them all with the soy marinade.

Dry-fry the five-spice powder with the sea salt and cracked black pepper in a frying pan only until they are fragrant — not burned.

lamb backstraps with vegetable crisps and beurre blanc

preparation time 20 minutes
cooking time 35 minutes
serves 4

½ small kumara (125g)
1 small parsnip (120g)
1 large beetroot (200g), trimmed
1 tablespoon olive oil
4 x 200g lamb backstraps
vegetable oil, for deep-frying

BEURRE BLANC
¼ cup (60ml) dry white wine
1 tablespoon lemon juice
¼ cup (60ml) cream
125g cold butter, chopped

1 Using vegetable peeler, slice kumara and parsnip into ribbons. Slice beetroot thinly.
2 Heat olive oil in large frying pan; cook lamb, in batches, about 5 minutes both sides or until cooked as desired. Cover to keep warm.
3 Make beurre blanc.
4 Heat vegetable oil in wok; deep-fry vegetables, in batches, about 2 minutes each batch or until crisp. Drain on absorbent paper.
5 Cut each piece of lamb into three pieces. Divide half of the sauce among serving plates; top with lamb, remaining sauce and vegetable crisps.
BEURRE BLANC
Combine wine and juice in medium saucepan; bring to a boil. Boil, without stirring, until reduced by two-thirds. Add cream; return to a boil. Whisk in cold butter, piece by piece, whisking between additions. Pour into medium jug; cover to keep warm.
per serving 60g total fat (30.5g saturated fat); 3189kJ (763 cal); 11.1g carbohydrate; 44.2g protein; 2.5g fibre

char kway teow

preparation time 25 minutes
cooking time 10 minutes
serves 6

1kg fresh rice noodles
500g small uncooked prawns
2 tablespoons peanut oil
340g chicken breast fillets, chopped coarsely
4 fresh red thai chillies, seeded, chopped finely
2 cloves garlic, crushed
4 cm piece fresh ginger (20g), grated
5 green onions, sliced thinly
2 cups (160g) bean sprouts
⅓ cup (80ml) soy sauce
¼ teaspoon sesame oil
1 teaspoon brown sugar

1 Place noodles in large heatproof bowl, cover with boiling water, gently separate with fork; drain.
2 Shell and devein prawns, leaving tails intact; halve prawns crossways.
3 Heat half of the peanut oil in wok; stir-fry chicken, chilli, garlic and ginger until chicken is cooked through. Remove from wok.
4 Heat remaining peanut oil in same wok; stir-fry prawns until they just change colour. Remove from wok. Stir-fry onion and sprouts in wok until onion is soft. Add noodles and combined remaining ingredients; stir-fry 1 minute.
5 Return chicken mixture and prawns to wok; stir-fry until heated through.
per serving 8.6g total fat (1.5g saturated fat); 1409kJ (337 cal); 37.6g carbohydrate; 26.5g protein; 2g fibre
TIP This recipe is best made just before serving.

seared calves liver with persillade and parsnip mash

preparation time 15 minutes
cooking time 30 minutes
serves 4

1kg parsnips, chopped coarsely
1 large potato (300g), chopped coarsely
3 cloves garlic
½ cup (125ml) cream
100g butter
250g asparagus, trimmed
400g piece calves liver, sliced thinly
1 shallot (25g), chopped finely
½ cup (125ml) chicken stock
1 tablespoon lemon juice
⅓ cup finely chopped fresh flat-leaf parsley

1 Boil, steam or microwave parsnip and potato, separately, until tender; drain. Crush 2 cloves of the garlic; mash in large bowl with parsnip, potato, cream and half of the butter. Cover to keep warm.
2 Boil, steam or microwave asparagus until just tender; drain. Cover to keep warm.
3 Pat liver dry with absorbent paper.
4 Melt about 1 tablespoon of the remaining butter in large frying pan; cook liver quickly, in batches, over high heat until browned both sides and cooked as desired (do not overcook). Remove from pan; cover, keep warm.
5 To make persillade, heat remaining butter in same pan. Finely chop remaining clove of garlic, add to pan with shallot; cook, stirring, until shallot softens. Add stock and juice; bring to a boil, stirring. Remove from heat; stir in parsley.
6 Serve sliced liver with parsnip mash and asparagus; top liver with persillade.

per serving 42.5g total fat (24.9g saturated fat); 2675kJ (640 cal); 35.5g carbohydrate; 29.5g protein; 8.1g fibre
TIP When peeling parsnips, make sure you remove all the bitter outer layer.

duck breasts with fig sauce and spinach risoni

preparation time 20 minutes
cooking time 25 minutes
serves 4

4 duck breast fillets (600g)
4 sprigs fresh rosemary
4 bay leaves
200g risoni
20g butter
200g baby spinach leaves, trimmed
1 small brown onion (80g), chopped finely
6 dried figs (90g), quartered
1 cup (250ml) port
1 cup (250ml) chicken stock
20g butter, extra

1 Using fingers, make pocket between meat and fat of each duck breast; press 1 sprig rosemary and 1 bay leaf into each pocket. Prick duck skins with fork several times. Cook duck, skin-side down, in heated lightly oiled large frying pan about 8 minutes or until browned and crisp. Turn duck; cook about 5 minutes or until cooked as desired. Remove from pan; cover to keep warm.
2 Cook pasta in large saucepan of boiling water, uncovered, until just tender; drain. Place pasta in large bowl with butter and spinach; toss gently to combine. Cover to keep warm.
3 Meanwhile, cook onion in same frying pan as duck, stirring, until soft. Add fig, port and stock; bring to a boil. Reduce heat; simmer, stirring, about 5 minutes or until sauce thickens. Whisk in extra butter until combined.
4 Slice duck thinly; serve with risoni and fig sauce.

per serving 17.6g total fat (8.1g saturated fat); 2441kJ (584 cal); 56g carbohydrate; 35.5g protein; 6.5g fibre

Grains
and Pulses

We have to thank generations of peasant cooks for many of today's delicious rice, grain, lentil and bean dishes. These great staples have always been foods of the poor, but, over time, cooks in many countries have found ways to build a world of splendid flavours and lovely textures into their basic sustenance. Today, top chefs and good cooks alike prize these ingredients because they offer such deeply enjoyable eating, and as a bonus, they're cheap and good for you too.

yellow coconut rice

spicy roasted pumpkin couscous

hummus

spiced lentils

yellow coconut rice

preparation time 5 minutes (plus standing time)
cooking time 15 minutes
serves 4

1¾ cups (350g) long-grain white rice
1¼ cups (310ml) water
400ml can coconut cream
½ teaspoon salt
1 teaspoon sugar
½ teaspoon ground turmeric
pinch saffron threads

1 Soak rice in large bowl of cold water for 30 minutes. Pour rice into strainer; rinse under cold water until water runs clear. Drain.
2 Place rice and remaining ingredients in large heavy-base saucepan; cover, bring to a boil, stirring occasionally. Reduce heat; simmer, covered, about 15 minutes or until rice is tender. Remove pan from heat; stand, covered, 5 minutes.
per serving 21.1g total fat (18.2g saturated fat); 2161kJ (517 cal); 74g carbohydrate; 7.7g protein; 2.4g fibre

spicy roasted pumpkin couscous

preparation time 10 minutes
cooking time 20 minutes
serves 4

1 tablespoon olive oil
2 cloves garlic, crushed
1 large red onion (200g), sliced thickly
500g pumpkin, peeled, chopped coarsely
3 teaspoons ground cumin
2 teaspoons ground coriander
1 cup (200g) couscous
1 cup (250ml) boiling water
20g butter
2 tablespoons coarsely chopped fresh
   flat-leaf parsley

1 Preheat oven to hot (220°C/200°C fan-forced).
2 Heat oil in medium flameproof baking dish; cook garlic, onion and pumpkin, stirring, until vegetables are browned lightly. Add spices; cook, stirring, about 2 minutes or until fragrant. Bake pumpkin mixture, uncovered, 15 minutes or until pumpkin is just tender.
3 Meanwhile, combine couscous, the water and butter in large heatproof bowl; cover, stand about 5 minutes or until water is absorbed, fluffing with fork occasionally.
4 Add pumpkin mixture to couscous; stir in parsley.
per serving 9.5g total fat (3.7g saturated fat); 1317kJ (315 cal); 47.8g carbohydrate; 9.4g protein; 2.7g fibre

hummus

preparation time 10 minutes (plus standing time)
cooking time 50 minutes
makes 2 cups (470g)

¾ cup (150g) dried chickpeas
1 teaspoon salt
1 clove garlic, quartered
⅓ cup (90g) tahini
¼ cup (60ml) lemon juice
pinch cayenne pepper
1 tablespoon finely chopped fresh flat-leaf parsley
2 teaspoons extra virgin olive oil

1 Place chickpeas in medium bowl, cover with cold water; stand overnight.
2 Drain chickpeas, place in medium saucepan, cover with fresh water. Bring to a boil; simmer, covered, about 50 minutes or until chickpeas are tender. Drain chickpeas over large heatproof bowl. Reserve ⅓ cup (80ml) chickpea liquid; discard remaining liquid.
3 Blend or process chickpeas with salt, garlic, tahini, juice and reserved liquid until almost smooth.
4 Spoon into serving bowl; sprinkle with pepper and parsley. Drizzle with olive oil.
per tablespoon 3g total fat (0.4g saturated fat); 184kJ (44 cal); 2.4g carbohydrate; 1.9g protein; 1.4g fibre
TIP Hummus can be made three days ahead; store, covered, in the refrigerator.
SERVING SUGGESTION Serve with warm pide or toasted pitta, or as an accompaniment to grilled kebabs or roast meat.

spiced lentils

preparation time 5 minutes
cooking time 15 minutes
serves 4

1½ cups (300g) red lentils
50g butter
1 small brown onion (80g), chopped finely
1 clove garlic, crushed
½ teaspoon ground coriander
½ teaspoon ground cumin
¼ teaspoon ground turmeric
¼ teaspoon cayenne pepper
½ cup (125ml) chicken stock
2 tablespoons coarsely chopped fresh
   flat-leaf parsley

1 Cook lentils, uncovered, in large saucepan of boiling water until just tender; drain.
2 Meanwhile, melt half of the butter in large frying pan; cook onion, garlic and spices, stirring, until onion softens.
3 Add lentils, stock and remaining butter; cook, stirring, until hot. Stir parsley into lentils off the heat.
per serving 11.9g total fat (7g saturated fat); 1225kJ (293 cal); 29.6g carbohydrate; 19g protein; 10.8g fibre

barley risotto with chicken and tarragon

preparation time 15 minutes
cooking time 40 minutes
serves 4

1 tablespoon olive oil
500g chicken breast fillets, sliced thinly
3 cups (750ml) chicken stock
2 cups (500ml) water
1 medium brown onion (150g), chopped finely
1 clove garlic, crushed
2 medium leeks (700g), sliced thinly
¾ cup (150g) pearl barley
⅓ cup (80ml) dry white wine
1 cup (120g) frozen peas
2 tablespoons finely shredded fresh tarragon

1 Heat half of the oil in large saucepan; cook chicken, in batches, until browned lightly and cooked through. Cover to keep warm.

2 Meanwhile, combine stock and the water in large saucepan; bring to a boil. Reduce heat; simmer, covered.

3 Meanwhile, heat remaining oil in same cleaned chicken pan; cook onion, garlic and leek, stirring, until onion softens. Add barley; stir to combine with onion mixture. Add wine; cook, stirring, until almost evaporated. Stir in ½ cup of the simmering stock mixture; cook, stirring, over low heat until liquid is absorbed. Continue adding stock mixture, in ½-cup batches, stirring until absorbed after each addition. Total cooking time should be about 30 minutes or until barley is just tender.

4 Add chicken and peas to risotto; cook, stirring, until peas are just tender. Remove from heat; stir in tarragon.

per serving 9.7g total fat (1.9g saturated fat); 1584kJ (379 cal); 31.6g carbohydrate; 38g protein; 9.8g fibre

almond coriander couscous

preparation time 10 minutes (plus standing time)
cooking time 10 minutes
serves 6

3 cups (600g) couscous
3 cups (750ml) boiling water
¼ cup (60ml) olive oil
1 clove garlic, crushed
2 green onions, chopped
¾ cup (105g) slivered almonds, toasted
⅓ cup (50g) dried currants
½ cup chopped fresh coriander

1 Combine couscous and the water in large heatproof bowl; stand, covered, 5 minutes or until water is absorbed. Fluff couscous with fork.
2 Heat oil in large frying pan; cook garlic and green onion, stirring, until onion is soft. Add couscous; stir until heated through.
3 Add nuts to pan with currants and coriander; stir until mixed through.
per serving 19.3g total fat (2.3g saturated fat); 2404kJ (575 cal); 83.1g carbohydrate; 16.8g protein; 3.2g fibre
TIP This recipe can be made three hours ahead; store, covered, in the refrigerator.

soft polenta

preparation time 10 minutes
cooking time 30 minutes
serves 4

1 litre (4 cups) milk
1 large brown onion (200g), quartered
4 bay leaves
4 cloves garlic, quartered
8 black peppercorns
1 cup (170g) instant polenta
40g butter, chopped
1 cup (80g) finely grated parmesan

1 Place milk, onion, bay leaves, garlic and peppercorns in large saucepan; bring to a boil. Strain milk mixture; discard solids. Return milk to same pan.
2 Gradually whisk in polenta; cook, stirring, over medium heat about 20 minutes.
3 Whisk in butter and cheese; season to taste with salt and freshly ground black pepper. Serve immediately.
per serving 25.4g total fat (16.1g saturated fat); 2015kJ (482 cal); 43.7g carbohydrate; 20.5g protein; 2.4g fibre
TIP This recipe is best made just before serving.

chicken, pea, sage and prosciutto risotto

preparation time 20 minutes
cooking time 45 minutes
serves 4

3 cups (750ml) chicken stock
3 cups (750ml) water
10g butter
2 tablespoons olive oil
1 small brown onion (80g), chopped finely
2 cups (400g) arborio rice
½ cup (125ml) dry white wine
350g chicken breast fillets, chopped coarsely
2 cloves garlic, crushed
1½ cups (180g) frozen peas
6 slices prosciutto (90g)
2 tablespoons finely shredded fresh sage

1 Place stock and the water in large saucepan; bring to a boil. Reduce heat; simmer, covered.

2 Heat butter and half of the oil in large saucepan; cook onion, stirring, until soft. Add rice; stir rice to coat in mixture. Add wine; cook, stirring, until liquid is almost evaporated.

3 Stir in 1 cup simmering stock mixture; cook, stirring, over low heat until liquid is absorbed. Continue adding stock mixture, in 1-cup batches, stirring, until absorbed after each addition. Total cooking time should be about 35 minutes or until rice is tender.

4 Meanwhile, heat remaining oil in medium frying pan; cook chicken, stirring, until cooked through. Add garlic; stir until fragrant. Add chicken mixture to risotto with peas; stir to combine.

5 Cook prosciutto in same frying pan until crisp; drain on absorbent paper then break into rough pieces. Stir sage and half of the prosciutto into risotto.

6 Divide risotto among serving bowls; sprinkle with remaining prosciutto.

per serving 18.8g total fat (5.1g saturated fat); 2784kJ (666 cal); 84.1g carbohydrate; 24.5g protein; 3.9g fibre
TIP The type of rice you use is the secret of a good risotto. If possible, get one of the traditional risotto rices: arborio, carnaroli or vialone nano. These short, almost opalescent grains release huge amounts of starch during cooking, causing them to absorb the amazing amount of liquid required to give the risotto its perfect creamy consistency.

Holding the root end of an onion half with the fingers of one hand, first slice in lengthways then crossways to achieve a very fine dice.

The simmering stock mixture and rice should maintain a consistent temperature throughout the whole cooking process.

balti biryani

preparation time 20 minutes (plus refrigeration time)
cooking time 1 hour 30 minutes
serves 4

¾ cup (225g) balti curry paste
750g skirt steak, cut into 2cm cubes
2 cups (400g) basmati rice
8 cloves garlic, unpeeled
20g ghee
4 cardamom pods, bruised
4 cloves
1 cinnamon stick
3 green onions, sliced thinly
2 cups (500ml) beef stock
¾ cup (100g) toasted slivered almonds
¼ cup loosely packed fresh coriander leaves
2 fresh red thai chillies, sliced thinly

1 Preheat oven to moderate (180°C/160°C fan-forced).
2 Place curry paste in medium bowl; add steak, toss to coat in paste. Cover; refrigerate 1 hour.
3 Meanwhile, place rice in medium bowl, cover with water; stand 30 minutes. Drain rice in strainer; rinse under cold water until water runs clear. Drain.
4 Place garlic in small baking dish; roast, uncovered, about 20 minutes or until softened.
5 Melt ghee in large saucepan; cook cardamom, cloves, cinnamon and onion, stirring, until fragrant. Add steak mixture, reduce heat; simmer, covered, stirring occasionally, about 45 minutes or until steak is tender.
6 Add rice to pan with stock; simmer, covered, stirring occasionally, about 15 minutes or until rice is just tender.
7 Peel roasted garlic; chop finely. Add garlic, almonds and coriander to biryani, cover; stand 5 minutes. Sprinkle with chilli; serve with raita and naan, if desired.
per serving 41.6g total fat (8.6g saturated fat); 4000kJ (957 cal); 86.3g carbohydrate; 59g protein; 10.1g fibre

chicken and thai basil fried rice

preparation time 15 minutes
cooking time 10 minutes
serves 4

¼ cup (60ml) peanut oil
1 medium brown onion (150g), chopped finely
3 cloves garlic, crushed
2 long green thai chillies, seeded, chopped finely
1 tablespoon brown sugar
500g chicken breast fillets, chopped coarsely
2 medium red capsicums (400g), sliced thinly
200g green beans, chopped coarsely
4 cups cooked jasmine rice
2 tablespoons fish sauce
2 tablespoons soy sauce
½ cup loosely packed fresh thai basil leaves

1 Heat oil in wok; stir-fry onion, garlic and chilli until onion softens. Add sugar; stir-fry until dissolved. Add chicken; stir-fry until lightly browned. Add capsicum and beans; stir-fry until vegetables are just tender and chicken is cooked through.
2 Add rice to wok with sauces; stir-fry, tossing gently to combine. Remove wok from heat; add basil leaves, toss gently to combine.
per serving 17.3g total fat (3.2g saturated fat); 2345kJ (561 cal); 63.4g carbohydrate; 37.2g protein; 5.1g fibre
TIPS You need to cook about 2 cups of jasmine rice the day before you want to make this recipe. Rice must be cold and quite dry, in order to prevent it sticking together in clumps when added to the wok.
Frozen rice is particularly good for frying: after it has partially thawed, break the rice apart and spread it on sheets of absorbent paper before you start cooking.
Picking up about a quarter of the rice at a time, break it up with your fingers so the grains are already separate when they hit the wok.

koshari

preparation time 15 minutes
cooking time 45 minutes
serves 4

2 cups (400g) brown lentils
¾ cup (150g) white long-grain rice
1 cup coarsely chopped fresh flat-leaf parsley

CARAMELISED ONION
2 tablespoons olive oil
5 large brown onions (1kg), sliced thinly
1½ teaspoons ground allspice
1 teaspoon ground coriander
2 teaspoons white sugar

TOMATO CHILLI SAUCE
2 teaspoons olive oil
3 cloves garlic, crushed
½ teaspoon ground cumin
½ teaspoon dried chilli flakes
⅓ cup (80ml) white vinegar
415ml can tomato juice

1 Make caramelised onion.
2 Meanwhile, cook lentils in medium saucepan of boiling water, uncovered, until just tender; drain.
3 Cook rice in medium saucepan of boiling water, uncovered, until just tender; drain.
4 Remove half of the caramelised onion from pan; reserve. Add lentils and rice to pan, stirring, until heated through. Remove from heat; stir in half of the parsley.
5 Make tomato chilli sauce.
6 Divide koshari among serving bowls; top with reserved caramelised onion, remaining parsley and tomato chilli sauce.

CARAMELISED ONION
Heat oil in large frying pan; cook onion, allspice and coriander, stirring, until onion softens. Add sugar; cook, uncovered, stirring occasionally, about 30 minutes or until onion caramelises.

TOMATO CHILLI SAUCE
Heat oil in small saucepan; cook garlic, cumin and chilli, stirring, until fragrant. Add vinegar and juice; bring to a boil. Boil, uncovered, 2 minutes.

per serving 13.9g total fat (2g saturated fat); 2416kJ (578 cal); 83.3g carbohydrate; 31.3g protein; 18.8g fibre

prawn and asparagus risotto

preparation time 25 minutes
cooking time 45 minutes
serves 4

500g uncooked medium king prawns
3 cups (750ml) chicken stock
3 cups (750ml) water
10g butter
1 tablespoon olive oil
1 small brown onion (80g), chopped finely
2 cups (400g) arborio rice
½ cup (125ml) dry sherry
10g butter, extra
2 teaspoons olive oil, extra
2 cloves garlic, crushed
500g asparagus, chopped coarsely
⅓ cup (25g) coarsely grated parmesan
⅓ cup coarsely chopped fresh basil

1 Shell and devein prawns; chop prawn meat coarsely.
2 Place stock and the water in large saucepan; bring to a boil. Reduce heat; simmer, covered.
3 Meanwhile, heat butter and oil in large saucepan; cook onion, stirring, until soft. Add rice; stir to coat in onion mixture. Add sherry; cook, stirring, until liquid is almost evaporated.
4 Stir in 1 cup simmering stock mixture; cook, stirring, over low heat until liquid is absorbed. Continue adding stock mixture, in 1-cup batches, stirring, until absorbed after each addition. Total cooking time should be about 35 minutes or until rice is tender.
5 Heat extra butter and extra oil in medium frying pan; cook prawn meat and garlic, stirring, until prawn just changes colour.
6 Boil, steam or microwave asparagus until just tender; drain. Add asparagus, prawn mixture and cheese to risotto; cook, stirring, until cheese melts. Stir in basil.
per serving 14.7g total fat (5.5g saturated fat); 2516kJ (602 cal); 82.8g carbohydrate; 26.3g protein; 2.6g fibre

cheesy pesto polenta

preparation time 10 minutes
cooking time 25 minutes
serves 4

2⅓ cups (580ml) water
2⅓ cups (580ml) milk
1 cup (170g) polenta
½ cup (40g) finely grated parmesan
30g butter, chopped

PESTO
2 tablespoons finely grated parmesan
2 tablespoons toasted pine nuts
2 tablespoons olive oil
1 clove garlic, crushed
1 cup firmly packed fresh basil leaves

1 Combine the water and milk in large saucepan; bring to a boil. Gradually sprinkle polenta over milk mixture; cook, stirring, until polenta thickens slightly.
2 Reduce heat; simmer, uncovered, about 20 minutes or until polenta is thickened, stirring occasionally.
3 Meanwhile, blend or process ingredients for pesto until mixture forms a paste.
4 Add cheese to polenta with butter and pesto, stirring until cheese melts.
per serving 31.3g total fat (12.3g saturated fat); 2032kJ (486 cal); 37.1g carbohydrate; 14.9g protein; 2.6g fibre

paella

preparation time 20 minutes (plus standing time)
cooking time 40 minutes
serves 4

500g clams
1 tablespoon coarse salt
1 pinch saffron threads
¼ cup (60ml) hot water
300g medium uncooked prawns
500g small black mussels
2 tablespoons olive oil
2 chicken thigh fillets (220g), chopped coarsely
200g chorizo sausage, sliced
1 large red onion (300g), chopped
1 medium red capsicum (200g), chopped
2 cloves garlic, crushed
2 teaspoons sweet paprika
1½ cups (300g) medium-grain white rice
3½ cups (875ml) chicken stock
1 cup (125g) frozen peas
2 medium tomatoes (380g), peeled, seeded,
    chopped finely

1 Rinse clams under cold water and place in large bowl. Sprinkle with salt, cover with cold water; soak 2 hours (this purges them of any grit). Discard water, rinse clams thoroughly; drain.
2 Meanwhile, shell and devein prawns, leaving tails intact. Scrub mussels and remove beards.
3 Combine saffron and the hot water in small bowl; stand for 30 minutes.
4 Heat oil in 40cm-wide shallow pan; cook chicken until browned. Remove from pan. Cook chorizo in same pan until browned; drain on absorbent paper.
5 Add onion to same pan with capsicum, garlic and paprika; cook, stirring, until soft. Add rice; stir to coat in onion mixture. Return chicken and chorizo to pan. Add stock and saffron mixture; stir until combined. Bring to a boil; simmer, uncovered, about 12 minutes or until rice is almost tender. Sprinkle peas and tomato over rice; simmer, uncovered, 3 minutes.
6 Place clams, mussels and prawns over rice mixture. Cover pan with foil; simmer 5 minutes or until clams and mussels have opened and prawns are cooked. Discard any unopened shells.

per serving 30.5g total fat (8.7g saturated fat); 3156kJ (755 cal); 73.3g carbohydrate; 47g protein; 5.5g fibre
TIPS Chorizo is a spicy pork sausage made with garlic and red capsicums. Saffron threads are available at specialty food stores and some supermarkets. If unavailable, substitute a tiny pinch of saffron powder.

When shelling the prawns, leave the tails intact and use your fingers to pull out and remove the main vein that runs along the top.

After the mussels have been scrubbed, grasp one in your fingers and give a sharp tug on the beard to pull it away then rinse the mussel again.

mixed dhal

preparation time 15 minutes
cooking time 1 hour 15 minutes
serves 8

60g ghee
2 medium brown onions (300g), chopped finely
2 cloves garlic, crushed
5 cm piece fresh ginger (25g), grated
2 tablespoons black mustard seeds
2 tablespoons ground cumin
1 tablespoon ground coriander
2 teaspoons ground turmeric
¾ cup (150g) brown lentils
¾ cup (150g) red lentils
¾ cup (150g) yellow split peas
¾ cup (150g) green split peas
2 x 400g cans tomatoes
1 litre (4 cups) vegetable stock
⅔ cup (160ml) coconut cream
½ cup coarsely chopped fresh coriander

1 Heat ghee in large heavy-based saucepan; cook onion, garlic and ginger, stirring, until onion is soft. Add seeds and spices; cook, stirring, until fragrant.
2 Add lentils and peas to pan; stir to combine. Add undrained crushed tomatoes and stock; bring to a boil. Simmer, covered, about 1 hour, stirring occasionally, until lentils are tender and mixture thickens.
3 Just before serving, add coconut cream and coriander; stir over low heat until dhal is heated through.
per serving 13.6g total fat (9g saturated fat); 1338kJ (320 cal); 33.1g carbohydrate; 17.3g protein; 9.3g fibre
TIP Clarify ordinary butter if ghee is unavailable by heating butter in small pan until white sediment comes to the surface; skim and discard sediment, using the remaining heavy 'oil'.
SERVING SUGGESTION Serve with steamed basmati rice and homemade roti.

pilaf with spinach and pine nuts

preparation time 10 minutes
cooking time 25 minutes
serves 4

2 tablespoons olive oil
50g vermicelli, broken roughly
1 cup (200g) white long-grain rice
1 small brown onion (80g), chopped finely
1 cup (250ml) vegetable stock
1½ cups (375ml) water
100g baby spinach leaves, shredded coarsely
½ cup (80g) toasted pine nuts

1 Heat oil in large saucepan; cook vermicelli, stirring, about 2 minutes or until vermicelli is golden brown. Add rice and onion; cook, stirring, until onion softens and rice is almost translucent.
2 Add stock and the water; bring to a boil. Reduce heat; simmer, covered with a tight-fitting lid, about 20 minutes or until liquid is absorbed and rice is just tender.
3 Just before serving, stir spinach and nuts into pilaf.
per serving 23.8g total fat (2.3g saturated fat); 1885kJ (451 cal); 50.4g carbohydrate; 8.9g protein; 2.8g fibre

beetroot risotto with rocket

preparation time 30 minutes
cooking time 45 minutes
serves 4

2 medium beetroot (350g), peeled, grated coarsely
3 cups (750ml) vegetable stock
3 cups (750ml) water
1 tablespoon olive oil
1 large brown onion (200g), chopped finely
2 cloves garlic, crushed
1½ cups (300g) arborio rice
¼ cup (20g) coarsely grated parmesan
50g baby rocket leaves
1 tablespoon finely chopped fresh flat-leaf parsley

1 Place beetroot, stock and the water in large saucepan; bring to a boil. Reduce heat; simmer, uncovered.
2 Meanwhile, heat oil in large saucepan; cook onion and garlic, stirring, until onion softens. Add rice; stir to coat in onion mixture. Stir in 1 cup simmering beetroot mixture; cook, stirring, over low heat until liquid is absorbed. Continue adding beetroot mixture, in 1-cup batches, stirring, until liquid is absorbed after each addition. Total cooking time should be about 35 minutes or until rice is just tender; gently stir in cheese.
3 Divide beetroot risotto among serving bowls; top with combined rocket and parsley.
per serving 7.6g total fat (2.1g saturated fat); 1643kJ (393 cal); 69.4g carbohydrate; 11.5g protein; 4.1g fibre

felafel burgers

preparation time 15 minutes
cooking time 10 minutes
serves 4

2 x 300g cans chickpeas, rinsed, drained
1 medium brown onion (150g), chopped coarsely
2 cloves garlic, quartered
½ cup coarsely chopped fresh flat-leaf parsley
2 teaspoons ground coriander
1 teaspoon ground cumin
1 teaspoon bicarbonate of soda
2 tablespoons plain flour
1 egg, beaten lightly
1 loaf turkish bread (430g)
1 large tomato (220g), sliced thinly
20g rocket leaves

YOGURT AND TAHINI SAUCE
¼ cup (70g) yogurt
2 tablespoons tahini
1 tablespoon lemon juice

1 Blend or process chickpeas, onion, garlic, parsley, coriander, cumin, soda, flour and egg until almost smooth. Using hands, shape mixture into four burgers. Cook burgers on heated oiled flat plate, uncovered, about 10 minutes or until browned both sides.
2 Cut bread into quarters; toast both sides on heated oiled grill plate (or grill or barbecue).
3 Meanwhile, combine ingredients for yogurt and tahini sauce in small bowl.
4 Split each piece of toasted bread in half horizontally; sandwich sauce, tomato, burgers and rocket between bread halves.
per serving 11.3g total fat (2.1g saturated fat); 1960kJ (469 cal); 69.4g carbohydrate; 21.5g protein; 10.2g fibre
TIP When cooking felafel, use two spatulas to turn them carefully.

Pasta

Every cook should have an insurance policy of a few pasta recipes that can be put together quickly, using ingredients you usually have on hand. In this chapter, Penne Puttanesca is one such recipe, Spaghetti with Tuna, Chilli and Fresh Tomato is another, and Pasta with Smoked Salmon is a third, if you keep one of those small supermarket packs of smoked salmon in the freezer. Marvellous as pasta is for quick meals, though, don't forget it for such sumptuous creations as Eggplant Pastitsio or Ricotta and Spinach Stuffed Pasta Shells, which are among the great party dishes of the world.

spaghetti alla vongole

ricotta and spinach stuffed pasta shells

baked three cheese pasta

rigatoni bolognese

spaghetti alla vongole

preparation time 30 minutes (plus standing time)
cooking time 40 minutes
serves 6

1.5kg clams
1 tablespoon coarse cooking salt
¼ cup (60ml) olive oil
1 medium brown onion (150g), chopped finely
2 cloves garlic, crushed
2 anchovy fillets, drained, chopped finely
1 fresh red thai chilli, chopped finely
2 teaspoons chopped fresh thyme
20 medium egg tomatoes (1.5kg), peeled,
    seeded, chopped finely
2 tablespoons chopped fresh flat-leaf parsley
500g spaghetti

1 Rinse clams under cold water and place in large bowl. Sprinkle with salt, cover with cold water and soak for 2 hours (this purges them of any grit). Discard water, then rinse clams thoroughly; drain.
2 Heat 2 tablespoons of the oil in large saucepan, add clams, cover with tight-fitting lid. Cook over high heat about 8 minutes or until all clams have opened.
3 Strain clam cooking liquid through fine cloth or tea-towel. Return liquid to same cleaned pan; cook, uncovered, until liquid is reduced to 1 cup (250ml). Reserve clam stock.
4 Heat remaining oil in another saucepan, add onion, garlic, anchovy, chilli and thyme; cook, stirring, until onion is soft. Add tomato and reserved clam stock; cook, uncovered, about 10 minutes or until sauce is thickened. Add clams, stir until heated through. Stir in parsley.
5 Meanwhile, cook pasta in large saucepan of boiling water, uncovered, until just tender, drain. Toss clam sauce through spaghetti.
per serving 10.6g total fat (1.5g saturated fat); 1848kJ (442 cal); 64.2g carbohydrate; 21.3g protein; 6.8g fibre

ricotta and spinach stuffed pasta shells

preparation time 20 minutes
cooking time 1 hour 5 minutes
serves 4

32 large pasta shells (280g)
500g spinach
250g low-fat ricotta
500g low-fat cottage cheese
600ml bottled tomato pasta sauce
1 cup (250ml) vegetable stock
1 tablespoon finely grated parmesan

1 Cook pasta in large saucepan of boiling water, uncovered, 3 minutes; drain. Cool slightly.
2 Preheat oven to moderate (180°C/160°C fan-forced). Oil shallow 2-litre (8-cup) ovenproof dish.
3 Boil, steam or microwave spinach until just wilted; drain. Chop spinach finely; squeeze out excess liquid.
4 Combine spinach and cheeses in large bowl; spoon spinach mixture into pasta shells.
5 Combine sauce and stock in prepared dish. Place pasta shells in dish; sprinkle with parmesan. Bake, covered, about 1 hour or until pasta is tender.
per serving 10.2g total fat (5.3g saturated fat); 2291kJ (548 cal); 70.3g carbohydrate; 43.4g protein; 9.1g fibre
SERVING SUGGESTION Accompany pasta shells with a loaf of ciabatta and a fresh green salad drizzled with a balsamic vinegar dressing.

baked three cheese pasta

preparation time 10 minutes
cooking time 30 minutes
serves 4

375g macaroni pasta
300ml cream
⅓ cup (80ml) vegetable stock
1¼ cups (150g) grated fontina cheese
⅓ cup (75g) crumbled gorgonzola cheese
1¼ cups (100g) coarsely grated parmesan
1 teaspoon dijon mustard
2 tablespoons chopped fresh flat-leaf parsley
1 tablespoon chopped fresh chives

1 Preheat oven to moderate (180°C/160°C fan-forced).
2 Cook pasta in large saucepan of boiling water, uncovered, until just tender; drain.
3 Meanwhile, heat cream and stock in a saucepan until hot. Remove pan from heat, add fontina, gorgonzola and half the parmesan; stir until melted. Add mustard and herbs; season to taste with freshly ground black pepper. Add salt, if necessary. Combine cream mixture with drained pasta.
4 Pour cheesy pasta mixture into 2.5-litre (10-cup) ovenproof dish. Top with remaining parmesan. Bake, uncovered, 20 minutes or until browned.
per serving 59.2g total fat (38g saturated fat); 3917kJ (937 cal); 66.4g carbohydrate; 35.4g protein; 3.3g fibre
TIP This recipe is best made close to serving.

rigatoni bolognese

preparation time 5 minutes
cooking time 30 minutes
serves 4

1 medium brown onion (150g), chopped coarsely
1 small carrot (70g), chopped coarsely
1 trimmed celery stalk (100g), chopped coarsely
1 tablespoon olive oil
50g butter
2 cloves garlic, crushed
2 italian-style sausages (170g)
500g veal and pork mince
2 tablespoons tomato paste
½ cup (125ml) dry white wine
¼ cup (60ml) beef stock
425g can crushed tomatoes
2 tablespoons finely chopped fresh basil
2 tablespoons finely chopped fresh flat-leaf parsley
500g rigatoni
¼ cup (20g) coarsely grated parmesan

1 Blend or process onion, carrot and celery until chopped finely.
2 Heat oil and butter in large saucepan; cook onion mixture and garlic, stirring occasionally, 5 minutes.
3 Meanwhile, squeeze filling from sausages; discard casings. Add sausage filling and mince to pan; cook, stirring, until meat is browned lightly.
4 Add paste to pan with wine, stirring to combine; bring to a boil. Reduce heat; simmer, uncovered, 2 minutes. Add stock and undrained tomatoes; return to a boil. Reduce heat; simmer, uncovered, about 20 minutes or until bolognese thickens. Stir in herbs.
5 Meanwhile, cook pasta in large saucepan of boiling water, uncovered, until just tender; drain.
6 Divide pasta among serving bowls, top with bolognese; sprinkle with parmesan.
per serving 36.9g total fat (16.5g saturated fat); 3933kJ (941 cal); 96.5g carbohydrate; 49.4g protein; 10.4g fibre

eggplant pastitsio

preparation time 40 minutes
cooking time 1 hour 20 minutes
serves 8

2 large eggplants (1kg)
150g bavette
30g butter, melted
3 eggs, beaten lightly
⅓ cup (25g) finely grated parmesan
¼ cup finely chopped fresh basil
¼ cup finely chopped fresh flat-leaf parsley
½ teaspoon ground nutmeg
500g lamb mince
1 teaspoon olive oil
1 medium brown onion (150g), chopped finely
1 clove garlic, crushed
½ teaspoon ground cinnamon
1 tablespoon tomato paste
¼ cup (60ml) dry red wine
¼ cup (60ml) beef stock
425g can crushed tomatoes

WHITE SAUCE
60g butter
⅓ cup (50g) plain flour
2 cups (500ml) milk

1 Preheat oven to hot (220°C/200°C fan-forced). Oil oven trays.

2 Cut eggplants lengthways into very thin slices; place eggplant, in single layer, on prepared trays, cover with foil. Bake about 25 minutes or until eggplant is softened and browned. Remove from oven.

3 Reduce oven to moderate (180°C/160°C fan-forced). Oil deep 22cm round cake pan.

4 Meanwhile, cook pasta in medium saucepan of boiling water, uncovered, until just tender; drain. Rinse under cold water; drain. Combine in medium bowl with butter, eggs, cheese, herbs and nutmeg.

5 Cook mince in heated large non-stick frying pan, stirring, until changed in colour; remove mince, drain pan.

6 Heat oil in same pan; cook onion and garlic, stirring, about 2 minutes or until onion softens. Return mince to pan with cinnamon and paste; cook, stirring, 2 minutes. Add wine, stock and undrained tomatoes; bring to a boil. Reduce heat; simmer, uncovered, stirring occasionally, about 15 minutes or until sauce thickens.

7 Meanwhile, make white sauce.

8 Line base and side of prepared cake pan with two-thirds of the eggplant. Place half of the pasta mixture in pan; cover with white sauce. Spread lamb sauce over white sauce; top with remaining pasta mixture. Use remaining eggplant to completely cover pastitsio; cover tightly with foil. Bake about 30 minutes or until heated through. Stand 10 minutes before serving.

WHITE SAUCE
Melt butter in medium saucepan, add flour; cook, stirring, about 2 minutes or until mixture thickens and bubbles. Gradually stir in milk; cook, stirring, until sauce boils and thickens.

per serving 20.3g total fat (11g saturated fat); 1618kJ (387 cal); 26.4g carbohydrate; 23.7g protein; 4.8g fibre
TIP Bucatini or macaroni can be used if bavette is not available.

Eggplant should be sliced lengthways as thinly as possible to result in enough pieces to adequately line the pan and cover the pastitsio.

Position the softened eggplant slices vertically, starting from just above the pan's top edge to toward the centre of the base.

pasta with smoked salmon

preparation time 5 minutes
cooking time 15 minutes
serves 4

500g casarecce or spiral pasta
1 cup (250ml) fish stock
300ml cream
200g smoked salmon off-cuts or strips,
    chopped coarsely
4 green onions, sliced thinly
2 tablespoons finely chopped fresh dill
1 teaspoon finely grated lemon rind
2 tablespoons lemon juice, optional

1 Cook pasta in large saucepan of boiling water, uncovered, until just tender; drain.
2 Meanwhile, place stock and cream in medium saucepan; bring to a boil. Reduce heat; simmer, uncovered, about 5 minutes or until thickened slightly.
3 Combine pasta with salmon, onion, dill, rind and cream mixture in large bowl; add juice and season to taste with freshly ground black pepper.
per serving 36.6g total fat (22.4g saturated fat); 3332kJ (797 cal); 88.5g carbohydrate; 27.9g protein; 4.4g fibre
TIP This recipe is best made just before serving.
SERVING SUGGESTION Serve with a green salad, if desired.

spaghetti with tuna, chilli and fresh tomato

preparation time 10 minutes
cooking time 10 minutes
serves 4

375g bavette or spaghetti
2 x 185g cans tuna in chilli oil
500g ripe tomatoes, chopped
1 fresh large red chilli, sliced
¼ cup loosely packed fresh oregano leaves
⅓ cup (80ml) lemon juice
¼ cup (60ml) extra virgin olive oil

1 Cook pasta in large saucepan of boiling water, uncovered, until just tender; drain.
2 Meanwhile, drain tuna, reserving 1 tablespoon of the oil. Place tuna in a large bowl; flake with a fork.
3 Add tomatoes to large bowl with chilli, oregano, juice, olive oil, reserved oil and pasta; toss gently to combine. Season to taste with salt.
per serving 25.1g total fat (3.8g saturated fat); 2592kJ (620 cal); 66.9g carbohydrate; 30.2g protein; 4.6g fibre
TIP This recipe is best made just before serving.

kumara gnocchi with rocket and basil pesto

preparation time 45 minutes (plus refrigeration time)
cooking time 25 minutes
serves 4

2 medium kumara (800g), unpeeled
4 small desiree potatoes (480g), unpeeled
1 cup (150g) plain flour
1 egg yolk

ROCKET AND BASIL PESTO
2 tablespoons olive oil
2 tablespoons finely grated parmesan
1 clove garlic, quartered
2 tablespoons lemon juice
50g baby rocket leaves
1 cup firmly packed fresh basil leaves

1 Boil, steam or microwave kumara and potatoes, separately, until tender; drain. Peel when cool enough to handle; chop coarsely. Using wooden spoon, push kumara and potato through fine sieve into large bowl.
2 Stir flour and yolk into kumara mixture then knead dough gently on floured surface until mixture comes together. Divide dough into four portions; roll each portion into 40cm log, cut each log into 24 pieces. Roll each piece into a ball; roll balls, one at a time, along the inside tines of a floured fork, pressing gently on top of dough with index finger to form gnocchi shape (grooved on one side and dimpled on the other). Place gnocchi, in single layer, on lightly floured trays, cover; refrigerate 1 hour.
3 Blend or process ingredients for rocket and basil pesto until smooth.
4 Cook gnocchi, in batches, in large saucepan of boiling water, uncovered, about 3 minutes or until gnocchi float to surface. Remove gnocchi from pan with slotted spoon. Gently toss gnocchi and pesto in large bowl; divide among serving bowls, serve topped with extra baby rocket leaves, if desired.
per serving 12.6g total fat (2.5g saturated fat); 1914kJ (458 cal); 71.8g carbohydrate; 13.4g protein; 8g fibre
TIP Gnocchi dough is very soft, so you'll need an extra half a cup of plain flour for the board when kneading and rolling to prevent it from sticking.

prawn ravioli with mint and pea puree

preparation time 40 minutes
cooking time 15 minutes
serves 4

1¼ cups (310ml) chicken stock
2½ cups (300g) frozen peas
½ cup loosely packed fresh mint leaves
40g butter
1 clove garlic, crushed
1kg uncooked medium king prawns
1 egg white
1 tablespoon sweet chilli sauce
2 tablespoons lemon juice
1 long green chilli, chopped finely
40 wonton wrappers
¼ cup (30g) frozen peas, extra

1 Bring stock to a boil in medium saucepan. Add peas, mint and butter; return to a boil. Reduce heat; simmer, uncovered, about 5 minutes or until peas are soft. Cool 10 minutes; blend or process with garlic until smooth.
2 Meanwhile, shell and devein prawns; chop half of the prawns coarsely. Blend or process remaining whole prawns with egg white, sauce and half of the juice until mixture is almost smooth. Combine prawn mixture with chopped prawn and chilli in large bowl.
3 Centre 1 level tablespoon of the prawn mixture on one wrapper; brush around edges with water. Top with another wrapper; press edges together to seal. Repeat with remaining prawn mixture and wrappers to make 20 ravioli. Cook ravioli, in batches, in large saucepan of boiling water, uncovered, until ravioli float to the surface and are cooked.
4 Meanwhile, return pea puree to same medium saucepan, add extra peas and remaining juice; stir over heat until peas are just tender.
5 Divide drained ravioli among serving bowls; top with pea puree.
per serving 10.8g total fat (6g saturated fat); 1613kJ (386 cal); 34g carbohydrate; 37.3g protein; 6.7g fibre

chicken and fresh pea risoni

preparation time 15 minutes
cooking time 30 minutes
serves 4

400g chicken breast fillets
1 litre (4 cups) chicken stock
300g sugar snap peas, trimmed
1 cup (160g) fresh shelled peas
1 tablespoon olive oil
1 small leek (200g), sliced thinly
1 clove garlic, crushed
500g risoni
½ cup (125ml) dry white wine
1 tablespoon white wine vinegar
1 tablespoon finely chopped fresh tarragon

1 Combine chicken and stock in medium frying pan; bring to a boil. Reduce heat; simmer, uncovered, about 10 minutes or until cooked through. Cool chicken in poaching liquid 10 minutes. Remove chicken from pan; reserve stock. Slice chicken thinly.
2 Meanwhile, boil, steam or microwave sugar snap and shelled peas, separately, until just tender; drain.
3 Heat oil in large saucepan; cook leek and garlic, stirring, until leek softens. Add risoni; stir to coat in leek mixture. Add wine; stir until wine is almost absorbed. Add reserved stock; bring to a boil. Reduce heat; simmer, uncovered, stirring occasionally, until stock is absorbed and risoni is just tender. Stir in vinegar; remove from heat. Gently stir in chicken, peas and tarragon. Serve in individual serving bowls.
per serving 9.6g total fat (2g saturated fat); 2801kJ (670 cal); 97.1g carbohydrate; 42.5g protein; 7.6g fibre

penne with char-grilled capsicum and pine nuts

preparation time 15 minutes
cooking time 20 minutes
serves 4

2 large red capsicums (700g)
375g penne
2 tablespoons olive oil
2 cloves garlic, crushed
½ cup (80g) toasted pine nuts
2 fresh small red thai chillies, chopped finely
¼ cup (60ml) lemon juice
100g baby rocket leaves
100g fetta, crumbled

1 Quarter capsicums; discard seeds and membranes. Roast under grill or in very hot oven, skin-side up, until skin blisters and blackens. Cover capsicum pieces in plastic or paper for 5 minutes; peel away skin, slice pieces thinly.
2 Cook pasta in large saucepan of boiling water, uncovered, until just tender; drain.
3 Meanwhile, heat oil in large frying pan; cook garlic, nuts and chilli, stirring, about 2 minutes or until fragrant. Add capsicum and juice; stir until hot.
4 Place pasta and capsicum mixture in large bowl with rocket and cheese; toss gently to combine.
per serving 30.5g total fat (6.2g saturated fat); 2755kJ (659 cal); 74.4g carbohydrate; 21g protein; 8.2g fibre
TIP A few hours spent in the kitchen on Sunday will go a long way towards simplifying a weeknight meal like this. Char-grill and peel several capsicums at one time then store the roasted sliced flesh, covered with olive oil in a tightly sealed glass jar and refrigerated, taking out only as much as you need for any given recipe.

creamy farfalle with fried zucchini

preparation time 10 minutes
cooking time 20 minutes
serves 4

375g farfalle
2 tablespoons olive oil
3 cloves garlic, crushed
6 small zucchini (540g), grated coarsely
2 teaspoons finely grated lemon rind
1 tablespoon finely chopped fresh flat-leaf parsley
3 green onions, sliced thinly
½ cup (40g) finely grated parmesan
300ml cream

1 Cook pasta in large saucepan of boiling water, uncovered, until just tender; drain.
2 Meanwhile, heat oil in large frying pan; cook garlic, stirring, about 2 minutes or until fragrant. Add zucchini; cook, stirring, 2 minutes.
3 Combine rind, parsley, onion and cheese in small bowl.
4 Add cream and hot pasta to zucchini mixture; stir gently over low heat until heated through. Serve pasta immediately, topped with cheese mixture.

per serving 46.6g total fat (25.2g saturated fat); 3189kJ (763 cal); 68.9g carbohydrate; 17.7g protein; 5.9g fibre

ricotta gnocchi in fresh tomato sauce

preparation time 10 minutes
cooking time 20 minutes
serves 4

500g firm ricotta
1 cup (80g) finely grated parmesan
½ cup (75g) plain flour
2 eggs, beaten lightly
1 tablespoon extra virgin olive oil
4 medium tomatoes (760g), chopped coarsely
6 green onions, sliced thinly
2 tablespoons coarsely chopped fresh oregano
2 tablespoons balsamic vinegar
2 tablespoons extra virgin olive oil, extra
½ cup (40g) shaved parmesan

1 Bring large saucepan of water to a boil.
2 Meanwhile, combine ricotta, grated parmesan, flour, eggs and oil in large bowl. Drop rounded tablespoons of mixture into boiling water; cook, without stirring, until gnocchi float to the surface. Remove from pan with slotted spoon; drain, cover to keep warm.
3 Combine tomato, onion, oregano and vinegar in medium bowl.
4 Divide warm gnocchi among serving bowls, top with fresh tomato sauce; drizzle with extra oil, sprinkle with shaved parmesan.

per serving 40.6g total fat (18g saturated fat); 2383kJ (570 cal); 19.4g carbohydrate; 32.1g protein; 3.3g fibre

pappardelle chicken and creamy mushroom sauce

preparation time 15 minutes
cooking time 15 minutes
serves 4

2 tablespoons olive oil
1 clove garlic, crushed
1 small brown onion (80g), chopped finely
250g swiss brown mushrooms, sliced thinly
¾ cup (180ml) cream
2 teaspoons finely chopped fresh rosemary
20g butter
500g pappardelle
3 cups (480g) coarsely shredded cooked chicken
½ cup (60g) coarsely chopped toasted walnuts
¼ cup coarsely chopped fresh flat-leaf parsley
¾ cup (60g) finely grated parmesan

1 Heat oil in large frying pan; cook garlic and onion, stirring, until onion softens. Add mushroom; cook, stirring, until just tender.
2 Add cream and rosemary to pan; bring to a boil. Reduce heat; simmer, uncovered, until sauce thickens slightly. Add butter; stir until butter melts.
3 Meanwhile, cook pasta in large saucepan of boiling water, uncovered, until just tender; drain. Return to pan.
4 Add hot cream sauce, chicken, nuts, parsley and half of the cheese to hot pasta; toss gently to combine. Serve immediately, sprinkled with remaining cheese.
per serving 54.9g total fat (24.1g saturated fat); 4523kJ (1082 cal); 88.8g carbohydrate; 48.5g protein; 7.2g fibre

penne puttanesca

preparation time 10 minutes
cooking time 20 minutes
serves 4

500g penne
⅓ cup (80ml) extra virgin olive oil
3 cloves garlic, crushed
1 teaspoon chilli flakes
5 medium tomatoes (950g), chopped coarsely
200g seeded kalamata olives
8 anchovy fillets, drained, chopped coarsely
⅓ cup (65g) rinsed drained capers
⅓ cup coarsely chopped fresh flat-leaf parsley
2 tablespoons finely shredded fresh basil

1 Cook pasta in large saucepan of boiling water, uncovered, until just tender; drain.
2 Meanwhile, heat oil in large frying pan, add garlic; cook, stirring, until fragrant. Add chilli and tomato; cook, stirring, 5 minutes. Add olives, anchovy, capers and herbs; cook, stirring occasionally, about 5 minutes or until sauce thickens slightly.
3 Add pasta to sauce; toss gently to combine.
per serving 21.2g total fat (3.1g saturated fat); 2855kJ (683 cal); 102.6g carbohydrate; 19.1g protein; 8.5g fibre

Vegetables

Vegetables can provide some of the most adventurous and satisfying ways to eat. In this chapter, you will find delicious and sustaining main courses as well as accompaniments with character, ready to add presence to plain meats, poultry or fish. Put two or three recipes together – for example, a curry plus Mixed Vegetables in Coconut Milk, or Stuffed Capsicums with Lentils followed by Steamed Spinach Dumplings and Stir-fried Cauliflower, Choy Sum and Snake Beans – and you have a vegetarian feast whose rich array of flavours and textures would certainly delight non-vegetarians too.

char-grilled vegetable salad with balsamic dressing

vegetable curry with yogurt

wok-tossed greens with oyster sauce

grilled vegetable and ricotta stack

char-grilled vegetable salad with balsamic dressing

preparation time 10 minutes
cooking time 20 minutes
serves 8

1 large red onion (300g)
8 medium egg tomatoes (600g)
8 baby eggplants (480g)
4 medium zucchini (480g)
4 medium yellow patty-pan squash (120g), halved
2 medium red capsicum (400g), sliced thickly

BALSAMIC DRESSING
¼ cup (60ml) extra virgin olive oil
¼ cup (60ml) balsamic vinegar
1 clove garlic, crushed

1 Cut onion and tomatoes into eight wedges each; thinly slice eggplants and zucchini lengthways.
2 Cook onion, tomato, eggplant and zucchini with squash and capsicum, in batches, on heated oiled grill plate (or grill or barbecue) until vegetables are browned lightly and just tender.
3 Meanwhile, place ingredients for balsamic dressing in screw-top jar; shake well.
4 Combine vegetables in large bowl or on serving platter. Drizzle with balsamic dressing; toss gently to combine.
per serving 7.4g total fat (1g saturated fat); 485kJ (116 cal); 8.5g carbohydrate; 3.8g protein; 4.8g fibre
TIP This recipe is just as good served at room temperature as it is eaten hot.

vegetable curry with yogurt

preparation time 25 minutes
cooking time 15 minutes
serves 4

2 teaspoons vegetable oil
4cm piece fresh ginger (20g), grated
3 green onions, sliced thinly
2 cloves garlic, crushed
1 long green chilli, chopped finely
¼ teaspoon ground cardamom
1 teaspoon garam masala
1 tablespoon curry powder
1 teaspoon ground turmeric
2 medium green apples (300g), grated coarsely
1 tablespoon lemon juice
2 cups (500ml) vegetable stock
½ small cauliflower (500g), cut into florets
4 yellow patty-pan squash (100g), halved
2 small green zucchini (180g), sliced thickly
150g baby spinach leaves
200g low-fat yogurt

1 Heat oil in large saucepan; cook ginger, onion, garlic, chilli, cardamom, garam masala, curry powder and turmeric until fragrant.
2 Add apple to pan with juice and stock; cook, uncovered, 5 minutes, stirring occasionally.
3 Add cauliflower to pan with squash and zucchini; cook, uncovered, until vegetables are just tender. Remove from heat; stir spinach and yogurt into curry just before serving.
per serving 3.8g total fat (0.6g saturated fat); 585kJ (140 cal); 15.9g carbohydrate; 9.9g protein; 6.6g fibre

wok-tossed greens with oyster sauce

preparation time 10 minutes
cooking time 10 minutes
serves 8

2 tablespoons peanut oil
4 cloves garlic, chopped finely
500g flat mushrooms, sliced thickly
1 tablespoon sesame seeds
400g baby bok choy, quartered
600g choy sum, chopped coarsely
4 green onions, chopped coarsely
2 tablespoons light soy sauce
⅓ cup (80ml) oyster sauce
1 teaspoon sesame oil

1 Heat half of the peanut oil in wok; stir-fry garlic, mushrooms and seeds until mushrooms just soften. Remove from wok.
2 Heat remaining peanut oil in same wok; stir-fry bok choy and choy sum until just wilted. Return mushroom mixture to wok with onion, combined sauces, and sesame oil; stir-fry until heated through.
per serving 6.6g total fat (1g saturated fat); 422kJ (101 cal); 3.4g carbohydrate; 4.8g protein; 3.7g fibre
TIPS You can use any leafy asian vegetable you like in this recipe. This recipe is best made just before serving.
SERVING SUGGESTION Serve with a side bowl of sambal oelek to add some spice to this recipe.

grilled vegetable and ricotta stack

preparation time 20 minutes
cooking time 30 minutes
serves 4

2 baby eggplants (120g), sliced thickly lengthways
1 medium green capsicum (200g),
   sliced thickly lengthways
1 medium red capsicum (200g),
   sliced thickly lengthways
2 large zucchini (300g), sliced thickly lengthways
4 x 175g flat mushrooms, stems removed
2 cups (400g) ricotta
2 cloves garlic, crushed
½ cup coarsely chopped fresh basil
2 tablespoons finely chopped fresh chives
1 tablespoon coarsely chopped fresh oregano
1 tablespoon finely grated lemon rind
2 tablespoons toasted pine nuts

SEMI-DRIED TOMATO PESTO
¼ cup (35g) drained semi-dried tomatoes, halved
½ cup firmly packed fresh basil leaves
2 tablespoons balsamic vinegar
2 tablespoons water

1 Cook eggplant, capsicums, zucchini and mushrooms, in batches, on heated oiled grill plate (or grill or barbecue) until tender.
2 Meanwhile, combine cheese, garlic, herbs and rind in medium bowl.
3 Make semi-dried tomato pesto.
4 Divide mushrooms, stem-side up, among serving plates; layer with cheese mixture then random slices of eggplant, zucchini and capsicums. Drizzle with pesto; sprinkle with nuts.
SEMI-DRIED TOMATO PESTO
Blend or process semi-dried tomato and basil until mixture forms a paste. With motor operating, gradually add combined vinegar and water in thin, steady stream until pesto is smooth.
per serving 17.9g total fat (7.6g saturated fat); 1242kJ (297 cal); 12.3g carbohydrate; 21.6g protein; 9.7g fibre

mixed vegetables in coconut milk

preparation time 25 minutes
cooking time 15 minutes
serves 4

6 cloves garlic, quartered
3 fresh small red thai chillies, chopped coarsely
2 tablespoons coarsely chopped fresh lemon grass
1 tablespoon coarsely chopped pickled galangal
4 cm piece fresh ginger (20g), chopped coarsely
4 cm piece fresh turmeric (20g), chopped coarsely
2 cups (500ml) coconut milk
2 whole kaffir lime leaves
4 medium zucchini (480g), chopped coarsely
6 yellow patty-pan squash (240g), chopped coarsely
200g cauliflower florets
100g baby corn, halved lengthways
2 tablespoons soy sauce
2 tablespoons lime juice
⅓ cup coarsely chopped fresh thai basil
2 kaffir lime leaves, shredded finely

1 Blend or process (or crush using mortar and pestle) garlic, chilli, lemon grass, galangal, ginger and turmeric until mixture forms a paste.
2 Place half of the coconut milk in wok or large saucepan; bring to a boil. Add garlic paste; whisk over high heat until smooth. Reduce heat, add remaining coconut milk and whole lime leaves; simmer, stirring, until coconut milk mixture thickens slightly.
3 Add zucchini, squash, cauliflower and corn; bring to a boil. Reduce heat; simmer, uncovered, 5 minutes or until vegetables are just tender. Remove from heat; remove and discard whole lime leaves. Stir sauce, juice and basil into vegetable mixture.
4 Divide among serving bowl; top with shredded lime leaves.
per serving 27g total fat (22.8g saturated fat); 1404kJ (336 cal); 15.1g carbohydrate; 8.7g protein; 8.7g fibre

maple-roast kumara

preparation time 5 minutes
cooking time 1 hour 10 minutes
serves 8

4 small kumara (1.25kg)
¼ cup (60ml) olive oil
¼ cup (60ml) maple syrup

1 Preheat oven to moderately slow (160°C/140°C fan-forced). Line medium baking dish with baking paper.
2 Cut kumara in half lengthways, then crossways; combine with oil and syrup in prepared dish. Roast, uncovered, 40 minutes.
3 Increase oven temperature to hot (220°C/200°C fan-forced). Roast, uncovered, further 30 minutes or until browned and cooked through.
per serving 7g total fat (1g saturated fat); 732kJ (175 cal); 25.9g carbohydrate; 2.6g protein; 2.5g fibre
TIP This recipe can be made several hours ahead; reheat just before serving.

steamed spinach dumplings with fresh tomato and herb sauce

preparation time 30 minutes (plus standing time)
cooking time 15 minutes
serves 4

2 x 250g packets frozen spinach, thawed
200g ricotta
1 clove garlic, crushed
1 egg white
1 tablespoon plain flour
¼ cup (20g) finely grated parmesan
1½ cups (110g) stale breadcrumbs
¼ teaspoon ground nutmeg
1 tablespoon finely chopped fresh chives
2 tablespoons finely grated parmesan, extra

FRESH TOMATO AND HERB SAUCE
½ cup (125ml) dry white wine
4 medium tomatoes (600g), chopped finely
2 tablespoons finely chopped flat-leaf parsley
1 teaspoon caster sugar

1 Squeeze excess liquid from spinach. Combine spinach in large bowl with ricotta, garlic, egg white, flour, parmesan, breadcrumbs, nutmeg and chives; roll level tablespoons of the mixture into balls. Place balls, in single layer, about 2cm apart in baking-paper-lined bamboo steamer fitted over large saucepan of boiling water; steam, covered, about 10 minutes or until dumplings are heated through.
2 Meanwhile, make fresh tomato and herb sauce.
3 Serve dumplings with sauce and extra parmesan.
FRESH TOMATO AND HERB SAUCE
Bring wine to a boil in medium saucepan. Reduce heat; simmer, uncovered, until reduced by half. Add tomato; return to a boil. Boil, uncovered, about 10 minutes or until thickened slightly. Stir in parsley and sugar.
per serving 10.2g total fat (5.5g saturated fat); 1237kJ (296 cal); 25.9g carbohydrate; 19.4g protein; 9.3g fibre

stir-fried cauliflower, choy sum and snake beans

preparation time 20 minutes
cooking time 10 minutes
serves 4

1 tablespoon peanut oil
2 cloves garlic, crushed
1 teaspoon ground turmeric
1 teaspoon finely chopped coriander root
   and stem mixture
4 green onions, sliced thinly
500g cauliflower florets
¼ cup (60ml) water
200g snake beans, cut into 5cm pieces
200g choy sum, chopped coarsely
1 tablespoon lime juice
1 tablespoon soy sauce
1 tablespoon coarsely chopped fresh coriander

1 Heat oil in wok; stir-fry garlic, turmeric, coriander mixture and onion until onion just softens. Remove from wok; keep warm.
2 Add cauliflower to same wok with the water; stir-fry until cauliflower is almost tender. Add beans and choy sum; stir-fry until vegetables are just tender.
3 Add juice, sauce, chopped coriander and onion mixture; stir-fry until heated through.
per serving 5.1g total fat (0.8g saturated fat); 368kJ (88 cal); 4.8g carbohydrate; 5.6g protein; 4.8g fibre

stuffed capsicums with lentils

preparation time 15 minutes
cooking time 30 minutes
serves 4

1 tablespoon olive oil
1 small brown onion (80g), chopped finely
1 clove garlic, crushed
1 small carrot (70g), chopped finely
1 small green zucchini (90g), chopped finely
¼ cup (60ml) water
¼ cup (50g) red lentils
¼ cup (55g) risoni
1 tablespoon tomato paste
1 cup (250ml) vegetable stock
12 baby red capsicums (540g)
2 tablespoons finely grated parmesan

1 Preheat oven to hot (220°C/200°C fan-forced). Line oven tray with baking paper.
2 Heat oil in large saucepan; cook onion and garlic, stirring, until onion softens. Add carrot and zucchini; cook, stirring, until vegetables are tender. Stir in the water, lentils, risoni, paste and stock; bring to a boil. Reduce heat; simmer, uncovered, about 10 minutes or until lentils are tender.
3 Meanwhile, carefully cut tops off capsicums; discard tops. Discard seeds and membranes, leaving capsicums intact. Place capsicums on prepared tray; roast, uncovered, about 15 minutes or until just softened.
4 Divide lentil mixture among capsicums; sprinkle with cheese. Place under hot grill until cheese melts.
per serving 6.7g total fat (1.5g saturated fat); 769kJ (184 cal); 21.8g carbohydrate; 9.3g protein; 5g fibre

potato and cheese kofta with tomato tamarind sauce

preparation time 30 minutes (plus standing time)
cooking time 35 minutes
serves 4

2 medium potatoes (400g)
2 tablespoons finely chopped fresh coriander
½ cup (75g) toasted unsalted cashews,
   chopped finely
½ cup (60g) frozen peas, thawed
vegetable oil, for deep-frying
4 hard-boiled eggs, halved

CHEESE
1 litre (4 cups) milk
2 tablespoons lemon juice

TOMATO TAMARIND SAUCE
1 tablespoon olive oil
1 clove garlic, crushed
3cm piece fresh ginger (15g), grated
½ teaspoon dried chilli flakes
1 teaspoon ground cumin
1 teaspoon ground coriander
½ teaspoon mustard seeds
¼ cup (60ml) tamarind concentrate
2 x 400g cans crushed tomatoes

1 Make cheese.
2 Meanwhile, boil, steam or microwave potato until tender; drain.
3 Make tomato tamarind sauce.
4 Mash potato in large bowl; stir in cheese, coriander, nuts and peas until combined. Heat oil in wok; deep-fry level tablespoons of the potato mixture, in batches, until cooked through. Drain on absorbent paper.
5 Add koftas to tomato tamarind sauce; simmer, uncovered, 5 minutes.
6 Divide koftas and tomato tamarind sauce among serving plates; top with egg.
CHEESE
Bring milk to a boil in medium saucepan. Remove from heat; stir in juice. Cool 10 minutes. Pour through muslin-lined sieve into medium bowl; stand cheese mixture in sieve over bowl 40 minutes. Discard liquid in bowl.
TOMATO TAMARIND SAUCE
Heat oil in large saucepan; cook garlic and ginger, stirring, until fragrant. Add chilli, spices and seeds; cook, stirring, 1 minute. Add tamarind and undrained tomatoes; bring to a boil. Reduce heat; simmer, uncovered, 5 minutes.
per serving 29.7g total fat (6.7g saturated fat); 2144kJ (513 cal); 37g carbohydrate; 25.3g protein; 6.2g fibre

To remove excess liquid, drain the cheese mixture in a fine sieve lined with muslin for 40 minutes before adding to the kofta mixture.

After deep-frying the kofta in batches, drain them well on layers of absorbent paper before adding them to the tomato tamarind sauce.

warm potato salad with caperberries

preparation time 10 minutes
cooking time 15 minutes
serves 8

2kg pontiac potatoes, unpeeled,
    diced into 2cm pieces
1 tablespoon dijon mustard
2 tablespoons red wine vinegar
½ cup (125ml) extra virgin olive oil
1 small white onion (80g), sliced thinly
¼ cup firmly packed fresh flat-leaf parsley leaves
2 tablespoons fresh dill sprigs
1 cup (200g) cornichons, halved lengthways
½ cup (80g) drained large caperberries, rinsed

1 Boil, steam or microwave potato until just tender; drain.
2 Meanwhile, whisk mustard, vinegar and oil in large bowl until combined.
3 Add hot potato to bowl with remaining ingredients; toss gently to combine.
per serving 14.5g total fat (2g saturated fat); 1195kJ (286 cal); 32.5g carbohydrate; 5.8g protein; 3.9g fibre

grilled tofu steaks with asian vegetables

preparation time 15 minutes
cooking time 15 minutes
serves 4

600g firm tofu, sliced thickly
2 tablespoons kecap manis
2 cloves garlic, crushed
1 tablespoon sesame oil
800g baby bok choy, halved lengthways
200g asparagus, trimmed, halved lengthways
100g enoki mushrooms
6 green onions, chopped coarsely

GINGER DRESSING
1 tablespoon soy sauce
1 tablespoon rice vinegar
1 tablespoon oyster sauce
1cm piece fresh ginger (5g), grated

1 Pat tofu slices both sides with absorbent paper to remove surface liquid. Combine kecap manis, garlic and oil in medium bowl; add tofu, toss gently to coat in mixture. Cook tofu on heated oiled flat plate, uncovered, until browned lightly both sides, brushing occasionally with mixture.
2 Meanwhile, place ingredients for ginger dressing in screw-top jar; shake well.
3 Cook bok choy, asparagus, mushrooms and onion on heated oiled flat plate until just tender.
4 Place vegetables in medium bowl, add dressing; toss gently to combine. Serve tofu with vegetables.
per serving 15.5g total fat (2.2g saturated fat); 1108kJ (265 cal); 7.5g carbohydrate; 23.5g protein; 7.3g fibre

chickpea vegetable braise with cumin couscous

preparation time 20 minutes (plus standing time)
cooking time 1 hour 25 minutes
serves 4

1 cup (200g) dried chickpeas
2 tablespoons olive oil
2 small leeks (400g), chopped coarsely
2 medium carrots (240g), cut into batons
2 cloves garlic, crushed
1 tablespoon finely chopped fresh rosemary
2 tablespoons white wine vinegar
2 cups (500ml) vegetable stock
100g baby spinach leaves
¼ cup (60ml) lemon juice
2 tablespoons olive oil, extra
2 cloves garlic, crushed, extra

CUMIN COUSCOUS
1 cup (250ml) boiling water
1 cup (200g) couscous
1 tablespoon olive oil
1 teaspoon ground cumin

TOMATO AND RED ONION SALAD
4 medium tomatoes (600g), sliced thinly
2 medium red onions (340g), sliced thinly
2 tablespoons red wine vinegar
1 tablespoon olive oil

1 Place chickpeas in medium bowl, cover with water; stand overnight, drain. Rinse under cold water; drain.
2 Place chickpeas in medium saucepan of boiling water. Return to a boil, reduce heat; simmer, uncovered, about 40 minutes or until chickpeas are tender. Drain.
3 Meanwhile, preheat oven to moderately slow (170°C/140°C fan-forced).
4 Heat oil in large deep flameproof baking dish; cook leek and carrot, stirring, until just tender. Add garlic, rosemary and chickpeas; cook, stirring, until fragrant. Add vinegar and stock; bring to a boil. Bake, covered, 30 minutes.
5 Meanwhile, make cumin couscous. Make tomato and red onion salad.
6 Remove dish from oven; stir in spinach, juice, extra oil and extra garlic. Serve chickpea vegetable braise with couscous and tomato and red onion salad.
CUMIN COUSCOUS
Combine the water and couscous in medium heatproof bowl, cover; stand about 5 minutes or until liquid is absorbed, fluffing with fork occasionally. Add oil and cumin; toss gently to combine.
TOMATO AND RED ONION SALAD
Arrange tomato and onion slices on serving platter; drizzle with vinegar and oil. Sprinkle with freshly cracked black pepper.
per serving 31.6g total fat (saturated fat 4.6g); 2717 kJ (650 cal); 68.7g carbohydrate; 21.3g protein; 13.8g fibre

soya bean and potato patties with teardrop tomato salsa

preparation time 20 minutes
cooking time 20 minutes
serves 4

700g potatoes, chopped coarsely
4 green onions, sliced thinly
1 clove garlic, crushed
300g can soya beans, rinsed, drained
1 teaspoon ground cumin
½ cup (60g) coarsely grated cheddar cheese
1 tablespoon plain flour

TEARDROP TOMATO SALSA
500g yellow teardrop tomatoes, halved
⅓ cup finely chopped fresh coriander
1 small red onion (100g), chopped finely
1 fresh long red chilli, seeded, sliced thinly
1 tablespoon red wine vinegar
1 tablespoon lime juice
1 tablespoon olive oil

1 Boil, steam or microwave potato until tender; drain.
2 Meanwhile, place ingredients for teardrop tomato salsa in medium bowl; toss gently to combine.
3 Coarsely mash potato in large bowl; stir in remaining ingredients until combined. Using hands, shape potato mixture into eight patties; cook on heated oiled flat plate, uncovered, until heated through.
4 Serve patties with salsa.
per serving 12.8g total fat (4.3g saturated fat); 1191kJ (285 cal); 27.5g carbohydrate; 13.5g protein; 7.8g fibre

mushroom burgers with the lot

preparation time 10 minutes
cooking time 15 minutes
serves 4

50g baby spinach leaves
1 tablespoon lemon juice
1 tablespoon olive oil
1 teaspoon dijon mustard
4 thick slices ciabatta (200g)
1 large brown onion (200g), cut into 4 slices
4 large flat mushrooms (400g), halved
1 large tomato (220g), cut into 4 slices
4 eggs

1 Place spinach and combined juice, oil and mustard in medium bowl; toss gently to combine.
2 Toast ciabatta, both sides, on heated oiled grill plate (or grill or barbecue); cook onion, mushrooms and tomato on same heated oiled grill plate, uncovered, until vegetables are just tender.
3 Meanwhile, cook eggs in lightly oiled egg rings on heated oiled flat plate, uncovered, until cooked as desired.
4 Divide ciabatta among serving plates; layer with mushroom, onion, tomato, egg and spinach mixture.
per serving 12.2g total fat (2.5g saturated fat); 1250kJ (299 cal); 30.9g carbohydrate; 16.2g protein; 5.9g fibre

celeriac mash

preparation time 10 minutes
cooking time 25 minutes
serves 4

800g lasoda potatoes, peeled, chopped coarsely
1kg celeriac, peeled, chopped coarsely
½ cup (125ml) hot cream
60g butter, softened

1 Boil, steam or microwave potato and celeriac, separately, until tender; drain.
2 Mash potato and celeriac in large bowl; stir in cream and butter until combined.
per serving 26.5g total fat (17.1g saturated fat); 1697kJ (406 cal); 34g carbohydrate; 8.1g protein; 11.6g fibre

spinach mash

preparation time 10 minutes
cooking time 20 minutes
serves 4

1kg lasoda potatoes, peeled, chopped coarsely
220g spinach leaves
40g butter, softened
½ cup (125ml) hot cream

1 Boil, steam or microwave potato until tender; drain.
2 Meanwhile, boil, steam or microwave spinach leaves until wilted; drain. Squeeze out excess liquid. Blend or process spinach with butter until almost smooth.
3 Mash potato in large bowl; stir in cream and spinach mixture until combined.
per serving 22.2g total fat (14.4g saturated fat); 1459kJ (349 cal); 30g carbohydrate; 7.2g protein; 5g fibre

kumara mash

preparation time 10 minutes
cooking time 20 minutes
serves 4

500g lasoda potatoes, peeled, chopped coarsely
500g kumara, peeled, chopped coarsely
¼ cup (60ml) hot chicken stock
40g butter, melted

1 Boil, steam or microwave potato and kumara,
together, until tender; drain.
2 Mash potato and kumara in large bowl; stir in
stock and butter.
per serving 8.5g total fat (5.4g saturated fat); 903kJ
(216 cal); 29.9g carbohydrate; 4.9g protein; 3.7g fibre

pea mash

preparation time 10 minutes
cooking time 20 minutes
serves 4

1kg lasoda potatoes, peeled, coarsely chopped
1½ cups (180g) frozen peas
¾ cup (180ml) hot milk
50g butter, softened

1 Boil, steam or microwave potato and peas,
separately, until tender; drain.
2 Mash potato in large bowl; stir in milk and butter.
3 Using fork, mash peas in small bowl; stir into potato
mixture until combined.
per serving 12.4g total fat (7.9g saturated fat); 1212kJ
(290 cal); 34.5g carbohydrate; 9.4g protein; 6.1g fibre

Pies and Tarts

You can make a pie or tart in one
rather lengthy session, including the
time it takes for the filling to cool,
if it is a cooked one, and the resting
times for the pastry before you roll
it out, and again before you bake it.
Many cooks prefer to work in
stages, making pastry and filling
a day ahead and leaving them to
chill overnight. This long resting
time actually makes for more tender
pastry – but remember to remove
it from the refrigerator at least
an hour before shaping so that
it will be pliable.

mini beef and guinness pies

roasted vegetable fillo tart

chicken pot pie

trevally mornay pies

mini beef and guinness pies

preparation time 20 minutes
cooking time 1 hour 50 minutes (plus refrigeration time)
makes 36

1 tablespoon vegetable oil
500g beef skirt steak, chopped finely
1 medium brown onion (150g), chopped finely
2 tablespoons plain flour
375ml bottle guinness stout
1 cup (250ml) beef stock
5 sheets ready-rolled shortcrust pastry
1 egg, beaten lightly

1 Heat oil in large saucepan; cook steak, stirring, until browned all over. Add onion; cook, stirring, until softened. Add flour; cook, stirring, until mixture bubbles and is well browned.

2 Gradually stir in stout and stock, stirring until gravy boils and thickens. Reduce heat; simmer, covered, stirring occasionally, 1 hour. Uncover; simmer, stirring occasionally, 30 minutes. Cool filling 10 minutes; refrigerate until cold.

3 Preheat oven to hot (220°C/200°C fan-forced). Lightly oil three 12-hole mini (1-tablespoon/20ml) muffin pans.

4 Using 6cm cutter, cut 36 rounds from pastry sheets; place 1 round in each of the muffin pan holes. Using 5cm pastry cutter, cut 36 rounds from remaining pastry sheets.

5 Spoon 1 heaped teaspoon of the cold filling into each muffin pan hole; brush around edges of pastry with a little egg. Top each pie with smaller pastry round; press gently around edge to seal, brush with remaining egg. Using sharp knife, make two small slits in top of each pie. Bake, uncovered, about 15 minutes or until browned lightly. Stand 5 minutes in pan before serving.
per pie 7.4g total fat (3.6g saturated fat); 564kJ (135 cal); 11.2g carbohydrate; 5.1g protein; 0.5g fibre

roasted vegetable fillo tart

preparation time 20 minutes
cooking time 55 minutes
serves 6

6 medium egg tomatoes (450g), quartered
1 small red onion (100g), sliced thickly
2 small yellow capsicums (300g)
2 small red capsicums (300g)
100g low-fat fetta, crumbled
1 tablespoon shredded fresh basil
9 sheets fillo pastry
cooking-oil spray

1 Preheat oven to moderately hot (200°C/180°C fan-forced). Lightly oil oven tray.

2 Combine tomato and onion in baking dish; roast, uncovered, about 40 minutes or until onion softens.

3 Meanwhile, quarter capsicums; remove and discard seeds and membranes. Roast under grill or in moderately hot oven, skin-side up, until skin blisters and blackens. Cover capsicum with plastic or paper 5 minutes; peel away and discard skin, then slice capsicum thinly. Place capsicum, cheese and basil in baking dish with tomato mixture; stir gently to combine.

4 Stack sheets of fillo on prepared tray; coat with cooking-oil spray every third sheet. Carefully fold over all four edges of the stack to create 18cm x 30cm tart 'shell'.

5 Fill tart shell with vegetable mixture, spreading it to an even thickness; bake, uncovered, about 15 minutes or until pastry is browned lightly.
per serving 4.7g total fat (1.8g saturated fat); 677kJ (162 cal); 20.4g carbohydrate; 9.3g protein; 2.8g fibre
TIP Cover fillo sheets with baking paper then damp tea towel to prevent the sheets from drying out before use.

chicken pot pie

preparation time 30 minutes
cooking time 30 minutes
serves 4

60g butter
400g kumara, chopped finely
1 medium leek (350g), sliced
600g chicken breast fillets, chopped coarsely
1 clove garlic, crushed
2 tablespoons plain flour
1½ cups (375ml) chicken stock
¼ cup (60ml) cream
1 tablespoon chopped chives
2 sheets ready-rolled butter puff pastry
1 egg, beaten lightly

1 Melt 20g butter in large frying pan; cook kumara and leek over medium heat, covered, stirring occasionally, until tender. Transfer to large bowl.

2 Cook chicken and garlic in same pan until browned and almost cooked. Add to kumara mixture.

3 Melt remaining butter in small saucepan, add flour; cook, stirring, until mixture bubbles. Gradually stir in stock, bring to a boil; simmer, stirring, until thickened. Stir in cream and chives.

4 Preheat oven to moderately hot (200°C/180°C fan-forced). Oil shallow 23cm-square ovenproof dish with a rim. Stand separated pastry sheets on kitchen bench for 5 minutes or until partially thawed.

5 Add sauce to chicken mixture; spread into prepared dish. Cut three 1cm-wide strips from one sheet of pastry. Brush rim of dish with a little water; press pastry strips onto rim of dish. Join strips with a little water. Top pie with second pastry sheet, pressing firmly to seal together; trim edge. Brush pastry with egg, place dish on oven tray. Bake, uncovered, about 30 minutes or until browned.

per serving 43.3g total fat (24.1g saturated fat); 3202kJ (766 cal); 49.6g carbohydrate; 45g protein; 5g fibre
TIP This recipe can be made a day ahead.

trevally mornay pies

preparation time 25 minutes
cooking time 35 minutes
serves 4

½ small brown onion (40g)
1 bay leaf
6 black peppercorns
2½ cups (625ml) milk
4 x 170g trevally fillets, skinned
3 large potatoes (900g), chopped coarsely
600g celeriac, chopped coarsely
1 egg yolk
½ cup (40g) finely grated parmesan
¾ cup (180ml) cream
60g butter
¼ cup (35g) plain flour
2 tablespoons coarsely chopped fresh
   flat-leaf parsley

1 Place onion, bay leaf, peppercorns and milk in large saucepan; bring to a boil. Add fish, reduce heat; simmer, covered, about 5 minutes or until cooked through. Remove fish from pan; divide among four 1½-cup (375ml) ovenproof dishes. Strain milk through sieve into medium jug. Discard solids; reserve milk.

2 Boil, steam or microwave potato and celeriac, separately, until tender; drain. Push potato and celeriac through sieve into large bowl; stir in egg yolk, cheese, ¼ cup (60ml) of the cream and half of the butter until smooth. Cover to keep warm.

3 Meanwhile, melt remaining butter in medium saucepan, add flour; cook, stirring, about 3 minutes or until mixture bubbles and thickens slightly. Gradually stir in reserved milk and remaining cream; cook, stirring, until mixture boils and thickens. Stir in parsley.

4 Divide mornay mixture among dishes; cover each with potato mixture. Place pies on oven tray; place under hot grill until browned lightly.

per serving 48g total fat (29g saturated fat); 3499kJ (837 cal); 47.6g carbohydrate; 54.3g protein; 9g fibre

onion and anchovy tartlets

preparation time 45 minutes
cooking time 35 minutes
serves 6

1 tablespoon olive oil
60g butter
3 medium brown onions (450g), halved, sliced thinly
2 cloves garlic, crushed
1 bay leaf
3 sprigs fresh thyme
⅓ cup coarsely chopped fresh flat-leaf parsley
8 anchovy fillets, drained, chopped finely
2 tablespoons coarsely chopped seeded
   kalamata olives
¾ cup (110g) self-raising flour
¾ cup (110g) plain flour
¾ cup (180ml) buttermilk

1 Heat oil and half of the butter in large frying pan; cook onion, garlic, bay leaf and thyme, stirring occasionally, about 20 minutes or until onion caramelises. Discard bay leaf and thyme; stir in parsley, anchovy and olives.
2 Meanwhile, blend or process flours and remaining butter until mixture resembles fine breadcrumbs. Add buttermilk; process until ingredients just come together. Knead dough on lightly floured surface until smooth.
3 Preheat oven to moderately hot (200°C/180°C fan-forced). Oil two oven trays.
4 Divide dough into six portions; roll each portion on floured surface into 14cm square. Fold edges over to form 1cm border.
5 Place squares on prepared trays; place rounded tablespoons of the onion mixture on each square. Bake, uncovered, about 15 minutes or until pastry browns lightly.
per serving 12.9g total fat (6.4g saturated fat); 1150kJ (275 cal); 31.8g carbohydrate; 7.7g protein; 2.7g fibre

Caramelising the onion with the herbs and garlic for about 20 minutes gives it a deliciously sweet flavour.

After dividing the dough into pieces, roll each one out into a square and fold the edges over to form a border.

beef bourguignon pies with chips

preparation time 30 minutes
cooking time 2 hours
serves 6

12 pickling onions (480g)
6 bacon rashers (420g), rind removed, sliced thinly
2 tablespoons olive oil
400g mushrooms
1kg gravy beef, trimmed, cut into 2cm pieces
¼ cup (35g) plain flour
1 tablespoon tomato paste
2 teaspoons fresh thyme leaves
1 cup (250ml) dry red wine
2 cups (500ml) beef stock
750g packet frozen potato chips
2 sheets ready-rolled butter puff pastry
cooking-oil spray
½ cup finely chopped fresh flat-leaf parsley

1 Peel onions, leaving roots intact; halve lengthways.
2 Cook bacon in heated large heavy-based saucepan, stirring, until crisp; drain on absorbent paper.
3 Cook onion in same pan, stirring, until browned all over; remove from pan. Heat 2 teaspoons of the oil in same pan; cook mushrooms, stirring, until just browned. Remove from pan.
4 Coat beef in flour; shake off excess. Heat remaining oil in same pan; cook beef, in batches, until browned all over.
5 Return bacon and onion to pan with tomato paste and thyme; cook, stirring, 2 minutes. Add wine and stock; bring to a boil. Reduce heat; simmer, covered, 1 hour. Add mushrooms; simmer, uncovered, about 40 minutes or until beef is tender, stirring occasionally.
6 Meanwhile, preheat oven to hot (220°C/200°C fan-forced). Cook chips according to directions on packet.
7 Place pastry sheets on board; using 1¼-cup (310ml) ovenproof dish, cut lid for one pie by tracing around upper-rim of dish with tip of sharp knife. Repeat process until you have six lids. Place lids on oiled oven tray, spray with cooking-oil spray; bake, uncovered, during last 4 minutes of chip cooking-time or until lids are browned lightly.
8 Meanwhile, stir parsley into beef bourguignon then divide among six 1¼-cup (310ml) ovenproof dishes; top each with pastry lid. Serve pies with hot chips.
per serving 42.4g total fat (13.5g saturated fat); 4101kJ (981 cal); 86.1g carbohydrate; 55.4g protein; 9.8g fibre

little chicken and leek pies

preparation time 30 minutes
cooking time 40 minutes (plus cooling time)
makes 36

¾ cup (180ml) chicken stock
½ cup (125ml) dry white wine
2 single chicken breast fillets (340g)
20g butter
1 medium leek (350g), chopped finely
1 trimmed celery stalk (100g), chopped finely
1 tablespoon plain flour
2 teaspoons fresh lemon thyme leaves
½ cup (125ml) cream
1 teaspoon dijon mustard
4 sheets ready-rolled shortcrust pastry
3 sheets ready-rolled puff pastry
1 egg yolk, beaten lightly
lemon thyme leaves, extra

1 Combine stock and wine in medium saucepan; bring to a boil. Add chicken, return to a boil, cover; reduce heat, simmer about 10 minutes or until chicken is just cooked through. Remove from heat, stand chicken in cooking liquid 10 minutes; remove chicken, reserve ¾ cup (180ml) cooking liquid; chop chicken finely.
2 Melt butter in medium saucepan; cook leek and celery, stirring, until soft. Add flour and thyme, stir until bubbling. Gradually stir in reserved liquid and cream; cook, stirring, until mixture boils and thickens. Stir in chicken and mustard. Remove from heat, cool slightly.
3 Preheat oven to hot (220°C/200°C fan-forced). Grease three 12-hole patty pans.
4 Using 7cm cutter, cut 36 rounds from shortcrust pastry; press into prepared pans. Spoon 1 tablespoon of chicken mixture into each pastry case. Using 6cm cutter, cut 36 rounds from puff pastry. Top chicken mixture with pastry lids, brush with egg yolk; sprinkle with extra thyme leaves. Bake, uncovered, 15 minutes or until browned.
per pie 10.6g total fat (5.8g saturated fat); 711kJ (170 cal); 13.9g carbohydrate; 4.5g protein; 0.8g fibre
TIP Chicken mixture can be made a day ahead. Cover; refrigerate.

Cut 7cm rounds from the shortcrust pastry to line the holes of the patty pans; the puff pastry sheets are used for the tops of the little pies.

Each hole of the patty pan holds about a tablespoon of the slightly cooled chicken and leek mixture; do not overfill or pies will overflow.

tomato tarte tatins with crème fraîche sauce

preparation time 40 minutes
cooking time 30 minutes
serves 6

9 small firm tomatoes (800g), peeled, quartered
30g butter
1 clove garlic, crushed
1 tablespoon brown sugar
2 tablespoons balsamic vinegar
1½ sheets ready-rolled butter puff pastry
1 egg, beaten lightly
vegetable oil, for deep-frying
6 sprigs fresh baby basil

CREME FRAICHE SAUCE
20g butter
2 shallots (50g), chopped finely
1 cup (240g) crème fraîche
⅓ cup (80ml) water

1 Preheat oven to moderately hot (200°C/180°C fan-forced). Oil six 1-cup (250ml) metal pie dishes.
2 Discard pulp and seeds from tomato quarters; gently flatten flesh.
3 Melt butter in large frying pan; cook garlic, stirring, over low heat, until fragrant. Add sugar and vinegar; cook, stirring, until sugar dissolves. Place tomato in pan, in single layer; cook, covered, turning once, 5 minutes or until tomato softens.
4 Cut six 11cm rounds from pastry sheets. Divide tomato among prepared dishes; top each with one pastry round, pressing down gently. Brush pastry with egg; bake, uncovered, about 15 minutes or until pastry is browned lightly and puffed.
5 Meanwhile, heat oil in small saucepan; using metal tongs, place thoroughly dry basil sprigs, one at a time, in pan. Deep-fry about 3 seconds or until basil is crisp. Drain on absorbent paper.
6 Make crème fraîche sauce.
7 Divide sauce among serving plates; turn tarts onto sauce, top with basil.
CREME FRAICHE SAUCE
Melt butter in small saucepan; cook shallot, stirring, about 3 minutes or until softened. Add crème fraîche; cook, stirring, over low heat, until heated through. Stir in the water.
per serving 33.8g total fat (20.4g saturated fat); 1714kJ (410 cal); 21g carbohydrate; 6g protein; 2.6g fibre
TIP Take care when deep-frying the basil sprigs as the hot oil is likely to splatter.

italian cottage pie

preparation time 25 minutes
cooking time 1 hour
serves 6

1 tablespoon olive oil
1 medium brown onion (150g), chopped finely
2 cloves garlic, crushed
200g mushrooms, sliced thinly
1 large carrot (180g), diced into 1cm pieces
1 medium eggplant (300g), diced into 1cm pieces
750g lamb mince
1 tablespoon plain flour
½ cup (125ml) dry red wine
425g can crushed tomatoes
2 tablespoons tomato paste
1 tablespoon worcestershire sauce
2 tablespoons finely chopped fresh oregano
800g potatoes, chopped coarsely
20g butter
⅓ cup (80ml) milk
¼ cup (20g) finely grated parmesan

SOFT POLENTA
1¼ cups (310ml) chicken stock
¾ cup (180ml) milk
½ cup (85g) polenta
¼ cup (20g) finely grated parmesan

1 Preheat oven to moderately hot (200°C/180°C fan-forced). Oil deep 2.5-litre (10-cup) casserole dish.
2 Heat oil in large frying pan; cook onion, garlic, mushrooms, carrot and eggplant, stirring, until onion softens. Add lamb; cook, stirring, until browned. Add flour; cook, stirring, 1 minute. Add wine; bring to a boil, stirring. Stir in undrained tomatoes, paste, sauce and oregano. Reduce heat; simmer, uncovered, 10 minutes or until mixture thickens slightly.
3 Meanwhile, make soft polenta.
4 Boil, steam or microwave potato until tender; drain. Mash potatoes with butter and milk in large bowl until smooth. Using wooden spoon, gently swirl hot polenta mixture into potato mixture.
5 Spoon mince mixture into prepared dish; top with potato polenta mixture, sprinkle with cheese. Cook, uncovered, in moderately hot oven about 25 minutes or until cheese browns lightly. Serve with baby rocket leaves in balsamic vinaigrette, if desired.
SOFT POLENTA
Combine stock and milk in large saucepan; bring to a boil. Gradually add polenta to stock mixture, stirring constantly. Reduce heat; cook, stirring, 10 minutes or until polenta thickens. Stir in cheese.
per serving 19.4g total fat (8.8g saturated fat); 2040kJ (488 cal); 37.1g carbohydrate; 37.5g protein; 6.7g fibre

Hot Desserts

Grandmotherly winter puddings
are stars in the smartest restaurants
now, and the height of fashion
for cold-weather dinner parties.
But that's not the only reason to
serve them – it's the smiles on
the faces round the table at the
prospect of tucking into a glorious
treat. Yes, proper puddings take
a bit of time to make, but you can
get most of the effort over hours
or, in some cases, a day or more
ahead. Really pushed for time?
Then turn to the recipe for luscious
grilled bananas, a quick dessert that
will still have everyone beaming.

pear and plum amaretti crumble

spiced apricot and plum pie

caramelised apple clafoutis

coffee and pecan puddings with caramel sauce

pear and plum amaretti crumble

preparation time 10 minutes
cooking time 15 minutes
serves 4

825g can plums in syrup, drained,
    halved, stoned
825g can pear halves in natural juice,
    drained, halved
1 teaspoon ground cardamom
125g amaretti, crushed
⅓ cup (50g) plain flour
⅓ cup (35g) almond meal
½ cup (70g) slivered almonds
100g butter, chopped

1 Preheat oven to moderately hot (200°C/180°C fan-forced). Grease deep 1.5-litre (6-cup) ovenproof dish.
2 Combine plums, pears and cardamom in prepared dish; toss gently to combine.
3 Combine amaretti, flour, almond meal and nuts in medium bowl. Using fingers, rub butter into amaretti mixture, sprinkle evenly over plum mixture. Bake, uncovered, about 15 minutes or until golden brown.
per serving 43.4g total fat (20.1g saturated fat); 2855kJ (683 cal); 66.5g carbohydrate; 9.5g protein; 9.8g fibre
TIP Crumble may also be made in four 1½-cup (375ml) individual dishes; bake 15 minutes.
SERVING SUGGESTION Serve with vanilla custard, if desired.

spiced apricot and plum pie

preparation time 30 minutes
cooking time 45 minutes (plus cooling time)
serves 8

2 x 825g cans dark plums in light syrup
2 cups (300g) dried apricots
1 cinnamon stick
3 cloves
½ teaspoon mixed spice
½ teaspoon ground ginger
2 sheets ready-rolled puff pastry
1 egg, beaten lightly
icing sugar, for dusting
SPICED YOGURT CREAM
½ cup (140g) yogurt
½ cup (120g) sour cream
1 tablespoon ground cinnamon
¼ teaspoon ground ginger

1 Preheat oven to moderately hot (200°C/180°C fan-forced). Grease 26cm pie dish or deep 1.25 litre (5-cup) rectangular dish.
2 Drain plums; reserve 1 cup (250ml) of the syrup. Halve plums, discard stones; place plums in prepared dish.
3 Combine reserved syrup, apricots, cinnamon, cloves, mixed spice and ginger in medium saucepan; simmer, uncovered, until liquid is reduced to ½ cup (125ml). Remove and discard cinnamon stick and cloves; cool to room temperature. Pour mixture over plums.
4 Cut pastry into 2.5cm strips. Brush edge of dish with a little of the egg; press pastry strips around edge of dish. Twist remaining strips, place over filling in a lattice pattern; trim ends, brush top with remaining egg. Bake, uncovered, 40 minutes or until pastry is browned lightly.
5 Combine ingredients for spiced yogurt cream in small bowl.
6 Dust pie generously with icing sugar and serve with spiced yogurt cream.
per serving 16.9g total fat (9.6g saturated fat); 1714kJ (410 cal); 58.8g carbohydrate; 6.4g protein; 6.4g fibre

caramelised apple clafoutis

preparation time 15 minutes
cooking time 50 minutes
serves 6

6 medium apples (900g)
50g unsalted butter
½ cup (110g) firmly packed brown sugar
⅓ cup (75g) caster sugar
⅓ cup (50g) plain flour
⅓ cup (50g) self-raising flour
4 eggs, beaten lightly
⅔ cup (160ml) milk
⅔ cup (160ml) cream
80g unsalted butter, melted, extra
1 teaspoon vanilla extract

1 Preheat oven to moderately hot (200°C/180°C fan-forced). Grease shallow 2.5-litre (10-cup) ovenproof dish.
2 Peel, core and halve apples; cut each half into four wedges. Melt butter in large frying pan; cook apple, stirring, about 5 minutes or until browned lightly. Add brown sugar; cook, stirring, about 5 minutes or until mixture thickens slightly. Place apple mixture into prepared dish; cool 5 minutes.
3 Meanwhile, combine caster sugar and flours in medium bowl; make well in centre. Gradually whisk in combined remaining ingredients until smooth. Pour batter over apple mixture; bake, uncovered, about 40 minutes.
4 Serve hot with double cream; dust with icing sugar, if desired.
per serving 34.5g total fat (21.3g saturated fat); 2345kJ (561 cal); 57.5g carbohydrate; 8.1g protein; 2.9g fibre

coffee and pecan puddings with caramel sauce

preparation time 15 minutes
cooking time 40 minutes
serves 6

¾ cup (90g) coarsely chopped toasted pecans
300ml cream
1½ cups (330g) firmly packed brown sugar
100g cold butter, chopped
125g butter, softened
1 teaspoon vanilla extract
½ cup (110g) caster sugar
2 eggs
1 cup (150g) self-raising flour
¼ cup (35g) plain flour
¼ cup (60ml) milk
1 tablespoon finely ground espresso coffee

1 Preheat oven to moderate (180°C/160°C fan-forced). Grease six ¾-cup (180ml) metal moulds or ovenproof dishes; line bases with baking paper.
2 Divide nuts among moulds; place moulds on oven tray.
3 Stir cream, brown sugar and chopped butter in small saucepan over heat, without boiling, until sugar dissolves. Reduce heat; simmer, uncovered, without stirring, about 5 minutes or until mixture thickens slightly. Spoon 2 tablespoons of the sauce over nuts in each mould; reserve remaining sauce.
4 Beat softened butter, extract and caster sugar in small bowl with electric mixer until light and fluffy. Add eggs, one at a time, beating until just combined between additions. Stir in sifted flours, milk and coffee; divide mixture among moulds. Bake, uncovered, 30 minutes. Stand puddings 5 minutes before turning onto serving plates.
5 Reheat reserved sauce. Serve puddings with sauce.
per serving 65.9g total fat (36.2g saturated fat); 4134kJ (989 cal); 96.3g carbohydrate; 8.4g protein; 2.4g fibre
TIP The caramel sauce and puddings can be made several hours ahead; reheat just before serving.
SERVING SUGGESTION Serve puddings with cream or ice-cream, if desired.

chocolate hazelnut self-saucing puddings

preparation time 15 minutes
cooking time 25 minutes
serves 4

½ cup (125ml) milk
40g dark cooking chocolate, chopped coarsely
50g butter
⅓ cup (35g) cocoa powder
½ cup (75g) self-raising flour
¼ cup (25g) hazelnut meal
⅓ cup (75g) caster sugar
⅔ cup (150g) firmly packed brown sugar
1 egg, beaten lightly
¾ cup (180ml) water
40g butter, chopped, extra
200g vanilla ice-cream

CHOCOLATE HAZELNUT SAUCE
½ cup (125ml) cream
2 tablespoons brown sugar
50g dark cooking chocolate, chopped finely
⅓ cup (110g) chocolate hazelnut spread
1 tablespoon frangelico

1 Preheat oven to moderate (180°C/160°C fan-forced). Grease four 1-cup (250ml) ovenproof dishes or cups.
2 Place milk, chocolate, butter and half of the cocoa in small saucepan; stir over low heat until smooth.
3 Combine flour, hazelnut meal, caster sugar and half of the brown sugar in medium bowl. Add chocolate mixture and egg; stir until combined. Divide mixture among prepared dishes.
4 Stir the water, extra butter, remaining brown sugar and remaining cocoa in small saucepan over low heat until smooth. Pour hot mixture gently and evenly over puddings; bake, uncovered, about 25 minutes. Stand 5 minutes.
5 Meanwhile, make chocolate hazelnut sauce.
6 Serve puddings with ice-cream; pour over sauce.
CHOCOLATE HAZELNUT SAUCE
Combine cream and sugar in small saucepan. Bring to a boil; remove from heat. Add chocolate; stir until smooth. Add spread and liqueur; stir until smooth.
per serving 61g total fat (33.6g saturated fat); 4485kJ (1073 cal); 121.9g carbohydrate; 12.9g protein; 2.4g fibre
TIP This dessert is best served hot because the sauce is quickly absorbed by the puddings.

Stir the warmed chocolate mixture and the egg into the dry ingredients until the pudding is well combined.

After the pudding is divided among dessert dishes, pour the hot sauce mixture evenly and carefully into each.

rhubarb galette

preparation time 10 minutes
cooking time 20 minutes
serves 4

20g butter, melted
2½ cups (275g) coarsely chopped rhubarb
⅓ cup (75g) firmly packed brown sugar
1 teaspoon finely grated orange rind
1 sheet ready-rolled puff pastry
2 tablespoons almond meal
10g butter, melted, extra

1 Preheat oven to hot (220°C/200°C fan-forced). Line oven tray with baking paper.
2 Place butter, rhubarb, sugar and rind in medium bowl; toss to combine.
3 Cut 24cm round from pastry sheet, place on prepared tray; sprinkle almond meal evenly over pastry. Spread rhubarb mixture over pastry, leaving a 4cm border. Fold 2cm of pastry edge up and around filling. Brush edge with extra butter. Bake, uncovered, about 20 minutes or until browned lightly.
per serving 18.2g total fat (9.3g saturated fat); 1325kJ (317 cal); 34.6g carbohydrate; 4.3g protein; 3.2g fibre
SERVING SUGGESTION Serve with scoops of vanilla ice-cream, if desired.

fig and brioche pudding

preparation time 15 minutes
cooking time 1 hour 15 minutes
serves 6

1½ cups (375ml) milk
600ml cream
1 cinnamon stick
1 vanilla bean
¾ cup (90g) honey
4 eggs
2 small brioche (200g)
3 medium fresh figs (180g)
1 tablespoon demerara sugar

1 Stir milk, cream, cinnamon, vanilla bean and honey in medium saucepan until hot; strain into large heatproof jug.
2 Whisk eggs in large bowl; whisking constantly, pour hot milk mixture into egg mixture.
3 Preheat oven to moderate (180°C/160°C fan-forced). Lightly grease shallow 2-litre (8 cup) ovenproof dish.
4 Cut each brioche into six slices and each fig into five slices. Layer brioche and figs, overlapping slightly, in prepared dish. Pour hot milk mixture over brioche and figs; sprinkle with sugar.
5 Place pudding dish in large baking dish; add enough boiling water to come halfway up sides of dish. Bake, uncovered, about 40 minutes or until pudding sets.
6 Remove pudding dish from baking dish; stand 5 minutes before serving.
per serving 53.7g total fat (33.3g saturated fat); 2817kJ (674 cal); 39.2g carbohydrate; 11.7g protein; 1.2g fibre
TIP Whole vanilla bean can be rinsed under warm water, dried, then stored in an airtight jar for future use. If you cannot find demerara sugar, use white sugar instead.

chocolate soufflé with raspberry coulis

preparation time 15 minutes
cooking time 20 minutes
serves 4

1 tablespoon caster sugar
50g butter
1 tablespoon plain flour
200g dark eating chocolate, melted
2 egg yolks
4 egg whites
¼ cup (55g) caster sugar, extra

RASPBERRY COULIS
150g frozen raspberries, thawed
2 tablespoons caster sugar
4 cloves
½ cup (125ml) dry red wine

1 Preheat oven to moderately hot (200°C/180°C fan-forced). Grease four ¾-cup (180ml) soufflé dishes. Sprinkle insides of dishes evenly with sugar; shake away excess. Place dishes on oven tray.
2 Melt butter in small saucepan; cook flour, stirring, about 2 minutes or until mixture thickens and bubbles. Remove from heat; stir in chocolate and egg yolks. Transfer to large bowl.
3 Beat egg whites in small bowl with electric mixer until soft peaks form. Gradually add extra sugar, one tablespoon at a time, beating until sugar dissolves between additions. Fold egg white mixture into chocolate mixture, in two batches.
4 Divide soufflé mixture among prepared dishes; bake, uncovered, about 15 minutes or until soufflés are puffed.
5 Meanwhile, make raspberry coulis.
6 Serve soufflés with coulis.
RASPBERRY COULIS
Combine raspberries and sugar in small saucepan; cook, without boiling, until sugar dissolves. Add cloves and wine; bring to a boil. Reduce heat; simmer, uncovered, about 5 minutes or until coulis thickens. Strain coulis into medium jug.
per serving 27.5g total fat (16.1g saturated fat); 2278kJ (545 cal); 63.6g carbohydrate; 8.6g protein; 2.7g fibre

chocolate bread and butter pudding

preparation time 20 minutes
cooking time 50 minutes
serves 6

1½ cups (375ml) milk
2 cups (500ml) cream
⅓ cup (75g) caster sugar
1 vanilla bean
4 eggs
2 small brioche (200g), sliced thickly
100g dark eating chocolate, chopped coarsely
⅓ cup (40g) coarsely chopped toasted pecans

1 Preheat oven to moderate (180°C/160°C fan-forced). Grease shallow 2-litre (8-cup) ovenproof dish.
2 Combine milk, cream and sugar in small saucepan. Split vanilla bean in half lengthways; scrape seeds into pan then place pod in pan. Stir over heat until hot; strain into large heatproof jug, discard pod.
3 Whisk eggs in large bowl; whisking constantly, pour hot milk mixture into eggs.
4 Layer brioche, chocolate and nuts, overlapping brioche slightly, in prepared dish. Pour hot milk mixture over brioche.
5 Place pudding dish in large baking dish; add enough boiling water to come halfway up sides of dish. Bake, uncovered, about 45 minutes or until pudding sets. Remove pudding from baking dish; stand 5 minutes before serving.
per serving 50.1g total fat (27.8g saturated fat); 2796kJ (669 cal); 45g carbohydrate; 12.6g protein; 1.4g fibre

roasted pear tart

preparation time 20 minutes
cooking time 40 minutes
serves 6

3 red sensation pears (900g)
1 tablespoon maple syrup
¼ cup (55g) raw sugar
40g butter, chopped
1 sheet ready-rolled butter-puff pastry
1 egg, beaten lightly
icing sugar, for serving

1 Preheat oven to moderate (180°C/160°C fan-forced).
2 Peel pears, leaving stems intact; halve lengthways. Remove cores carefully. Place pears in baking dish, cut-side up, and top with syrup, raw sugar and butter. Bake, uncovered, about 20 minutes or until tender, brushing pears occasionally with juices and turning pears over after 10 minutes.
3 Increase oven to moderately hot (200°C/180°C fan-forced). Grease oven tray.
4 Cut pastry sheet in half; place halves about 2cm apart on prepared tray.
5 Place 3 pear halves, with cut-side down, on each pastry strip; reserve syrup in baking dish. Brush pears and pastry with reserved syrup; brush pastry with a little of the egg. Bake, uncovered, 20 minutes or until puffed and browned.
6 Dust with sifted icing sugar and serve with cream or ice-cream, if desired.
per serving 12.8g total fat (7.3g saturated fat); 1145kJ (274 cal); 38.3g carbohydrate; 3.1g protein; 2.6g fibre
TIP Pears can be roasted several hours ahead; the tart is best cooked close to serving.

quince tarte tatin

preparation time 20 minutes (plus refrigeration time)
cooking time 3 hours
serves 6

4 medium quinces (1.2kg)
1 cup (220g) caster sugar
1 litre (4 cups) water
¼ cup (60ml) orange juice
1 teaspoon finely grated orange rind
40g butter

PASTRY
1 cup (150g) plain flour
¼ cup (40g) icing sugar
100g butter, chopped
1 egg yolk
1 tablespoon cold water, approximately

1 Peel and core quinces; quarter lengthways. Place quince in large saucepan with sugar, the water, juice and rind; bring to a boil. Reduce heat; simmer, covered, about 2½ hours or until quince is rosy in colour. Using slotted spoon, remove quinces from syrup; bring syrup to a boil. Boil, uncovered, until syrup reduces to ¾ cup. Stir in butter.
2 Meanwhile, make pastry.
3 Preheat oven to moderately hot (200°C/180°C fan-forced). Line base of deep 22cm-round cake pan with baking paper.
4 Place quince, rounded-sides down, in prepared pan; pour syrup over quince.
5 Roll pastry between sheets of baking paper until large enough to line base of prepared pan. Lift pastry into pan, tucking pastry down side of pan. Bake, uncovered, 30 minutes or until pastry is browned lightly. Cool 5 minutes; turn tart onto serving plate, serve with vanilla ice-cream, if desired.
PASTRY
Blend or process flour, sugar and butter until crumbly. Add egg yolk and enough of the water to make the ingredients just come together. Shape dough into ball, enclose in plastic wrap; refrigerate 30 minutes.
per serving 20.7g total fat (12.9g saturated fat); 2098kJ (502 cal); 77.5g carbohydrate; 4.1g protein; 11.3g fibre

After quinces are quite rosy in colour, place them, rounded-side down, in the prepared cake pan.

Carefully lift the pastry and place it on top of the quinces, tucking the edges in around the side of pan.

grilled bananas with vanilla cream

preparation time 10 minutes
cooking time 10 minutes
serves 4

4 medium bananas (800g), halved lengthways
¼ cup (55g) brown sugar
20g butter
2 tablespoons coconut-flavoured liqueur
1 vanilla bean
⅔ cup (160ml) thickened cream
1 tablespoon icing sugar

1 Sprinkle banana with 1 tablespoon of the brown sugar; place under hot grill until browned lightly.
2 Meanwhile, stir remaining brown sugar, butter and liqueur in small saucepan over low heat until smooth.
3 Split vanilla bean in half lengthways, scrape seeds into small bowl; discard pod. Add cream and icing sugar; beat with electric mixer until soft peaks form.
4 Serve banana with vanilla cream; drizzle with sauce.
per serving 19g total fat (12.4g saturated fat); 1392kJ (333 cal); 35.4g carbohydrate; 3.2g protein; 3g fibre

orange and raspberry self-saucing pudding

preparation time 5 minutes
cooking time 15 minutes
serves 4

¼ cup (20g) flaked almonds
30g butter
¾ cup (110g) self-raising flour
⅓ cup (80ml) milk
⅔ cup (150g) firmly packed brown sugar
2 teaspoons finely grated orange rind
¾ cup (110g) frozen raspberries
¼ cup (60ml) orange juice
¾ cup (180ml) boiling water

1 Grease shallow 1.5-litre (6-cup) microwave-safe dish.
2 Place nuts in small microwave-safe bowl; cook, uncovered, in microwave oven on HIGH (100%) about 2 minutes or until browned lightly.
3 Place butter in medium microwave-safe bowl; cook, uncovered, in microwave oven on HIGH (100%) 30 seconds. Add flour, milk and half of the sugar; whisk until smooth. Stir in rind and raspberries; spread into prepared dish.
4 Sprinkle remaining sugar over raspberry mixture; carefully pour over combined juice and boiling water.
5 Place pudding on microwave-safe rack; cook, uncovered, in microwave oven on MEDIUM-HIGH (70%–80%) about 12 minutes. Stand 5 minutes.
6 Sprinkle pudding with nuts. Serve with cream or ice-cream, if desired.
per serving 10.4g total fat (4.8g saturated fat); 1451kJ (347 cal); 59.8g carbohydrate; 4.9g protein; 3g fibre
TIPS If cooking in a conventional oven, grease 1.5-litre (6-cup) ovenproof dish. Bake, uncovered, in moderately hot (200°C/180°C fan-forced) oven about 20 minutes. This recipe is best made close to serving.

raspberry bombe alaska

preparation time 20 minutes
  (plus freezing and cooling time)
cooking time 10 minutes
serves 4

1.5 litres vanilla ice-cream, softened slightly
1 cup (135g) frozen raspberries
1 tablespoon caster sugar
200g madeira cake
4 egg whites
1 cup (220g) firmly packed brown sugar
1 teaspoon vanilla extract
1 teaspoon cornflour

1 Line four ¾-cup (180ml) moulds with plastic wrap. Press quarter of the ice-cream firmly up and around inside of each mould to form a cavity. Cover with foil; freeze about 2 hours or until firm.

2 Preheat oven to very hot (240°C/220°C fan-forced).

3 Combine raspberries and caster sugar in small saucepan; stir gently over low heat about 5 minutes or until sugar dissolves. Cool 15 minutes.

4 Cut cake into four thick slices; cut one round from each slice, large enough to cover top of mould.

5 Beat egg whites in small bowl with electric mixer until soft peaks form. Gradually add brown sugar, 1 tablespoon at a time, beating until sugar dissolves between additions. Fold in extract and cornflour.

6 Spoon a quarter of the raspberry sauce into one mould; turn mould onto one cake round on oven tray, peel away plastic wrap. Spread a quarter of the meringue mixture over cake to enclose bombe completely; repeat with remaining raspberry sauce, moulds, cake rounds and meringue mixture. Bake, uncovered, about 3 minutes or until browned lightly.

per serving 28.4g total fat (15.7g saturated fat); 3143kJ (752 cal); 116.3g carbohydrate; 13.1g protein; 2.3g fibre

Cold Desserts

Summer's gorgeous fruits are naturals
for refreshing hot-weather desserts.
The easiest way, and possibly the
most perfect, is simply to arrange
them in jewel-like salads. But then,
it would be a shame to let summer
go by without sharp-sweet fruit ices,
real fruit jellies and decorative fruit
tarts. Other beautiful thoughts: cool
new cheesecake ideas, a knockout
variation on tiramisu, or amazing Italian
ice-cream. Or perhaps you'll want to
delight chocolate fanciers with cool
concoctions starring lavish amounts
of their favourite ingredient.

balsamic strawberries with black pepper wafers

fresh figs in honey and fennel syrup with muscat granita

frozen passionfruit yogurt

white chocolate and pistachio parfait

balsamic strawberries with black pepper wafers

preparation time 15 minutes
(plus standing and refrigeration time)
cooking time 5 minutes
serves 4

750g strawberries, halved
¼ cup (55g) caster sugar
2 tablespoons balsamic vinegar
¼ cup (35g) plain flour
2 tablespoons caster sugar, extra
1 egg white
30g butter, melted
½ teaspoon vanilla extract
½ teaspoon freshly ground black pepper

1 Preheat oven to moderate (180°C/160°C fan-forced). Line oven tray with baking paper.
2 Combine strawberries, sugar and vinegar in medium bowl, cover; refrigerate 1 hour.
3 Meanwhile, using wooden spoon, beat flour, extra sugar, egg white, butter and extract in small bowl until smooth.
4 Place 1 level teaspoon of the wafer mixture on prepared tray; using back of spoon, spread mixture into 8cm circle. Repeat with remaining wafer mixture, allowing 2cm between each wafer. Sprinkle each wafer with pepper; bake, uncovered, about 5 minutes or until browned lightly. Cool 15 minutes.
5 Serve strawberry mixture with wafers.
per serving 6.5g total fat (4.1g saturated fat); 899kJ (215 cal); 34.5g carbohydrate; 5.1g protein; 4.5g fibre

fresh figs in honey and fennel syrup with muscat granita

preparation time 15 minutes
cooking time 10 minutes
(plus cooling and freezing time)
serves 4

1 cup (250ml) water
½ cup (125ml) muscat
½ cup (110g) caster sugar
1 teaspoon black peppercorns
1 teaspoon finely grated lemon rind
1 tablespoon lemon juice
1 tablespoon fennel seeds
½ cup (125ml) water, extra
¼ cup (90g) honey
8 large fresh figs (640g)

1 Combine the water, muscat, sugar, peppercorns, rind and juice in small saucepan; bring to a boil. Cool 10 minutes; strain into 14cm x 21cm loaf pan. Cover with foil; freeze 4 hours or until firm, scraping granita from bottom and sides of pan with fork every hour.
2 Dry-fry seeds in small saucepan until fragrant. Add the extra water and honey; bring to a boil. Reduce heat; simmer, uncovered, without stirring, about 5 minutes or until mixture thickens slightly. Strain through sieve into small jug; discard seeds. Cool syrup 10 minutes.
3 Cut figs lengthways into five slices; divide among serving plates, drizzle with syrup, top with granita.
per serving 0.5g total fat (0g saturated fat); 1196kJ (286 cal); 61.7g carbohydrate; 2.1g protein; 3.2g fibre

frozen passionfruit yogurt

preparation time 10 minutes (plus freezing time)
cooking time 5 minutes
serves 4

½ cup (110g) caster sugar
¼ cup (60ml) water
1 teaspoon gelatine
2 cups (560g) low-fat yogurt
½ cup (125ml) passionfruit pulp

1 Combine sugar and the water in small saucepan, stirring over low heat until sugar dissolves; transfer to medium jug.
2 Sprinkle gelatine over sugar syrup, stirring until gelatine dissolves.
3 Combine yogurt and pulp in jug with syrup. Pour yogurt mixture into loaf pan, cover tightly with foil; freeze 3 hours or until almost set. Scrape yogurt from bottom and sides of pan with fork; return to freezer until firm.
per serving 0.4g total fat (0.1g saturated fat); 966kJ (231 cal); 46.2g carbohydrate; 9.9g protein 4.3g fibre

white chocolate and pistachio parfait

preparation time 30 minutes
cooking time 10 minutes
*   (plus refrigeration and freezing time)*
serves 8

¾ cup (180ml) thickened cream
250g white eating chocolate, chopped coarsely
6 egg yolks
2 eggs
½ cup (110g) caster sugar
1⅔ cups (400ml) thickened cream, extra
½ cup (125ml) irish cream liqueur
1 cup (150g) toasted shelled pistachios, chopped finely

BERRY COMPOTE
300g frozen mixed berries
2 tablespoons caster sugar
1 tablespoon water

1 Combine cream and chocolate in medium saucepan; stir over low heat until smooth. Beat yolks, whole eggs and sugar in small bowl with electric mixer until thick and creamy; with motor operating, gradually beat hot chocolate mixture into egg mixture. Transfer parfait mixture to large bowl, cover; refrigerate 30 minutes or until mixture thickens slightly.
2 Meanwhile, cut eight 30cm squares of baking paper; fold one square in half diagonally. Place triangle on bench with centre point towards you; curl one point towards you, turning it under where it meets the centre point. Hold these two points together with one hand then roll remaining point towards you to meet the other two, turning it under to form a cone. Staple or tape the cone securely to hold its shape; stand cone upright in tall glass. Repeat with remaining paper squares, standing each in a tall glass; place glasses on tray.
3 Beat extra cream in small bowl with electric mixer until soft peaks form; fold into parfait mixture with liqueur and nuts. Divide mixture among cones. Cover cones loosely with plastic wrap; freeze overnight.
4 Make berry compote.
5 Place parfaits on individual serving plates; carefully remove and discard paper. Serve with berry compote.
BERRY COMPOTE
Combine ingredients in small saucepan; stir over low heat until sugar dissolves. Cool 10 minutes.
per serving 54.1g total fat (28.4g saturated fat); 3014kJ (721 cal); 45.4g carbohydrate; 12.8g protein; 2.7g fibre

roast nectarine tart

preparation time 40 minutes (plus refrigeration time)
cooking time 45 minutes
serves 8

8 nectarines (1.5kg), halved, stone removed
¼ cup (60ml) orange juice
½ cup (110g) firmly packed brown sugar

PASTRY

1⅔ cups (250g) plain flour
⅔ cup (110g) icing sugar
125g cold butter, chopped
1 egg yolk
1½ tablespoons cold water, approximately

CREME PATISSIERE

300ml thickened cream
1 cup (250ml) milk
½ cup (110g) caster sugar
1 vanilla bean
3 egg yolks
2 tablespoons cornflour
90g unsalted butter, chopped

1 Grease 19cm x 27cm loose-based flan tin.
Make pastry.
2 Make crème pâtissière while pastry case is cooling.
3 Increase oven temperature to hot (220°C/200°C fan-forced). Place nectarines, in single layer, in large shallow baking dish; sprinkle with juice and sugar. Roast, uncovered, about 20 minutes or until nectarines are soft. Cool.
4 Meanwhile, spoon crème pâtissière into pastry case, cover; refrigerate about 30 minutes or until firm. Top with nectarines.

PASTRY
Blend or process flour, sugar and butter until combined. Add egg yolk and enough of the water to make ingredients just come together. Knead dough on floured surface until smooth. Cover; refrigerate 30 minutes. Preheat oven to moderate (180°C/160°C fan-forced). Roll dough between sheets of baking paper until large enough to line prepared tin. Ease dough into prepared tin, press into sides; trim edges. Cover; refrigerate 30 minutes. Cover pastry case with baking paper, fill with dried beans or rice; place on oven tray. Bake, uncovered, 10 minutes. Remove paper and beans; bake, uncovered, about 10 minutes or until pastry case is browned lightly. Cool.

CREME PATISSIERE
Combine cream, milk and sugar in medium saucepan. Split vanilla bean in half lengthways, scrape seeds into saucepan, then add pod; bring to a boil. Remove from heat; discard pod. Beat egg yolks in small bowl with electric mixer until thick and creamy; beat in cornflour. Gradually beat in hot cream mixture. Strain mixture into same cleaned saucepan; stir over heat until mixture boils and thickens. Remove from heat; whisk in butter. Cover surface of custard with plastic wrap; cool to room temperature.

per serving 40.6g total fat (25.4g saturated fat); 2997kJ (717 cal); 81.7g carbohydrate; 8.8g protein; 5.2g fibre
TIP Uncooked rice or dried beans used to weigh down the pastry are not suitable for eating. Use them every time you bake blind; store in an airtight storage jar.

ice-cream with espresso and irish cream

preparation time 15 minutes
serves 4

2 tablespoons finely ground espresso coffee
⅔ cup (160ml) boiling water
500ml vanilla ice-cream
½ cup (125ml) irish cream liqueur
4 chocolate-coated rolled wafer sticks (15g)

1 Place coffee and the water in coffee plunger; stand 2 minutes, plunge coffee. Cool 5 minutes.
2 Divide ice-cream among serving glasses; pour liqueur, then coffee over ice-cream. Serve with wafer sticks.
per serving 12.9g total fat (8.4g saturated fat); 1012kJ (242 cal); 21.6g carbohydrate; 3.3g protein; 0.1g fibre
TIP We used Bailey's Irish Cream in this recipe, but you can use any irish cream liqueur.

cookies and cream cheesecake

preparation time 20 minutes (plus refrigeration time)
cooking time 5 minutes
serves 12

250g plain chocolate biscuits
150g butter, melted
2 teaspoons gelatine
¼ cup (60ml) water
1½ cups (360g) packaged cream cheese, softened
300ml thickened cream
1 teaspoon vanilla extract
½ cup (110g) caster sugar
180g white eating chocolate, melted
150g cream-filled chocolate biscuits, quartered
50g dark eating chocolate, melted

1 Line base of 23cm springform tin with baking paper.
2 Blend or process plain chocolate biscuits until mixture resembles fine breadcrumbs. Add butter; process until just combined. Using hand, press biscuit mixture evenly over base and 3cm up side of prepared tin, cover; refrigerate 20 minutes.
3 Sprinkle gelatine over the water in small heatproof jug; stand jug in small saucepan of simmering water. Stir until gelatine dissolves; cool 5 minutes.
4 Beat cheese, cream, extract and sugar in medium bowl with electric mixer until smooth. Stir in gelatine mixture and white chocolate; fold in quartered biscuits. Pour cheesecake mixture over biscuit mixture in tin, cover; refrigerate about 3 hours or until set. Drizzle with dark chocolate to serve.
per serving 41.9g total fat (26.7g saturated fat); 2362kJ (565 cal); 42.8g carbohydrate; 6.8g protein; 0.8g fibre
TIP Place the dark chocolate in a small plastic bag with the corner snipped off to help you drizzle the chocolate evenly over the cheesecake.

nougat semifreddo with orange honey syrup

preparation time 20 minutes (plus freezing time)
cooking time 5 minutes
serves 4

1 vanilla bean
3 eggs, separated
⅓ cup (75g) caster sugar
1½ cups (375ml) thickened cream
200g nougat, chopped finely
½ cup (75g) coarsely chopped toasted
  shelled pistachios
1 tablespoon honey

ORANGE HONEY SYRUP
¼ cup (90g) honey
1 tablespoon finely grated orange rind
2 tablespoons orange juice

1 Split vanilla bean in half lengthways; scrape seeds into small bowl, reserve pod for another use. Add yolks and sugar; beat with electric mixer until thick and creamy. Transfer mixture to large bowl.
2 Beat cream in small bowl with electric mixer until soft peaks form; gently fold cream into yolk mixture.
3 Beat egg whites in separate small bowl with electric mixer until soft peaks form. Gently fold half of the egg white into cream mixture; fold in nougat, nuts, honey and remaining egg white. Transfer mixture to 14cm x 21cm loaf pan, cover with foil; freeze 3 hours or until just firm.
4 Make orange honey syrup.
5 Stand semifreddo at room temperature 10 minutes before serving with syrup.
ORANGE HONEY SYRUP
Place ingredients in small saucepan; bring to a boil. Reduce heat; simmer, uncovered, 2 minutes.
per serving 51.6g total fat (25.5g saturated fat); 3532kJ (845 cal); 87g carbohydrate; 13.3g protein; 2.2g fibre
TIP Using the actual bean imparts the real taste of aromatic vanilla to a recipe. But since the beans aren't cheap, make them do double-duty; after the seeds are scraped out of one, place the empty vanilla pod in a jar then cover it with caster sugar. Keep sealed, in the refrigerator, for whenever you require a flavoured sugar.

Use the tip of a sharp knife to split the vanilla bean lengthways in half then prise out the minuscule seeds.

Fold half of the beaten egg whites into cream mixture before adding nougat, nuts, honey and remaining whites.

marsala and almond mascarpone

preparation time 10 minutes
serves 4

250g mascarpone
2 tablespoons marsala
⅓ cup (55g) sugared almonds, chopped coarsely
½ cup (125ml) thickened cream, whipped
1 tablespoon honey
4 savoiardi sponge finger biscuits

1 Combine mascarpone, marsala, almonds, cream and honey in medium bowl.
2 Spoon mascarpone mixture into individual serving glasses; serve with biscuits.
per serving 46.7g total fat (28.4g saturated fat); 2241kJ (536 cal); 22.3g carbohydrate; 6.4g protein; 0.9g fibre

white chocolate, irish cream and berry trifle

preparation time 25 minutes
* (plus cooling and refrigeration time)*
serves 10

5 eggs
¾ cup (165g) caster sugar
500g mascarpone
300ml thickened cream
⅓ cup (25g) ground espresso coffee
2 cups (500ml) boiling water
1 cup (250ml) irish cream liqueur
2 x 250g packets savoiardi sponge finger biscuits
75g white eating chocolate, grated
500g strawberries
300g fresh raspberries
75g white eating chocolate, extra

1 Beat eggs and sugar in medium bowl with electric mixer about 10 minutes or until thick and creamy.
2 Beat mascarpone and cream in large bowl with electric mixer until thick. Fold egg mixture into mascarpone mixture.
3 Place coffee and boiling water in coffee plunger; stand 2 minutes before plunging. Strain coffee through a fine sieve into a medium heatproof bowl; stir in liqueur.
4 Dip half of the biscuits, one at a time, briefly in coffee mixture until just starting to soften. Line the base of two shallow 2 litre (8 cup) or one 3.5 litre (14 cup) capacity serving dish with biscuits.
5 Spread half the mascarpone mixture over biscuits; top with grated chocolate. Slice half of the strawberries and place over chocolate. Repeat layering process with remaining biscuits, coffee mixture and mascarpone mixture. Cover; refrigerate several hours or overnight.
6 Slice remaining strawberries; place on top of trifle with raspberries. Using vegetable peeler, make chocolate curls from extra white chocolate. Just before serving, sprinkle curls over berries.
per serving 48.8g total fat (30.7g saturated fat); 3202kJ (766 cal); 65.4g carbohydrate; 13.4g protein; 3.3g fibre
TIP This recipe is best made a day ahead.

hazelnut praline tiramisu

preparation time 40 minutes (plus cooling time)
cooking time 10 minutes
  (plus refrigeration and standing time)
serves 15

¼ cup (30g) ground espresso coffee
2 cups (500ml) boiling water
1 cup (250ml) marsala
4 egg yolks
¼ cup (55g) caster sugar
1kg (4 cups) mascarpone
¼ cup (60ml) marsala, extra
½ cup (110g) caster sugar, extra
500g savoiardi sponge finger biscuits
100g coarsely grated dark eating chocolate

HAZELNUT PRALINE
¼ cup (35g) hazelnuts
⅓ cup (75g) caster sugar
2 tablespoons water

1 Place coffee and the boiling water in coffee plunger; stand 2 minutes before plunging. Pour into large jug, stir in liqueur.

2 Beat egg yolks and sugar in small bowl with electric mixer until fluffy.

3 Beat mascarpone, extra liqueur and extra sugar in large bowl until slightly thickened. Gently fold in egg yolk mixture.

4 Pour half the coffee mixture into shallow bowl. Dip half the biscuits, a couple at a time, into coffee mixture until beginning to soften. Line base of 3-litre (12-cup) rectangular serving dish with biscuits; brush with any unused coffee mixture. Spread biscuits with half the mascarpone mixture and sprinkle with half the grated chocolate. Repeat with remaining biscuits, coffee mixture and mascarpone. Cover; refrigerate overnight.

5 Make hazelnut praline.

6 Just before serving, sprinkle with remaining chocolate and chopped hazelnut praline.

HAZELNUT PRALINE
Preheat oven to moderate (180°C/160°C fan-forced). Place hazelnuts in shallow baking dish; bake about 8 minutes or until skins split. Rub nuts in tea towel to remove most of the skin; cool. Lightly grease oven tray. Combine sugar and water in small saucepan; stir over low heat until sugar is dissolved. Brush sides of pan with pastry brush dipped in water to remove sugar crystals. Bring to a boil; boil, uncovered, without stirring, about 5 minutes or until mixture turns a toffee colour. Remove from heat, stir in nuts then quickly pour onto prepared tray. Stand until set.

per serving 38.1g total fat (24.5g saturated fat); 2353kJ (563 cal); 44.7g carbohydrate; 7.6g protein; 1.3g fibre
TIPS Tiramisu is best prepared a day ahead. Hazelnut praline can be made several days ahead; store in an airtight container. Use a blender or food processor to roughly chop the praline.

berries with white chocolate sauce

preparation time 10 minutes
cooking time 5 minutes
serves 4

½ cup (125ml) cream
125g white eating chocolate, chopped finely
1 tablespoon Malibu
500g strawberries, quartered
300g blueberries

1 Bring cream to a boil in medium saucepan; remove from heat. Add chocolate; stir until smooth. Stir in liqueur.
2 Divide combined berries among serving bowls; pour warm sauce over berries.

per serving 24.2g total fat (15.6g saturated fat); 1517kJ (363 cal); 29.8g carbohydrate; 5.4g protein; 4.1g fibre

poached nectarines with orange almond bread

preparation time 25 minutes
   (plus refrigeration and cooling time)
cooking time 1 hour 20 minutes
serves 4

1 cup (220g) caster sugar
1 star anise
10cm strip orange rind
3 cups (750ml) water
8 small nectarines (800g)
⅔ cup (190g) greek-style yogurt

ORANGE ALMOND BREAD
2 egg whites
⅓ cup (75g) caster sugar
¾ cup (110g) plain flour
1 teaspoon finely grated orange rind
¾ cup (120g) blanched almonds

1 Make orange almond bread.
2 Combine sugar, star anise, rind and the water in medium saucepan, stir over medium heat until sugar dissolves; bring to a boil. Boil, uncovered, 2 minutes.
3 Add nectarines to same pan, reduce heat; simmer, uncovered, 20 minutes. Cool nectarines 10 minutes in poaching liquid.
4 Using slotted spoon, transfer nectarines from pan to serving dishes; bring liquid in pan to a boil. Boil, uncovered, about 5 minutes or until syrup reduces to 1 cup; strain into small bowl.
5 Cool syrup to room temperature; pour ¼ cup of the syrup over nectarines in each dish. Serve with yogurt and almond bread.

ORANGE ALMOND BREAD
Preheat oven to moderate (180°C/160°C fan-forced). Grease 8cm x 25cm bar cake pan; line base with baking paper. Beat egg whites in small bowl with electric mixer until soft peaks form. Gradually add sugar, 1 tablespoon at a time, beating until sugar dissolves between additions; transfer to medium bowl. Gently fold in flour, rind and nuts; spread into prepared pan. Bake, uncovered, about 30 minutes or until browned lightly; cool in pan. Wrap in foil; refrigerate 3 hours or overnight. Preheat oven to slow (150°C/130°C fan-forced). Using serrated knife, cut bread into 3mm slices; place slices on baking-paper-lined oven trays. Bake, uncovered, 15 minutes or until crisp.

per serving 20.6g total fat (3.3g saturated fat); 2867kJ (686 cal); 112.6g carbohydrate; 15.5g protein; 7.9g fibre

passionfruit and coconut crème brûlée

preparation time 15 minutes (plus refrigeration time)
cooking time 40 minutes
serves 8

2 eggs
4 egg yolks
¼ cup (55g) caster sugar
½ cup (125ml) passionfruit pulp
1⅔ cups (400ml) coconut cream
300ml thickened cream
2 tablespoons brown sugar

1 Preheat oven to moderate (180°C/160°C fan-forced).
2 Combine eggs, egg yolks, caster sugar and passionfruit in medium heatproof bowl.
3 Combine coconut cream and cream in small saucepan; bring to a boil. Gradually whisk hot cream mixture into egg mixture. Place bowl over medium saucepan of simmering water; stir over heat about 10 minutes or until custard mixture thickens slightly and coats the back of a spoon.
4 Divide custard among eight ½-cup (125ml) heatproof dishes or cups; place dishes in large baking dish. Pour enough boiling water into baking dish to come halfway up sides of dishes; bake 20 minutes or until custards are just set. Remove custards from water; cool to room temperature. Cover; refrigerate 3 hours or overnight.
5 Place custards in shallow flameproof dish filled with ice cubes; sprinkle each with 1 teaspoon brown sugar. Using finger, distribute sugar evenly over surface, pressing in gently; place under preheated hot grill until sugar caramelises.

per serving 28.3g total fat (19.4g saturated fat); 1371kJ (328 cal); 14g carbohydrate; 5.5g protein; 3g fibre
TIPS You will need about eight passionfruit for this recipe. Preheat grill on highest setting for about 5 minutes. It is important the sugar on the custard browns as quickly as possible (the ice in the baking dish helps keep the custards cold while the sugar is caramelising).

Working quickly, whisk the hot cream mixture into the bowl containing the egg yolk and passionfruit pulp.

If running a finger through custard coating a spoon leaves a trail, the mixture has thickened adequately.

Gently press the brown sugar onto top of custards before caramelising them under the preheated grill.

red fruit salad with lemon mascarpone

preparation time 20 minutes
serves 4

1kg seedless watermelon
250g strawberries, hulled, quartered
150g raspberries
2 medium plums (225g), sliced thinly
1 tablespoon caster sugar
⅓ cup (80ml) kirsch

LEMON MASCARPONE
250g mascarpone
2 teaspoons finely grated lemon rind
2 teaspoons caster sugar
1 tablespoon lemon juice

1 Cut watermelon into bite-sized pieces.
2 Place watermelon pieces in large serving bowl with strawberries, raspberries, plums, sugar and liqueur; toss gently to combine. Cover; refrigerate until ready to serve.
3 Combine ingredients for lemon mascarpone in small bowl.
4 Serve fruit salad with lemon mascarpone.
per serving 30.3g total fat (20.3g saturated fat); 2002kJ (479 cal); 34.9g carbohydrate; 5.3g protein; 5.4g fibre
TIP Use a melon baller to scoop watermelon into bite-sized balls, if desired, for a more decorative look.

gourmet chocolate tart

preparation time 40 minutes (plus refrigeration time)
cooking time 30 minutes
serves 8

2 eggs
2 egg yolks
¼ cup (55g) caster sugar
250g dark eating chocolate, melted
200g butter, melted

TART SHELL
1½ cups (240g) plain flour
½ cup (110g) caster sugar
140g cold butter, chopped
1 egg, beaten lightly

1 Make tart shell.
2 Reduce oven temperature to moderate (180°C/160°C fan-forced).
3 Whisk whole eggs, egg yolks and sugar in medium heatproof bowl over medium saucepan of simmering water about 15 minutes or until light and fluffy. Gently whisk chocolate and butter into egg mixture.
4 Pour mixture into tart shell. Bake, uncovered, about 10 minutes or until filling is set; cool 10 minutes. Refrigerate 1 hour. Serve dusted with cocoa powder, if desired.
TART SHELL
Blend or process flour, sugar and butter until crumbly; add egg, process until ingredients just come together. Knead dough on floured surface until smooth. Enclose in plastic wrap; refrigerate 30 minutes. Grease 24cm-round loose-base flan tin. Roll dough between sheets of baking paper until large enough to line prepared tin. Lift dough onto tin; press into side, trim edge, prick base all over with fork. Cover; refrigerate 30 minutes. Preheat oven to moderately hot (200°C/180°C fan-forced). Place tin on oven tray; cover dough with baking paper, fill with dried beans or rice. Bake, uncovered, 10 minutes. Carefully remove paper and beans; bake, uncovered, about 5 minutes or until pastry browns lightly. Cool to room temperature.
per serving 48.1g total fat (32.7g saturated fat); 2897kJ (693 cal); 60.4g carbohydrate; 8g protein; 2.6g fibre

asian fruit salad

preparation time 20 minutes
cooking time 15 minutes
   (plus cooling and refrigeration time)
serves 8

1 litre (4 cups) water
1 cup (270g) grated palm sugar
1 vanilla bean
2cm piece fresh ginger (10g), chopped finely
3 star anise
1 tablespoon finely grated lime rind
⅓ cup (80ml) lime juice
½ cup coarsely chopped fresh vietnamese mint
2 large mangoes (1.2kg), chopped coarsely
3 star fruit (450g), sliced thinly
2 large oranges (600g), segmented
1 large pineapple (2kg), chopped coarsely
1 medium papaya (1kg), chopped coarsely
½ cup (125ml) passionfruit pulp
12 rambutans (500g), halved
12 lychees (300g), halved

1 Stir the water and sugar in medium saucepan over high heat until sugar dissolves; bring to a boil. Reduce heat; simmer without stirring, uncovered, 5 minutes. Split vanilla bean in half lengthways; scrape seeds into pan. Add pod, ginger and star anise; simmer, uncovered, about 10 minutes or until syrup thickens. Discard pod; cool to room temperature. Stir in rind, juice and mint.
2 Combine remaining ingredients in large bowl. Pour syrup over fruit; stir gently to combine. Cover; refrigerate until cold.
per serving 0.9g total fat (0g saturated fat); 1488kJ (356 cal); 82.9g carbohydrate; 5.2g protein; 12.4g fibre
TIP You need about six passionfruit for this recipe.

mango-passionfruit sorbet with grilled mango

preparation time 30 minutes (plus freezing time)
cooking time 25 minutes
serves 4

½ cup (125ml) passionfruit pulp
1 cup (250ml) water
½ cup (110g) caster sugar
1 large mango (600g), chopped coarsely
2 tablespoons orange-flavoured liqueur
3 egg whites
4 small mangoes (1.2kg)
2 tablespoons brown sugar
1 lime, cut into 8 wedges

1 Strain passionfruit pulp over small jug; reserve seeds.
2 Stir the water and caster sugar in small saucepan over heat, without boiling, until sugar dissolves; bring to a boil. Reduce heat; simmer, uncovered, without stirring, about 10 minutes or until mixture thickens. Cool.
3 Blend or process chopped mango until smooth; transfer to small bowl. Stir in pulp, syrup and liqueur. Pour mixture into 14cm x 21cm loaf pan, cover with foil; freeze about 3 hours or until just firm.
4 Process sorbet with egg whites until almost smooth. Stir in 2 tablespoons reserved passionfruit seeds; discard remaining seeds. Return sorbet to pan, cover; freeze overnight.
5 Just before serving, slice cheeks from small mangoes; score each cheek in shallow criss-cross pattern, taking care not to cut through skin. Sprinkle brown sugar over cheeks; place under hot grill until browned lightly. Serve sorbet with mango cheeks and lime wedges.
per serving 0.8g total fat (0g saturated fat); 1538kJ (368 cal); 80.1g carbohydrate; 6.9g protein; 9.4g fibre
TIPS You need about six passionfruit for this recipe. You can use Cointreau, Grand Marnier, Curaçao or any other orange-flavoured liqueur in this recipe.

Cakes

Never underestimate the power of
a homemade cake to thrill even
the most sophisticated people.
A number of the cakes in this
chapter could appear as the
crowning glory of an important
celebration. Others are the kind
that enrich family life, from Sunday
morning muffins to healthy cakes
for lunch-boxes and uncomplicated
but delicious offerings for afternoon
tea or supper. Some will keep well,
others are best the day they are
baked. If you should have any of
the second kind left over, slice
and freeze them for another day.
They will thaw almost as new.

blackberry and orange mascarpone cake

citrus poppy seed muffins

maple pecan cake

vanilla pear almond cake

blackberry and orange mascarpone cake

preparation time 30 minutes (plus refrigeration time)
cooking time 50 minutes
serves 10

185g butter
1 tablespoon finely grated orange rind
1 cup (220g) caster sugar
3 eggs, beaten lightly
1 cup (150g) self-raising flour
⅓ cup (40g) almond meal
½ cup (125ml) orange juice
350g blackberries
⅓ cup (110g) blackberry jam, warmed
1 tablespoon orange-flavoured liqueur
1 tablespoon icing sugar

MASCARPONE CREAM
⅔ cup (160ml) thickened cream
1 cup (250g) mascarpone cheese
⅓ cup (55g) icing sugar
1 teaspoon finely grated orange rind
1 tablespoon orange-flavoured liqueur

1 Preheat oven to moderately slow (170°C/150°C fan-forced). Grease deep 22cm-round cake pan; line base and side with baking paper.
2 Beat butter, rind and caster sugar in medium bowl with electric mixer until light and fluffy. Add eggs, one at a time, beating until combined between additions. Fold flour, almond meal and juice, in two batches, into butter mixture. Pour into prepared pan; bake, uncovered, about 50 minutes. Stand cake 5 minutes; turn, top-side up, onto wire rack to cool.
3 Meanwhile, make mascarpone cream.
4 Reserve 10 blackberries.
5 Using large serrated knife, split cake into three layers. Place one layer of cake on serving plate; spread with half of the combined jam and liqueur. Spread with half of the mascarpone cream, then top with half of the blackberries. Repeat layering process, finishing with layer of cake. Cover; refrigerate 1 hour.
6 Serve cake sprinkled with sifted icing sugar and reserved blackberries.
MASCARPONE CREAM
Beat cream, cheese and sugar in small bowl with electric mixer until soft peaks form; stir in rind and liqueur.
per serving 41.1g total fat (25.2g saturated fat); 2654kJ (635 cal); 60g carbohydrate; 7.2g protein; 3.7g fibre
TIP You can use Cointreau, Grand Marnier, Curaçao or any other orange-flavoured liqueur in this recipe.

citrus poppy seed muffins

preparation time 15 minutes
cooking time 20 minutes
makes 12

125g softened butter, chopped
2 teaspoons finely grated lemon rind
2 teaspoons finely grated lime rind
2 teaspoons finely grated orange rind
⅔ cup (150g) caster sugar
2 eggs, beaten lightly
2 cups (300g) self-raising flour
1 cup (250ml) milk
2 tablespoons poppy seeds
1 medium orange (240g)
icing sugar, for dusting

1 Preheat oven to moderately hot (200°C/180°C fan-forced). Grease 12-hole (⅓-cup/80ml) muffin pan.
2 Combine butter, rinds, caster sugar, egg, sifted flour and milk in medium bowl; beat with electric mixer until just combined. Increase speed to medium, beat until mixture is just changed in colour; stir in poppy seeds. Divide mixture among holes of prepared pan. Bake, uncovered, about 20 minutes. Stand muffins in pan for a few minutes before turning onto wire rack.
3 Peel rind thinly from orange, avoiding any white pith. Cut rind into thin strips. To serve, dust muffins with icing sugar; top with orange strips.
per muffin 11.4g total fat (6.6g saturated fat); 1041kJ (249 cal); 32.5g carbohydrate; 4.8g protein; 1.7g fibre
TIP Tiny, blue-grey poppy seeds add texture and a slightly nutty taste.

maple pecan cake

preparation time 15 minutes
cooking time 1 hour
serves 10

cooking-oil spray
1 cup (100g) pecans
⅓ cup (80ml) maple syrup
1¼ cups (310ml) boiling water
1¼ cups (235g) coarsely chopped dried figs
1 teaspoon bicarbonate of soda
60g butter
¾ cup (150g) firmly packed brown sugar
2 eggs
1 cup (150g) self-raising flour

MAPLE BUTTERSCOTCH SAUCE
1 cup (250ml) maple syrup
½ cup (125ml) cream
100g butter, chopped

1 Preheat oven to moderate (180°C/160°C fan-forced). Grease deep 20cm-round cake pan; line base with baking paper, coat with cooking-oil spray.
2 Arrange nuts over base of prepared pan; drizzle with maple syrup.
3 Combine the water, figs and soda in bowl of food processor. Cover with lid; stand 5 minutes. Add butter and sugar; process until almost smooth. Add eggs and flour; process until just combined. Pour into prepared pan; bake about 55 minutes. Stand cake 5 minutes; turn onto wire rack.
4 Before serving, make butterscotch sauce.
5 Serve cake with sauce and, if desired, ice-cream.
MAPLE BUTTERSCOTCH SAUCE
Stir ingredients in small saucepan over heat until smooth; bring to a boil. Boil, uncovered, about 2 minutes or until mixture thickens slightly.
per serving 27.6g total fat (13.1g saturated fat); 2215kJ (530 cal); 68.4g carbohydrate; 5g protein; 4.8g fibre
TIP Either maple syrup or maple-flavoured syrup can be used in this recipe.

vanilla pear almond cake

preparation time 30 minutes (plus cooling time)
cooking time 2 hours 15 minutes
serves 8

8 corella pears (800g)
1 strip lemon rind
1¾ cups (385g) caster sugar
2½ cups (625ml) water
1 vanilla bean
125g butter, chopped
3 eggs
⅔ cup (160g) sour cream
⅔ cup (100g) plain flour
⅔ cup (100g) self-raising flour
¼ cup (40g) blanched almonds, toasted, chopped coarsely
40g dark eating chocolate, chopped coarsely
½ cup (60g) almond meal

1 Peal pears, leaving stems intact.
2 Combine rind, 1 cup of the sugar and the water in medium saucepan. Split vanilla bean in half lengthways; scrape seeds into pan, then add pod. Stir over heat, without boiling, until sugar dissolves. Add pears; bring to a boil. Reduce heat; simmer, covered, about 30 minutes or until pears are just tender. Transfer pears to medium bowl; bring syrup to a boil. Boil, uncovered, until syrup reduces by half. Cool completely.
3 Preheat oven to moderately slow (170°C/150°C fan-forced). Insert base of 23cm springform tin upside down in tin to give a flat base; grease tin.
4 Beat butter and remaining sugar in medium bowl with electric mixer until light and fluffy. Add eggs, one at a time, beating until just combined between each addition. Add sour cream; beat until just combined. Mixture may curdle at this stage but will come together later. Stir in 2 tablespoons of the syrup, then flours, nuts, chocolate and almond meal.
5 Spread cake mixture into prepared tin; place pears upright around edge of tin, gently pushing to the bottom. Bake, uncovered, about 1 hour 35 minutes. Stand 10 minutes; remove from tin.
6 Serve cake warm, brushed with remaining syrup.
per serving 31.5g total fat (15.6g saturated fat); 2633kJ (630 cal); 81.8g carbohydrate; 8.6g protein; 3.7g fibre

rhubarb and coconut cake

preparation time 25 minutes
cooking time 1 hour 30 minutes
serves 8

1½ cups (225g) self-raising flour
1¼ cups (275g) caster sugar
1¼ cups (110g) desiccated coconut
125g butter, melted
3 eggs, beaten lightly
½ cup (125ml) milk
½ teaspoon vanilla extract
1 cup (110g) finely chopped rhubarb
5 trimmed rhubarb stalks (300g)
2 tablespoons demerara sugar

1 Preheat oven to slow (150°C/130°C fan-forced). Grease 14cm x 21cm loaf pan; line base of pan with baking paper.
2 Combine flour, caster sugar and coconut in medium bowl; stir in butter, eggs, milk and extract until combined.
3 Spread half the cake mixture into prepared pan; sprinkle evenly with chopped rhubarb, spread remaining cake mixture over rhubarb.
4 Cut rhubarb stalks into 12cm lengths. Arrange rhubarb pieces over top of cake; sprinkle with demerara sugar. Bake, uncovered, about 1 hour 30 minutes. Stand cake in pan 5 minutes; turn, top-side up, onto wire rack to cool.

per serving 24.8g total fat (17.4g saturated fat); 2044kJ (489 cal); 61g carbohydrate; 7.5g protein; 4.7g fibre
TIPS You need about seven large stalks of rhubarb for this recipe. When you buy a bunch, cut off and discard all the leaves, as they are poisonous. The taste of rhubarb stalks themselves is enhanced by combining them with certain other flavours such as orange, strawberry or the vanilla used here, to name a few.

little lime friands

preparation time 20 minutes
cooking time 15 minutes (plus cooling time)
makes 30

6 egg whites
185g butter, melted
1 cup (125g) almond meal
1½ cups (240g) icing sugar
½ cup (75g) plain flour
1 tablespoon finely grated lime rind
1 tablespoon lime juice
30 whole blanched almonds (60g)

1 Preheat oven to moderately hot (200°C/180°C fan-forced). Grease 30 x 1½-tablespoon (30ml) mini muffin pan holes.
2 Place egg whites in medium bowl; whisk lightly until combined. Add butter, almond meal, sifted icing sugar and flour, then rind and juice. Whisk until just combined. Divide mixture among prepared pans; top mixture with an almond.
3 Bake, uncovered, about 15 minutes. Turn, top-side up, onto wire racks to cool. Serve warm or at room temperature.
per friand 8g total fat (3.5g saturated fat); 493kJ (118 cal); 10.1g carbohydrate; 1.8g protein; 0.6g fibre
TIP This recipe can be made 2 days ahead.

coffee friands

preparation time 15 minutes
cooking time 20 minutes
makes 12

6 egg whites
2 teaspoons instant coffee powder
2 teaspoons hot water
185g butter, melted
1 cup (100g) hazelnut meal
1½ cups (240g) icing sugar
½ cup (75g) plain flour
24 whole coffee beans

1 Preheat oven to moderately hot (200°C/180°C fan-forced). Grease 12 x ½-cup (125ml) rectangular or oval friand pans; stand on oven tray.
2 Place egg whites in medium bowl; whisk lightly with fork until combined. Dissolve coffee powder in the hot water; add to egg-white mixture.
3 Add butter, hazelnut meal, sugar and flour to egg-white mixture; using wooden spoon, stir until just combined.
4 Divide mixture among prepared pans; top each friand with two coffee beans. Bake, uncovered, about 25 minutes. Stand friands in pans 5 minutes; turn, top-side up, onto wire rack to cool.
per friand 17.8g total fat (8.6g saturated fat); 1133kJ (271 cal); 25.2g carbohydrate; 3.9g protein; 1.2g fibre

dark chocolate and almond torte

preparation time 20 minutes (plus standing time)
cooking time 55 minutes
serves 14

160g dark eating chocolate, chopped coarsely
160g unsalted butter
5 eggs, separated
¾ cup (165g) caster sugar
1 cup (125g) almond meal
⅔ cup (50g) toasted flaked almonds, chopped
⅓ cup (35g) coarsely grated dark eating chocolate
1 cup (140g) vienna almonds

DARK CHOCOLATE GANACHE
125g dark eating chocolate, chopped coarsely
⅓ cup (80ml) thickened cream

1 Preheat oven to moderate (180°C/160°C fan-forced). Grease deep 22cm round cake pan; line base and side with two layers of baking paper.
2 Stir chopped chocolate and butter in small saucepan over low heat until smooth; cool to room temperature.
3 Beat egg yolks and sugar in small bowl with electric mixer until thick and creamy. Transfer to large bowl; fold in chocolate mixture, almond meal, flaked almonds and grated chocolate.
4 Beat egg whites in small bowl with electric mixer until soft peaks form; fold into chocolate mixture, in two batches. Pour mixture into prepared pan; bake, uncovered, about 45 minutes. Stand cake in pan 15 minutes; turn cake, top-side up, onto wire rack to cool.
5 Meanwhile, make dark chocolate ganache.
6 Spread ganache over cake, decorate cake with vienna almonds; stand 30 minutes before serving.
DARK CHOCOLATE GANACHE
Stir ingredients in small saucepan over heat until smooth.
per serving 30.5g total fat (12.9g saturated fat); 1747kJ (418 cal); 30.6g carbohydrate; 7.6g protein; 2g fibre

The pan should be lined with two layers of baking paper, both base and side, for this torte recipe.

After egg whites are beaten enough to hold soft peaks, fold them, in two batches, into chocolate mixture.

Pour warm ganache onto torte, then spread it to cover surface entirely, allowing it to drip down the sides.

raspberry hazelnut cake

preparation time 30 minutes
cooking time 1 hour 30 minutes
serves 12

250g butter, softened
2 cups (440g) caster sugar
6 eggs
1 cup (150g) plain flour
½ cup (75g) self-raising flour
1 cup (110g) hazelnut meal
⅔ cup (160g) sour cream
300g fresh or frozen raspberries

MASCARPONE CREAM
250g mascarpone cheese
¼ cup (40g) icing sugar
2 tablespoons frangelico
½ cup (120g) sour cream
½ cup (75g) roasted hazelnuts, chopped finely

1 Preheat oven to moderate (180°C/160°C fan-forced). Grease deep 22cm-round cake pan; line base and side with baking paper.
2 Beat butter and sugar in medium bowl with electric mixer until light and fluffy; add eggs, one at a time, beating until just combined between additions. Mixture will curdle at this stage, but will come together later.
3 Transfer mixture to large bowl; using wooden spoon, stir in flours, hazelnut meal, sour cream and raspberries. Spread mixture into prepared pan. Bake, uncovered, about 1½ hours. Stand cake 10 minutes; turn onto wire rack, turn top-side up to cool.
4 Make mascarpone cream.
5 Place cake on serving plate. Using metal spatula, spread cake all over with mascarpone cream.
MASCARPONE CREAM
Combine mascarpone, icing sugar, liqueur and sour cream in medium bowl. Using wooden spoon, stir until smooth; stir in nuts.
per serving 48.7g total fat (25.4g saturated fat); 2959kJ (708 cal); 59.1g carbohydrate; 9.6g protein; 3.7g fibre
TIP If using frozen raspberries, don't thaw them; frozen berries are less likely to 'bleed' into the cake mixture.

chocolate fudge cake

preparation time 20 minutes
cooking time 40 minutes
serves 8

85g dark chocolate, chopped finely
½ cup (50g) cocoa powder
1 cup (200g) firmly packed brown sugar
½ cup (125ml) boiling water
2 egg yolks
¼ cup (30g) almond meal
⅓ cup (50g) wholemeal plain flour
4 egg whites

1 Preheat oven to moderate (180°C/160°C fan-forced). Line base and side of deep 20cm-round cake pan.
2 Combine chocolate, cocoa, sugar and the water in large bowl; stir until smooth. Add egg yolks; whisk to combine. Fold in almond meal and flour.
3 Beat egg whites in small bowl with electric mixer until firm peaks form. Gently fold egg white mixture into chocolate mixture, in two batches; pour into prepared pan. Bake, uncovered, about 40 minutes. Stand in pan 5 minutes; turn onto wire rack, remove paper.
per serving 7.5g total fat (2.9g saturated fat); 966kJ (231 cal); 36.4g carbohydrate; 5.9g protein; 1.4g fibre
SERVING SUGGESTION Serve cake warm, dusted with icing sugar and dotted with fresh strawberries.

white chocolate mud cakes

preparation time 1 hour 30 minutes
cooking time 40 minutes
makes 24 cakes

24 silver muffin cases
250g butter, chopped coarsely
150g white eating chocolate, chopped coarsely
2 cups (440g) caster sugar
1 cup (250ml) milk
1½ cups (225g) plain flour
½ cup (75g) self-raising flour
1 teaspoon vanilla essence
2 eggs, beaten lightly
small flowers and silver cachous, for decorating

FLUFFY FROSTING
1 cup (220g) caster sugar
⅓ cup (80ml) water
2 egg whites

1 Preheat oven to moderately slow (160°C/140°C fan-forced). Line two 12-hole (⅓-cup/80ml) muffin pans with silver cases.
2 Combine butter, chocolate, sugar and milk in a medium pan; with a wooden spoon, stir over low heat, without boiling, until smooth. Transfer mixture to a bowl; cool 15 minutes.
3 Whisk in sifted flours, then essence and eggs. Pour mixture evenly into prepared pans. Bake, uncovered, about 35 minutes or until cooked when tested. Cool.
4 Make fluffy frosting. Spread cakes with fluffy frosting; decorate with the flowers and cachous. Arrange on cake stand, if desired.

FLUFFY FROSTING
Combine sugar and water in small saucepan; stir with wooden spoon over low heat, without boiling, until sugar dissolves. Boil, uncovered, without stirring, for 3–5 minutes or until syrup is slightly thick. If a candy thermometer is available, the syrup will be ready at 114°C. Otherwise, when syrup is thick, remove pan from the heat, allow bubbles to subside, then test the syrup by dropping 1 teaspoon of it into a cup of cold water. The syrup should form a ball of soft sticky toffee when rolled between fingertips. (Syrup should not colour; if it does, discard it.) Just before the syrup reaches the correct temperature, beat egg whites in a small bowl with an electric mixer until firm. When the syrup is ready, allow bubbles to subside, then pour in a thin stream onto egg whites, with electric mixer operating on medium speed. If syrup is added too quickly to the egg whites, frosting will not thicken. Continue to beat on high speed for about 5 minutes or until thick. Frosting should be barely warm by now.
per cake 11.6g total fat (7.4g saturated fat); 1137kJ (272 cal); 40.5g carbohydrate; 3g protein; 0.5g fibre
TIP Un-iced cakes can be frozen.

mixed berry buttermilk muffins

preparation time 5 minutes
cooking time 20 minutes
makes 12

2½ cups (375g) self-raising flour
¾ cup (165g) caster sugar
1 egg, beaten lightly
1 teaspoon vanilla essence
⅔ cup (160ml) vegetable oil
¾ cup (180ml) buttermilk
200g frozen mixed berries

1 Preheat oven to moderately hot (200°C/180°C fan-forced). Line 12-hole (⅓-cup/80ml) muffin pan with paper cases or grease holes of pan.
2 Sift flour and sugar together into large bowl; stir in remaining ingredients.
3 Divide mixture among muffin holes; bake, uncovered, about 20 minutes. Stand 5 minutes; turn, top-side up, onto wire rack to cool.

per muffin 13.4g total fat (2g saturated fat); 1191kJ (285 cal); 37.1g carbohydrate; 4.6g protein; 1.6g fibre
TIPS Be careful not to overmix the muffin mixture; it should be slightly lumpy. Using still-frozen berries will minimise 'bleeding' of colour into the muffin mixture. These muffins freeze well; wrap them individually in plastic wrap so you only need to defrost a certain number of them at any time.
SERVING SUGGESTIONS Serve the muffins hot with a scoop of vanilla ice-cream. Dust the tops of warm muffins with icing sugar and serve with fresh fruit jam.

mixed berry cake with vanilla bean syrup

preparation time 20 minutes
cooking time 40 minutes
serves 8

125g butter, chopped
1 cup (220g) caster sugar
3 eggs
½ cup (75g) plain flour
¼ cup (35g) self-raising flour
½ cup (60g) almond meal
⅓ cup (80g) sour cream
1½ cups (225g) frozen mixed berries
½ cup (100g) drained canned seeded
  black cherries

VANILLA BEAN SYRUP
½ cup (110g) caster sugar
½ cup (125ml) water
2 vanilla beans

1 Preheat oven to moderate (180°C/160°C fan-forced). Grease 20cm baba pan thoroughly.
2 Beat butter and sugar in small bowl with electric mixer until light and fluffy. Add eggs, one at a time, beating until just combined between additions. Mixture may curdle at this stage but will come together later.
3 Transfer mixture to large bowl; stir in sifted flours, almond meal, sour cream, berries and cherries. Pour mixture into prepared pan; bake, uncovered, about 40 minutes. Stand cake 5 minutes; turn onto wire rack placed over a large tray.
4 Make vanilla bean syrup. Pour hot syrup over hot cake.
VANILLA BEAN SYRUP
Combine sugar and the water in small saucepan. Split vanilla beans in half lengthways; scrape seeds into pan then add pods. Stir over heat, without boiling, until sugar dissolves. Simmer, uncovered, without stirring, 5 minutes. Using tongs, remove pods from syrup.

per serving 23.1g total fat (12g saturated fat); 1852kJ (443 cal); 54.9g carbohydrate; 6.4g protein; 2g fibre

pistachio and polenta cake with blood orange syrup

preparation time 10 minutes
cooking time 1 hour 15 minutes
serves 12

300g sour cream
125g butter, softened
1 cup (220g) caster sugar
2 cups (300g) self-raising flour
½ teaspoon bicarbonate of soda
⅔ cup (110g) polenta
1 teaspoon finely grated blood orange rind
¾ cup (180ml) water
⅔ cup (100g) toasted shelled pistachios

BLOOD ORANGE SYRUP
1 cup (250ml) blood orange juice
1 cup (220g) caster sugar
1 cinnamon stick

1 Preheat oven to moderately slow (170°C/150°C fan-forced). Grease deep 20cm-round cake pan; line base and side with baking paper.
2 Make blood orange syrup.
3 Place sour cream, butter, sugar, sifted flour and soda, polenta, rind and the water in large bowl; beat on low speed with electric mixer until just combined. Beat on medium speed until mixture changes to a slightly lighter colour. Stir in nuts.
4 Spread cake mixture into prepared pan; bake, uncovered, about 1 hour. Stand cake in pan 10 minutes; turn cake, top-side up, onto wire rack to cool. Serve cake warm or cold with strained blood orange syrup.
BLOOD ORANGE SYRUP
Combine ingredients in small saucepan; bring to a boil, stirring. Reduce heat; simmer, uncovered, 15 minutes or until syrup thickens. Cool to room temperature.
per serving 15.2g total fat (7.6g saturated fat); 1714kJ (412 cal); 64.3g carbohydrate; 5.6g protein; 2.1g fibre

After the sugar dissolves, cook the blood orange syrup over low heat, without stirring, until it's thickened.

Cake mixture will be quite thick so spread it wih a rubber spatula to level the surface before baking.

coffee and walnut cake

preparation time 20 minutes
cooking time 45 minutes
   (plus cooling and standing time)
serves 8

30g butter
1 tablespoon brown sugar
2 teaspoons ground cinnamon
200g walnuts, toasted
½ cup (125ml) milk
1 tablespoon dry instant coffee
185g butter, extra
1⅓ cups (300g) caster sugar
3 eggs
1 cup (150g) self-raising flour
¾ cup (110g) plain flour

TOFFEE
½ cup (110g) caster sugar
2 tablespoons water
3 teaspoons cream

1 Preheat oven to moderately slow (170°C/150°C fan-forced). Thoroughly grease 22cm-baba cake pan; lightly flour base and side with flour, shake out excess.
2 Melt butter in small saucepan, add brown sugar, cinnamon and walnuts; stir well. Cool.
3 Combine milk and coffee in small bowl; stir until coffee dissolves.
4 Beat extra butter and caster sugar in small bowl with electric mixer until light and fluffy. Beat in eggs one at a time, beating until just combined between additions. Fold in sifted flours, then milk mixture.
5 Spread one-third of the cake mixture in base of prepared pan, sprinkle with half walnut mixture, top with remaining cake mixture. Bake, uncovered, about 45 minutes or until cooked when tested. Stand cake 5 minutes before turning onto wire rack to cool.
6 Make toffee.
7 Place cake on wire rack over oven tray. Drizzle some of the toffee on top of cake, press on remaining walnut mixture; drizzle with remaining toffee.
TOFFEE
Combine sugar and the water in small saucepan; stir over low heat until sugar dissolves. Bring to a boil, simmer, uncovered, until sugar browns slightly. Add cream and stir 1 minute or until thickened slightly.
per serving 43.1g total fat (17.2g saturated fat); 3031kJ (725 cal); 77.8g carbohydrate; 10.2g protein; 2.9g fibre
TIP This recipe is best made on the day of serving.

double-decker mud cake

preparation time 30 minutes (plus standing time)
cooking time 1 hour
serves 10

250g butter, chopped
150g white eating chocolate, chopped coarsely
2 cups (440g) caster sugar
1 cup (250ml) milk
1½ cups (225g) plain flour
½ cup (75g) self-raising flour
1 teaspoon vanilla essence
2 eggs, beaten lightly
2 tablespoons cocoa powder
600g milk eating chocolate, chopped coarsely
1 cup (250ml) cream

1 Preheat oven to slow (150°C/130°C fan-forced). Grease two deep 20cm-round cake pans; line bases and sides with baking paper.
2 Combine butter, white chocolate, sugar and milk in medium saucepan; stir over heat, without boiling, until smooth. Transfer mixture to large bowl; cool 15 minutes.
3 Whisk sifted flours into white chocolate mixture then whisk in essence and egg; pour half of the mixture into one of the prepared pans. Whisk sifted cocoa into remaining mixture; pour into other prepared pan. Bake cakes, uncovered, about 50 minutes. Cool cakes in pans 5 minutes; turn cakes, top-side up, onto wire rack to cool.
4 Combine milk chocolate and cream in medium saucepan; stir over low heat until smooth. Transfer to medium bowl. Cover; refrigerate, stirring occasionally, until chocolate mixture is of spreadable consistency. Reserve 1 cup of the chocolate mixture for spreading over cake.
5 Split each cooled cake in half. Centre one layer of cake on serving plate; spread with ½ cup of the remaining milk chocolate mixture. Repeat layering, alternating colours. Cover top and sides of cake with reserved chocolate mixture.
per serving 55.4g total fat (35.1g saturated fat); 4092kJ (979 cal); 113.4g carbohydrate; 12.3g protein; 1.7g fibre
TIP You can also melt the milk chocolate and cream in a microwave oven; cook on HIGH (100%) about 90 seconds, pausing to stir every 30 seconds.

flourless hazelnut chocolate cake

preparation time 20 minutes (plus standing time)
cooking time 1 hour
serves 9

⅓ cup (35g) cocoa powder
⅓ cup (80ml) hot water
150g dark chocolate, melted
150g butter, melted
1⅓ cups (275g) firmly packed brown sugar
1 cup (125g) hazelnut meal
4 eggs, separated
1 tablespoon cocoa powder, extra

1 Preheat oven to moderate (180°C/160°C fan-forced). Grease deep 19cm-square cake pan; line base and sides with baking paper.
2 Blend cocoa with the hot water in large bowl until smooth. Stir in chocolate, butter, sugar, hazelnut meal and egg yolks.
3 Beat egg whites in small bowl with electric mixer until soft peaks form; fold into chocolate mixture in two batches.
4 Pour mixture into prepared pan; bake, uncovered, about 1 hour or until firm. Stand cake 15 minutes; turn, top-side up, onto wire rack, to cool. Dust with sifted extra cocoa to serve.
per serving 29.9g total fat (13.3g saturated fat); 1898kJ (454 cal); 42g carbohydrate; 7g protein; 1.9g fibre
TIP This cake can be made up to 4 days ahead, cover; refrigerate. It can also be frozen for up to 3 months.

chocolate banana bread

preparation time 15 minutes
cooking time 1 hour
serves 12

1 cup mashed banana
¾ cup (165g) caster sugar
2 eggs, beaten lightly
¼ cup (60ml) extra light olive oil
¼ cup (60ml) milk
⅔ cup (100g) self-raising flour
⅔ cup (100g) wholemeal self-raising flour
¾ cup (90g) coarsely chopped toasted walnuts
¼ cup (45g) finely chopped dark eating chocolate

WHIPPED NUT BUTTER
100g butter
¼ cup (30g) finely chopped toasted walnuts

1 Preheat oven to moderate (180°C/160°C fan-forced). Grease 14cm x 21cm loaf pan; line base and long sides with baking paper.
2 Combine banana and sugar in large bowl; stir in eggs, oil and milk. Add flours, nuts and chocolate; stir until combined.
3 Spread mixture into prepared pan; bake, uncovered, about 1 hour. Stand bread in pan 5 minutes; turn onto wire rack to cool.
4 Make whipped nut butter. Serve bread warm with whipped nut butter.
WHIPPED NUT BUTTER
Beat butter in small bowl with electric mixer until light and fluffy; stir in nuts.
per serving 20.7g total fat (6.7g saturated fat); 1371kJ (328 cal); 31.7g carbohydrate; 5.1g protein; 2.4g fibre
TIP Leftover banana bread can be toasted if desired.

chocolate ganache and raspberry cake

preparation time 25 minutes
cooking time 1 hour 25 minutes (plus standing time)
serves 12

⅓ cup (35g) cocoa powder
⅓ cup (80ml) water
150g dark eating chocolate, melted
150g butter, melted
1⅓ cups (300g) firmly packed brown sugar
1 cup (125g) almond meal
4 eggs, separated
200g dark eating chocolate, chopped coarsely
⅔ cup (160ml) thickened cream
300g raspberries

1 Preheat oven to moderately slow (170°C/150°C fan-forced). Grease deep 22cm-round cake pan; line base and side with baking paper.
2 Blend sifted cocoa powder with the water in large bowl until smooth. Stir in melted chocolate, butter, sugar, almond meal and egg yolks.
3 Beat egg whites in small bowl with electric mixer until soft peaks form; fold egg whites, in two batches, into chocolate mixture.
4 Pour mixture into prepared pan; bake, uncovered, about 1¼ hours. Stand cake 15 minutes, turn onto wire rack; turn cake top-side up to cool.
5 Stir chopped chocolate and cream in small saucepan over low heat until smooth.
6 Place raspberries on top of cake; drizzle chocolate mixture over raspberries. Stand cake at room temperature until chocolate sets.
per serving 31.5g total fat (16.1g saturated fat); 2019kJ (483 cal); 45.7g carbohydrate; 7.1g protein; 2.8g fibre
TIPS Undecorated cake is suitable to freeze. The cake can be made up to three days in advance. Top cake with raspberries and chocolate on the day of serving.

upside-down toffee banana cake

preparation time 15 minutes
cooking time 55 minutes
serves 8

1 cup (220g) caster sugar
1 cup (250ml) water
2 medium bananas (400g), sliced thinly
2 eggs, beaten lightly
⅔ cup (160ml) vegetable oil
¾ cup (165g) firmly packed brown sugar
1 teaspoon vanilla extract
⅔ cup (100g) plain flour
⅓ cup (50g) wholemeal self-raising flour
2 teaspoons mixed spice
1 teaspoon bicarbonate of soda
1 cup mashed banana

1 Preheat oven to moderate (180°C/160°C fan-forced). Grease deep 22cm-round cake pan; line base with baking paper.
2 Stir caster sugar and the water in medium saucepan over heat, without boiling, until sugar dissolves; bring to a boil. Boil, uncovered, without stirring, 10 minutes or until caramel in colour. Pour toffee into prepared pan; top with sliced banana.
3 Combine egg, oil, brown sugar and extract in medium bowl. Stir in sifted dry ingredients, then mashed banana. Pour mixture into prepared pan; bake, uncovered, about 40 minutes. Turn onto wire rack, peel off baking paper; turn cake top-side up.
4 Serve cake warm or at room temperature with thick cream, if desired.
per serving 20g total fat (2.8g saturated fat); 2011kJ (481 cal); 73.5g carbohydrate; 4.7g protein; 2.1g fibre

yogurt and lemon syrup cake

preparation time 25 minutes
cooking time 50 minutes
serves 12

250g butter, softened
3 teaspoons finely grated lemon rind
1 cup (220g) caster sugar
3 eggs
½ cup (45g) desiccated coconut
¼ cup (30g) almond meal
2 tablespoons lemon juice
2½ cups (375g) self-raising flour
¾ cup (200g) yogurt
1 medium lemon (140g)
½ cup (125ml) water
¼ cup (90g) honey
4 cardamom pods, bruised

1 Preheat oven to moderate (180°C/160°C fan-forced). Grease 20cm baba pan.
2 Beat butter, rind and sugar in small bowl with electric mixer until light and fluffy. Add eggs, one at a time, beating well between additions.
3 Transfer mixture to large bowl; using wooden spoon stir in coconut, almond meal and juice, then flour and yogurt. Spoon mixture into prepared pan; spread evenly with plastic spatula. Bake, uncovered, about 50 minutes. Stand cake 5 minutes in pan then turn onto wire rack over tray.
4 Meanwhile, using vegetable peeler, remove rind from lemon; slice rind finely. Squeeze juice from lemon; you need ¼ cup (60ml) juice.
5 Combine rind, juice, the water, honey and cardamom in small saucepan; stir over heat, without boiling, until honey melts. Bring to a boil; reduce heat then simmer, uncovered, 5 minutes. Using slotted spoon, carefully remove and discard cardamom. Pour hot syrup over hot cake.
per serving 23.2g total fat (14.3g saturated fat); 1764kJ (422 cal); 48g carbohydrate; 6.5g protein; 2.1g fibre

Biscuits
and Slices

Home-made biscuits speak of
continuity: your grandmother
may have made some of these.
Their calm pleasures are never out
of fashion. They are often the first
thing that children learn to cook,
and we've included two recipes,
Snickers Rocky Road and Apricot
Muesli Slice, that are designed
especially for beginners in the
kitchen. Crisp biscuits keep best
in an airtight glass jar; airtight plastic
boxes are good for slices and
brownies. Don't store them for too
long though (not that that's usually
a problem), as they do gradually
get 'tired' after a week or so.

snickers rocky road

hazelnut caramel slice

honey snap biscuits

raspberry and white chocolate brownies

snickers rocky road

preparation time 15 minutes (plus refrigeration time)
cooking time 5 minutes
makes 54 squares

4 x 60g snickers bars, chopped coarsely
1 cup (35g) rice bubbles
150g toasted marshmallows, chopped coarsely
1 cup (150g) roasted unsalted peanuts
400g milk eating chocolate, chopped coarsely
2 teaspoons vegetable oil

1 Grease 19cm x 29cm slice pan. Line base and two long sides with baking paper, extending paper 2cm above sides.
2 Combine snickers, rice bubbles, marshmallows and nuts in large bowl. Stir chocolate and oil in small saucepan over low heat until smooth; cool 5 minutes.
3 Pour chocolate mixture into snickers mixture; mix until well combined. Spoon rocky road mixture into prepared pan, cover; refrigerate about 30 minutes or until set. Remove from pan, trim edges of mixture; cut into 3cm squares. Store, covered, in the refrigerator.
per square 4.9g total fat (2.3g saturated fat); 368kJ (88 cal); 9.5g carbohydrate; 1.9g protein; 0.6g fibre

hazelnut caramel slice

preparation time 25 minutes
cooking time 45 minutes
  (plus cooling and refrigeration time)
makes 30

200g butter, chopped
½ cup (50g) cocoa powder
2 cups (440g) firmly packed brown sugar
1 teaspoon vanilla essence
2 eggs, beaten lightly
1½ cups (225g) plain flour
200g dark eating chocolate, melted, cooled
1 tablespoon vegetable oil

CARAMEL FILLING
180g butter, chopped
½ cup (110g) caster sugar
2 tablespoons golden syrup
¾ cup (180ml) sweetened condensed milk
1¼ cups (185g) whole hazelnuts, toasted

1 Preheat oven to moderately slow (170°C/150°C fan-forced). Grease 20cm x 30cm lamington pan; line base and two sides with baking paper, extending paper 2cm above sides of pan.
2 Combine butter and cocoa powder in medium saucepan, stir over low heat until smooth. Add sugar; stir until dissolved.
3 Remove pan from heat, add essence, egg and sifted flour; mix well. Spread mixture into prepared pan, bake 20 minutes; cool.
4 Meanwhile, make caramel filling. Quickly spread caramel filling evenly over base; refrigerate at least 30 minutes or until firm.
5 Combine chocolate and oil in small bowl, spread over caramel filling; refrigerate until set, cut into pieces.
CARAMEL FILLING
Combine butter, sugar, syrup and condensed milk in medium saucepan; stir over low heat until butter is melted. Increase heat to medium; simmer, stirring, about 13 minutes or until mixture is dark caramel in colour. Remove from heat, stir in nuts.
per slice 18.1g total fat (9g saturated fat); 1279kJ (306 cal); 34g carbohydrate; 3.6g protein; 1.1g fibre
TIP This recipe can be made two days ahead; store in an airtight container in refrigerator.

honey snap biscuits

preparation time 15 minutes
cooking time 30 minutes
makes about 45

80g butter
⅓ cup (115g) honey
½ cup (110g) firmly packed brown sugar
½ teaspoon vanilla extract
¾ cup (110g) plain flour
½ teaspoon ground ginger

1 Preheat the oven to moderate (180°C/160°C fan-forced). Grease oven trays.
2 Combine butter, honey and sugar in small saucepan; stir over medium heat until butter is melted. Remove from heat, stir in extract.
3 Sift flour and ginger into large bowl; using a wooden spoon, stir in butter mixture, beating until smooth.
4 Drop heaped teaspoons of mixture, about 8cm apart, onto prepared trays, about six at a time. The biscuits will spread during cooking.
5 Bake about 8 minutes or until golden brown. You can cook two trays at a time in a fan-forced oven. In a conventional oven, alternate the trays' positions halfway through cooking.
6 Stand biscuits on trays 5 minutes; transfer to wire rack to cool. These biscuits are delicious served with ice-cream or fruit desserts.
per biscuit 1.5g total fat (1g saturated fat); 159kJ (38 cal); 6g carbohydrate; 0.3g protein; 0.1g fibre
TIP This recipe can be made a week ahead; store in an airtight container or glass jar.

raspberry and white chocolate brownies

preparation time 20 minutes
cooking time 40 minutes
makes 18

150g butter, chopped
200g dark cooking chocolate, chopped
1 cup (220g) caster sugar
1 teaspoons vanilla extract
3 eggs, beaten lightly
½ cup (75g) plain flour
½ cup (75g) self-raising flour
100g white eating chocolate, chopped
150g raspberries

1 Preheat the oven to moderate (180°C/160°C fan-forced). Grease deep 19cm square cake pan; line base and two opposite sides with baking paper, extending paper 2cm above sides.
2 Melt butter and dark chocolate in medium heatproof bowl over a saucepan of simmering water.
3 Stir in sugar and extract, then eggs, sifted flours, white chocolate and raspberries. Spread mixture into prepared pan. Bake, uncovered, about 35 minutes or until just firm. Cool in pan. Turn out; cut into squares.
per brownie 12.9g total fat (7.8g saturated fat); 995kJ (238 cal); 28.7g carbohydrate; 3.1g protein; 0.9g fibre
TIP This recipe can be made five days ahead; store, covered, in refrigerator.

coffee snaps

preparation time 15 minutes
cooking time 10 minutes per tray
makes about 70

125g butter, softened
1¼ cups (250g) firmly packed brown sugar
3 teaspoons ground espresso coffee
3 teaspoons vanilla extract
1 egg
¾ cup (110g) plain flour
¾ cup (110g) self-raising flour
2 tablespoons coffee beans (70 beans)

1 Preheat oven to moderate (180°C/160°C fan-forced). Grease oven trays.
2 Beat butter, sugar, coffee and extract in small bowl with electric mixer until pale and fluffy. Add egg; beat until just combined. Stir in sifted flours.
3 Roll rounded teaspoons of the mixture into balls. Place 3cm apart on prepared trays. Top each with a coffee bean. Bake, uncovered, about 10 minutes or until browned. Stand 5 minutes; transfer to a wire rack to cool.

per biscuit 1.6g total fat (1g saturated fat); 159kJ (38 cal); 5.7g carbohydrate; 0.4g protein; 0.1g fibre
TIP This recipe can be made a week ahead; store in an airtight or glass container.

chocolate melting moments

preparation time 15 minutes
cooking time 10 minutes
makes 28

125g butter, chopped
2 tablespoons icing sugar
¾ cup (110g) plain flour
2 tablespoons cornflour
2 tablespoons cocoa powder
¼ cup (85g) chocolate hazelnut spread

1 Preheat oven to moderate (180°C/160°C fan-forced). Lightly grease two oven trays.
2 Beat butter and sugar in small bowl with electric mixer until light and fluffy. Stir in sifted dry ingredients, in two batches.
3 Spoon mixture into piping bag fitted with 5mm fluted tube; pipe directly onto prepared trays, allowing 3cm between each biscuit. Bake, uncovered, about 10 minutes or until biscuits are firm. Stand biscuits 5 minutes; transfer to wire rack to cool.
4 Sandwich biscuits with spread to serve.
per melting moment 4.8g total fat (2.8g saturated fat); 293kJ (70 cal); 6.2g carbohydrate; 0.7g protein; 0.2g fibre
TIP Strawberry or raspberry jam can also be used instead of chocolate hazelnut spread.

triple-choc cookies

preparation time 10 minutes
cooking time 10 minutes
makes 36

125g butter, chopped
½ teaspoon vanilla essence
1¼ cups (250g) firmly packed brown sugar
1 egg
1 cup (150g) plain flour
¼ cup (35g) self-raising flour
1 teaspoon bicarbonate of soda
⅓ cup (35g) cocoa powder
½ cup (85g) chopped raisins
½ cup (95g) milk choc bits
½ cup (75g) white chocolate melts, halved
½ cup (75g) dark chocolate melts, halved

1 Preheat oven to moderate (180°C/160°C fan-forced). Lightly grease two oven trays.
2 Beat butter, essence, sugar and egg in small bowl with electric mixer until smooth; do not overbeat. Stir in sifted dry ingredients, then raisins and all chocolates.
3 Drop level tablespoons of mixture onto prepared trays, allowing 5cm between each cookie. Bake, uncovered, about 10 minutes. Stand 5 minutes; transfer to wire rack to cool.
per cookie 74.4g total fat (46.8g saturated fat); 5108kJ (1222 cal); 130g carbohydrate; 16.3g protein; 0.4g fibre
TIP For a firmer cookie, bake an extra 2 minutes. Choc bits are made of cocoa liquor, cocoa butter, sugar and an emulsifier; these hold their shape in baking. Chocolate melts are discs of compounded chocolate ideal for melting and moulding.

choc nut biscotti

preparation time 35 minutes
cooking time 50 minutes (plus cooling time)
makes 60

1 cup (220g) caster sugar
2 eggs
1⅔ cups (250g) plain flour
1 teaspoon baking powder
1 cup (150g) shelled pistachios, toasted
½ cup (70g) slivered almonds
¼ cup (25g) cocoa powder

1 Preheat oven to moderate (180°C/160°C fan-forced). Lightly grease oven tray.
2 Whisk sugar and eggs in medium bowl. Stir in sifted flour, baking powder and nuts; mix to a sticky dough.
3 Knead dough on lightly floured surface until smooth; divide into two portions. Using floured hands, knead one portion on lightly floured surface until smooth, but still slightly sticky. Divide this portion into four pieces; roll each piece into 25cm log shape.
4 Knead remaining portion with cocoa until smooth; divide into two pieces. Roll each piece of chocolate mixture into a 25cm log shape.
5 Place one chocolate log on prepared tray; place a plain log each side, press gently together to form a slightly flattened shape. Repeat with remaining chocolate and plain logs. Bake, uncovered, about 30 minutes or until browned lightly. Cool on tray 10 minutes.
6 Reduce oven to slow (150°C/130°C fan-forced).
7 Using a serrated knife, cut logs diagonally into 5mm slices. Place slices, in single layer, on ungreased oven trays. Bake, uncovered, about 20 minutes or until dry and crisp, turning over halfway through cooking. Cool on wire racks.
per biscotti 2.1g total fat (0.3g saturated fat); 226kJ (54 cal); 7.3g carbohydrate; 1.5g protein; 0.5g fibre
TIP Store biscotti in an airtight container for up to four weeks. Not suitable to freeze.

Knead the second portion of dough with the cocoa then divide it in half and roll each half into a 25cm log.

Centre one chocolate log between two of the plain logs; pressing them gently together to flatten slightly.

After the first baking, slice the slightly cooled biscotti on the diagonal then bake again until dry and crisp.

chocolate macadamia slice

preparation time 15 minutes (plus refrigeration time)
cooking time 5 minutes
makes 30

200g butter
⅓ cup (115g) golden syrup
⅓ cup (35g) drinking chocolate
¼ cup (25g) cocoa powder
500g plain sweet biscuits, chopped finely
½ cup (75g) toasted macadamias,
   chopped coarsely
200g dark eating chocolate

1 Line 20cm x 30cm lamington pan with plastic wrap.
2 Combine butter, syrup, drinking chocolate and sifted cocoa in medium saucepan; stir over medium heat until smooth. Add biscuits and nuts; stir to combine.
3 Press mixture into prepared pan, cover; refrigerate until firm.
4 Stir chocolate in medium heatproof bowl over medium saucepan of simmering water until smooth. Spread chocolate over slice; refrigerate, uncovered, until firm. Cut into 4cm x 5cm pieces to serve.
per piece 12.2g total fat (6.4g saturated fat); 811kJ (194 cal); 20.1g carbohydrate; 1.9g protein; 0.6g fibre
TIP Macadamias can be replaced with any other variety of nut.

pistachio bread

preparation time 20 minutes
cooking time 45 minutes
makes 40

3 egg whites
⅓ cup (75g) sugar
¼ teaspoon ground cardamom
1 teaspoon finely grated orange rind
¾ cup (110g) plain flour
¾ cup (110g) shelled pistachios

1 Preheat oven to moderate (180°C/160°C fan-forced). Grease 8cm x 26cm bar cake pan; line base and sides with baking paper, extending paper 2cm above long sides.
2 Beat egg whites in small bowl with electric mixer until soft peaks form. With motor operating, gradually add sugar, beating until dissolved between additions. Fold in cardamom, rind, flour and nuts; spread mixture into prepared pan.
3 Bake, uncovered, about 30 minutes or until browned lightly. Cool in pan; wrap in foil, stand overnight.
4 Preheat oven to slow (150°C/130°C fan-forced).
5 Using a serrated or electric knife, cut bread into 3mm diagonal slices. Place slices on ungreased oven trays. Bake, uncovered, about 15 minutes or until dry and crisp; turn onto wire racks to cool.
per slice 1.4g total fat (0.2g saturated fat); 117kJ (28 cal); 2.5g carbohydrate; 1.3g protein; 0.4g fibre

cashew ginger squares

preparation time 15 minutes
cooking time 20 minutes
makes about 12

125g butter
¼ cup (55g) caster sugar
1 cup (150g) self-raising flour
1 teaspoon ground ginger

TOPPING
½ cup (80g) icing sugar
60g butter
2 tablespoons golden syrup
1 cup (150g) unsalted roasted cashews,
  chopped coarsely
¼ cup (50g) finely chopped glacé ginger

1 Preheat oven to moderate (180°C/160°C fan-forced). Grease 20cm x 30cm lamington pan; line base and two long sides with baking paper, extending paper 2cm above edge.
2 Beat butter and sugar in small bowl with electric mixer until light and fluffy; stir in sifted flour and ginger. Spread mixture evenly over base of prepared pan. Bake, uncovered, about 20 minutes or until lightly browned; cool in pan.
3 Make topping. Spread hot topping evenly over cold base; cool.
TOPPING
Combine sifted icing sugar, butter and syrup in small saucepan; stir over heat until butter is melted. Stir in nuts and ginger.
per square 19.2g total fat (9.4g saturated fat); 1216kJ (291 cal); 27.2g carbohydrate; 3.5g protein; 1.1g fibre
TIP This recipe can be made a week ahead; store, covered, in the refrigerator.

snickerdoodles

preparation time 25 minutes (plus refrigeration time)
cooking time 12 minutes per tray (plus cooling time)
makes 50

250g butter, softened
1 teaspoon vanilla extract
½ cup (110g) firmly packed brown sugar
1 cup (220g) caster sugar
2 eggs
2¾ cups (410g) plain flour
1 teaspoon bicarbonate of soda
½ teaspoon ground nutmeg
1 tablespoon caster sugar, extra
2 teaspoons ground cinnamon

1 Beat butter, extract and sugars in small bowl with electric mixer until light and fluffy. Add eggs, one at a time, beating until just combined. Transfer to large bowl.
2 Stir combined sifted flour, soda and nutmeg, in two batches, into egg mixture. Cover; refrigerate 30 minutes.
3 Meanwhile, preheat oven to moderate (180°C/160°C fan-forced).
4 Combine extra caster sugar and cinnamon in small shallow bowl. Roll level tablespoons of dough into balls; roll balls in cinnamon sugar. Place balls on ungreased oven trays, 7cm apart. Bake, uncovered, 12 minutes. Cool biscuits on trays.
per biscuit 4.4g total fat (2.8g saturated fat); 393kJ (94 cal); 12.8g carbohydrate; 1.2g protein; 0.3g fibre
TIPS Store biscuits in an airtight container for up to three weeks. Suitable to freeze for up to three months.

apricot muesli slice

preparation time 25 minutes
cooking time 30 minutes
makes 20

100g butter
½ cup (110g) caster sugar
1 egg yolk
⅔ cup (100g) plain flour
¼ cup (35g) self-raising flour
1 tablespoon custard powder
½ cup (160g) apricot jam, warmed

MUESLI TOPPING
¼ cup (90g) honey
50g butter
1½ cups (135g) rolled oats
1 cup (40g) cornflakes
½ cup (35g) shredded coconut
½ cup (75g) finely chopped dried apricots

1 Preheat oven to moderate (180°C/160°C fan-forced). Grease 20cm x 30cm lamington pan; line base with baking paper.
2 Beat butter, sugar and egg yolk in small bowl with electric mixer until light and fluffy. Stir in sifted combined flours and custard powder. Using fingers, press mixture over base of prepared pan. Bake, uncovered, about 15 minutes or until browned lightly.
3 Meanwhile, make muesli topping.
4 Remove slice from oven, spread with jam. Sprinkle muesli topping over jam, pressing gently with fingers. Bake, uncovered, another 15 minutes. Cool in pan; cut into 5cm x 6cm pieces to serve.
MUESLI TOPPING
Heat honey and butter in small saucepan until butter melts; transfer to large bowl. Stir in remaining ingredients.
per piece 8.4g total fat (5.3g saturated fat); 798kJ (191 cal); 27.4g carbohydrate; 2.2g protein; 1.5g fibre

greek almond biscuits

preparation time 30 minutes
cooking time 15 minutes per tray (plus cooling time)
makes 25

3 cups (375g) almond meal
1 cup (220g) caster sugar
3 drops almond essence
3 egg whites, beaten lightly
1 cup (80g) flaked almonds

1 Preheat oven to moderate (180°C/160°C fan-forced). Line oven trays with baking paper.
2 Combine almond meal, sugar and essence in large bowl. Add egg white; stir until mixture forms firm paste.
3 Roll level tablespoons of mixture into flaked almonds; roll into 8cm logs. Press on any remaining almonds. Shape logs to form crescents; place on prepared trays. Bake, uncovered, about 15 minutes or until browned lightly. Cool on trays.
per biscuit 10.1g total fat (0.7g saturated fat); 594kJ (142 cal); 9.6g carbohydrate; 4.1g protein; 1.6g fibre
TIP Store biscuits in an airtight container for up to one week. Suitable to freeze for up to three months.

passionfruit melting moments

preparation time 40 minutes
cooking time 15 minutes
makes about 25

3 passionfruit
250g butter, softened
1 teaspoon vanilla extract
½ cup (80g) soft icing sugar
1⅔ cups (250g) plain flour
½ cup (75g) cornflour

PASSIONFRUIT BUTTER CREAM
80g butter, softened
⅔ cup (110g) soft icing sugar

1 Preheat oven to moderately slow (170°C/150°C fan-forced). Line three baking trays with baking paper.
2 Remove pulp from passionfruit, place in fine sieve; press down with back of a spoon. Reserve 1 tablespoon of passionfruit juice for passionfruit butter cream.
3 Beat butter, extract and sifted icing sugar in medium bowl with electric mixer until pale. Stir in combined sifted flours in two batches; stir in passionfruit pulp.
4 With lightly floured hands, roll 2 level teaspoons of mixture into balls; place on prepared trays about 3cm apart. Dip fork into a little extra flour, press biscuits lightly.
5 Bake, uncovered, about 15 minutes or until biscuits are a pale straw colour. Cool biscuits on trays 5 minutes; transfer to wire racks to cool.
6 Meanwhile, make passionfruit butter.
7 Sandwich biscuits with 1 teaspoon of the passionfruit butter cream. Dust with a little extra sifted icing sugar, if desired.
PASSIONFRUIT BUTTER CREAM
Beat butter and sifted icing sugar in small bowl with electric mixer until pale and fluffy. Beat in reserved passionfruit juice.
per melting moment 11g total fat (7.2g saturated fat); 719kJ (172 cal); 17.7g carbohydrate; 1.2g protein; 0.7g fibre
TIP Biscuits can be made a week ahead; store in an airtight container or glass jar. Sandwich with passionfruit butter cream close to serving.

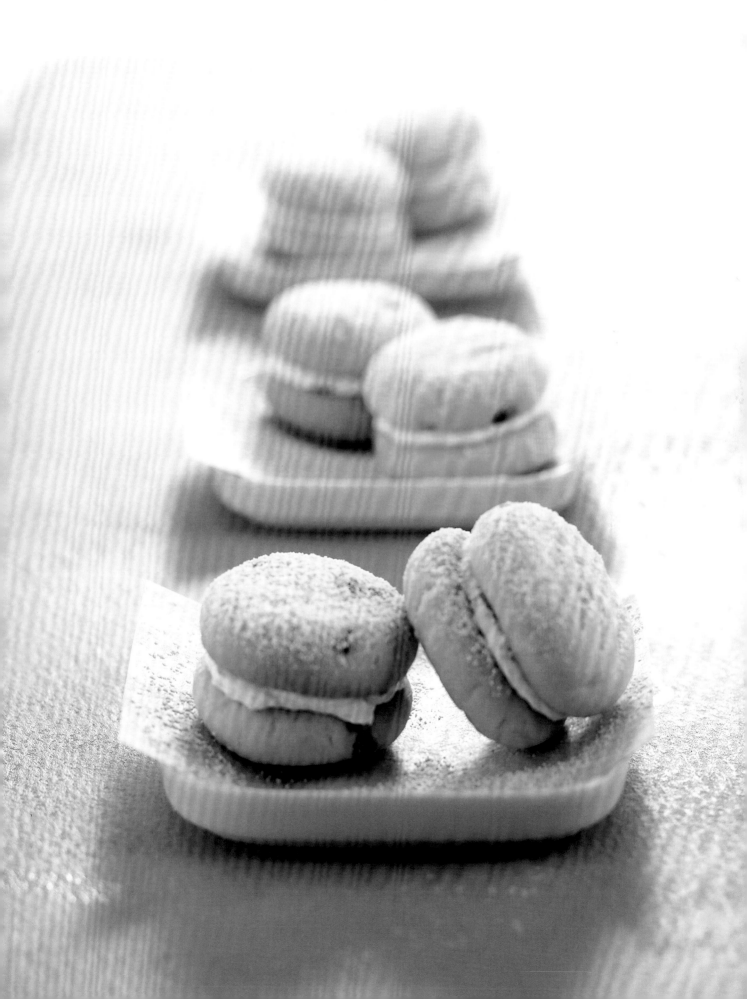

pepita and sesame slice

preparation time 20 minutes
cooking time 20 minutes (plus cooling time)
makes 16

90g butter
1 teaspoon grated lemon rind
2 tablespoons caster sugar
1 egg
⅔ cup (100g) plain flour
½ cup (80g) wholemeal plain flour
½ cup (80g) unsalted pepitas, chopped coarsely
¼ cup (80g) apricot jam
2 tablespoons sesame seeds, toasted

1 Preheat oven to moderately hot (200°C/180°C fan-forced). Grease 23cm-square slab pan; line base and two long sides with baking paper, extending paper 2cm above edge.
2 Beat butter, rind, sugar and egg in medium bowl with electric mixer until light and fluffy. Stir in sifted flours and pepitas; press mixture evenly into prepared pan.
3 Spread slice with jam; sprinkle with seeds.
4 Bake, uncovered, about 20 minutes or until browned lightly; cool slice in pan before cutting.
per piece 7.2g total fat (3.2g saturated fat); 552kJ (132 cal); 12.2g carbohydrate; 1.9g protein; 1.4g fibre
TIP Store in an airtight container for up to one week.

caramel coconut slice

preparation time 20 minutes
cooking time 35 minutes
makes about 12

½ cup (75g) plain flour
½ cup (75g) self-raising flour
½ cup (45g) desiccated coconut
½ cup (110g) caster sugar
100g butter, melted

CARAMEL FILLING
395g can sweetened condensed milk
2 tablespoons golden syrup
¼ cup (55g) firmly packed brown sugar
60g butter, melted

COCONUT TOPPING
4 eggs, beaten lightly
⅔ cup (150g) caster sugar
4 cups (360g) desiccated coconut

1 Preheat oven to moderate (180°C/160°C fan-forced). Grease 25cm x 30cm swiss roll pan.
2 Sift flours into medium bowl, stir in coconut, sugar and butter; press mixture evenly over base of prepared pan. Bake, uncovered, about 10 minutes or until lightly browned; cool.
3 Combine ingredients for caramel filling in small bowl; mix well.
4 Combine ingredients for coconut topping in medium bowl; mix well.
5 Spread caramel filling evenly over base; sprinkle with coconut topping. Bake, uncovered, about 25 minutes or until topping is lightly browned; cool in pan.
per piece 37.9g total fat (29.2g saturated fat); 2496kJ (597 cal); 59.2g carbohydrate; 8.5g protein; 5.4g fibre
TIP This recipe can be made a week ahead; store in an airtight container.

apricot and pine nut biscotti

preparation time 25 minutes
cooking time 50 minutes (plus cooling time)
makes 50

1¼ cups (275g) caster sugar
2 eggs
1 teaspoon vanilla extract
1½ cups (225g) plain flour
½ cup (75g) self-raising flour
½ cup (125g) coarsely chopped glacé apricots
¼ cup (40g) pine nuts, toasted
2 teaspoons water

1 Preheat oven to moderate (180°C/160°C fan-forced). Lightly grease oven tray.
2 Whisk sugar, eggs and extract in medium bowl. Stir in sifted flours, apricots, nuts and the water; mix to a sticky dough.
3 Knead dough on lightly floured surface until smooth; divide into two portions. Using floured hands, roll each portion into 30cm log. Place logs on prepared tray. Bake, uncovered, about 25 minutes or until browned lightly. Cool on tray 10 minutes.
4 Reduce oven to slow (150°C/130°C fan-forced).
5 Using a serrated knife, cut logs diagonally into 1cm slices. Place slices, in single layer, on ungreased oven trays. Bake, uncovered, about 25 minutes or until dry and crisp, turning over halfway through cooking; cool on wire racks.

per biscotto 0.8g total fat (0.1g saturated fat); 238kJ (57 cal); 11.5g carbohydrate; 1g protein; 0.3g fibre
TIPS To toast nuts, place in a heavy-base frying pan; stir constantly over medium-to-high heat until they are evenly browned. Remove from pan immediately.
Store biscotti in an airtight container for up to one month. Not suitable to freeze.

aniseed biscotti

preparation time 20 minutes (plus refrigeration time)
cooking time 45 minutes
makes 40

125g butter, chopped
¾ cup (165g) caster sugar
3 eggs
2 tablespoons brandy
1 tablespoon grated lemon rind
1½ cups (225g) plain flour
¾ cup (110g) self-raising flour
¾ cup (120g) blanched almonds, toasted, chopped coarsely
1 tablespoon ground aniseed

1 Beat butter and sugar in large bowl until just combined; add eggs, one at a time, beating well after each addition. Add brandy and rind; mix well. Stir in flours, nuts and aniseed. Cover; refrigerate 1 hour.
2 Preheat oven to moderate (180°C/160°C fan-forced). Lightly grease oven tray.
3 Halve dough; shape each half into a 30cm log. Place on prepared tray. Bake, uncovered, 20 minutes or until lightly browned and firm. Cool on tray 10 minutes.
4 Reduce oven to slow (150°C/130°C fan-forced).
5 Using serrated or electric knife, cut logs diagonally into 1cm slices. Place slices, in one layer, on ungreased oven trays. Bake, uncovered, about 25 minutes or until dry and crisp, turning over halfway through cooking; cool on wire racks.

per biscotto 4.7g total fat (1.9g saturated fat); 389kJ (93 cal); 10.3g carbohydrate; 2g protein; 0.6g fibre
TIP Store biscotti in an airtight container for up to one month.

coconut macaroons

preparation time 15 minutes
cooking time 45 minutes (plus cooling time)
makes 18

1 egg, separated
1 egg yolk
¼ cup (55g) caster sugar
1⅔ cups (120g) shredded coconut

1 Preheat oven to slow (150°C/130°C fan-forced). Grease oven trays.
2 Beat egg yolks and sugar in small bowl until creamy; stir in coconut.
3 Beat egg white in small bowl until firm peaks form; stir gently into coconut mixture.
4 Drop heaped teaspoons of mixture onto prepared trays. Bake, uncovered, 15 minutes.
5 Reduce oven to very slow (120°C/100°C fan-forced); bake further 30 minutes or until biscuits are golden brown. Loosen biscuits; cool on trays.
per macaroon 5g total fat (4g saturated fat); 255kJ (61 cal); 3.5g carbohydrate; 1g protein; 1g fibre
TIP Store biscuits in an airtight container for up to three weeks. Suitable to freeze for up to three months.

semolina slice

preparation time 15 minutes (plus refrigeration time)
cooking time 1 hour 50 minutes
makes 28

1kg coarsely ground semolina
2½ cups (550g) sugar
1 cup (250ml) milk
125g butter
¼ cup (40g) blanched almonds

SUGAR SYRUP
3 cups (750ml) water
2 teaspoons lemon juice
1½ cups (330g) caster sugar
2 teaspoons orange flower water

1 Make sugar syrup.
2 Preheat oven to moderately slow (170°C/150°C fan-forced). Grease 20cm x 30cm lamington pan.
3 Combine semolina and sugar in large bowl. Place milk and butter in small saucepan; stir over low heat until butter melts. Pour into semolina mixture; stir to combine.
4 Spread mixture into prepared pan; smooth the top with a wet hand. Score slice into 4cm diamond shapes; centre one almond on each diamond. Bake, uncovered, about 1 hour 20 minutes or until slice is golden brown and slightly firm to the touch.
5 Cut through diamond shapes to bottom of slice; gradually pour cooled syrup over hot slice. Cool in pan.
SUGAR SYRUP
Combine the water, juice and sugar in medium saucepan; bring to a boil. Reduce heat; simmer, uncovered, about 20 minutes or until syrup reduces to about 2½ cups. Cool to room temperature. Add orange flower water, cover; refrigerate 3 hours or overnight. (Syrup is best made the day before, covered and refrigerated; remove from refrigerator when slice goes into oven so that syrup is room temperature cool before pouring over hot slice.)
per piece 5.2g total fat (2.8g saturated fat); 1179kJ (282 cal); 55.6g carbohydrate; 4.5g protein; 1.3g fibre
TIP Cover slice loosely with aluminium foil if it starts to overbrown during cooking.

After-dinner Treats

They'll all say they can't eat another thing. Don't argue, just leave a plate of delicious-looking little treats within their reach and let human nature do the rest. Each bite provides just the right chocolatey, fruity, spicy or nutty sweetness to offset, to perfection, coffee's bitter kick. Confections like these are best made when you are feeling unhurried enough to take care over their decorative looks, but you can schedule this well ahead of time: they'll keep a week in airtight containers (leaving the meringues for Meringue Kisses unfilled and sandwiching them together shortly before they're needed).

craisin, port and dark chocolate truffles

peanut butter and milk chocolate truffles

gourmet rocky road

meringue kisses with passionfruit cream

craisin, port and dark chocolate truffles

preparation time 40 minutes (plus refrigeration time)
cooking time 5 minutes
makes 30

¼ cup (60ml) thickened cream
200g dark eating chocolate, chopped coarsely
2 tablespoons port
⅓ cup (50g) craisins, chopped coarsely
300g dark eating chocolate, melted

1 Combine cream and chopped chocolate in small saucepan; stir over low heat until smooth, stir in port and craisins. Transfer to small bowl, cover; refrigerate 3 hours or overnight.
2 Working with a quarter of the chocolate mixture at a time (refrigerate remaining mixture until needed), roll rounded teaspoons into balls; place on ungreased oven tray. Freeze truffles until firm.
3 Working quickly, dip truffles in melted chocolate then roll gently in hands to coat evenly, return to tray; refrigerate until firm.
per truffle 5.7g total fat (4.4g saturated fat); 410kJ (98 cal); 11.3g carbohydrate; 0.8g protein; 0.6g fibre

peanut butter and milk chocolate truffles

preparation time 40 minutes (plus refrigeration time)
cooking time 5 minutes
makes 30

⅓ cup (80ml) thickened cream
200g milk eating chocolate, chopped coarsely
¼ cup (70g) unsalted crunchy peanut butter
¾ cup (110g) crushed peanuts

1 Place cream and chocolate in small saucepan, stirring over low heat until smooth; stir in peanut butter. Transfer to small bowl. Cover; refrigerate 3 hours or overnight.
2 Working with a quarter of the chocolate mixture at a time (refrigerate remaining mixture until needed), roll rounded teaspoons into balls; place on ungreased oven tray. Refrigerate truffles until firm.
3 Working quickly, roll balls in peanuts, return to tray; refrigerate truffles until firm.
per truffle 5.7g total fat (2.2g saturated fat); 322kJ (77 cal); 4.8g carbohydrate; 2.1g protein; 0.6g fibre

gourmet rocky road

preparation time 20 minutes (plus refrigeration time)
makes 30

300g toasted marshmallow with coconut,
   chopped coarsely
400g turkish delight, chopped coarsely
¼ cup (40g) toasted blanched almonds,
   chopped coarsely
½ cup (75g) toasted shelled pistachios
450g white eating chocolate, melted

1 Grease two 8cm x 26cm bar cake pans; line base and sides with baking paper, extending paper 5cm above long sides.
2 Combine marshmallow, turkish delight and nuts in large bowl. Working quickly, stir in chocolate.
3 Spread mixture into prepared pans, push mixture down firmly to flatten the top. Refrigerate until set; cut as desired.
per piece 7.8g total fat (4g saturated fat); 727kJ (174 cal); 24.8g carbohydrate; 2.5g protein; 0.4g fibre

meringue kisses with passionfruit cream

preparation time 20 minutes
cooking time 30 minutes
makes 35

1 egg white
½ teaspoon white vinegar
⅓ cup (75g) caster sugar
1 teaspoon icing sugar
¼ cup (60ml) thickened cream
1 tablespoon icing sugar, extra
1 tablespoon passionfruit pulp

1 Preheat oven to very slow (120°C/100°C fan-forced). Grease oven trays; dust with cornflour, shake off excess.
2 Beat egg white, vinegar and sugar in small bowl with electric mixer about 10 minutes or until sugar dissolves; fold in icing sugar.
3 Place meringue mixture in piping bag fitted with a small plain nozzle; pipe 1.5cm rounds 3cm apart on prepared trays. Bake, uncovered, about 30 minutes or until crisp and dry. Cool meringues on trays.
4 Beat cream, 2 teaspoons of the extra icing sugar and passionfruit pulp in small bowl with electric mixer until stiff peaks form.
5 Sandwich meringues with passionfruit cream; dust with remaining extra icing sugar.
per kiss 0.6g total fat (0.4g saturated fat); 67kJ (16 cal); 2.6g carbohydrate; 0.2g protein; 0.1g fibre

chocolate panforte

preparation time 15 minutes
cooking time 55 minutes
makes 30

2 sheets rice paper
¾ cup (110g) plain flour
2 tablespoons cocoa powder
½ teaspoon ground cinnamon
½ teaspoon ground ginger
½ cup (150g) coarsely chopped glacé figs
½ cup (85g) dates, halved
½ cup (125g) coarsely chopped glacé peaches
¼ cup (50g) red glacé cherries, halved
¼ cup (50g) green glacé cherries, halved
½ cup (80g) blanched almonds, toasted
½ cup (75g) unsalted cashews, toasted
½ cup (75g) hazelnuts, toasted
½ cup (75g) macadamia nuts, toasted
⅓ cup (115g) honey
⅓ cup (75g) caster sugar
⅓ cup (75g) firmly packed brown sugar
2 tablespoons water
100g dark eating chocolate, melted

1 Preheat oven to moderately slow (170°C/160°C fan-forced). Grease 20cm sandwich pan; line base with rice paper sheets.
2 Sift flour, cocoa and spices into large bowl; stir in fruit and nuts.
3 Combine honey, sugars and the water in small saucepan; stir over heat, without boiling, until sugars dissolve. Simmer, uncovered, without stirring, 5 minutes. Pour hot syrup, then chocolate into nut mixture; stir until well combined. Press mixture firmly into prepared pan. Bake, uncovered, about 45 minutes; cool in pan.
4 Remove panforte from pan; wrap in foil. Stand overnight; cut into thin wedges to serve.
per wedge 7.4g total fat (1.3g saturated fat); 627kJ (150 cal); 19.1g carbohydrate; 2.4g protein; 1.5g fibre

chocolate cream fudge

preparation time 5 minutes (plus standing time)
cooking time 40 minutes
makes 49

1½ cups (330g) caster sugar
½ cup (100g) firmly packed brown sugar
60g dark eating chocolate, chopped coarsely
2 tablespoons glucose syrup
½ cup (125ml) cream
¼ cup (60ml) milk
40g butter

1 Grease deep 15cm-square cake pan.
2 Combine sugars, chocolate, syrup, cream and milk in small saucepan; stir over heat, without boiling, until sugar dissolves. Using pastry brush dipped in hot water, brush down side of pan to dissolve any sugar crystals; bring to a boil. Boil, uncovered, without stirring, about 10 minutes or until syrup reaches 116°C on candy thermometer. Remove pan immediately from heat, leaving candy thermometer in syrup; add butter, do not stir. Cool fudge, about 20 minutes or until syrup drops to 40°C on candy thermometer.
3 Using a wooden spoon, stir fudge about 10 minutes or until a small amount dropped from the spoon holds its shape. Spread fudge into prepared pan; cover with foil. Stand at room temperature about 3 hours or until fudge sets. Turn fudge out of pan; trim edges. Cut into 2cm squares.
per piece 2.2g total fat (1.4g saturated fat); 251kJ (60 cal); 10.5g carbohydrate; 0.2g protein; 0g fibre

mini florentines

preparation time 10 minutes
cooking time 6 minutes per tray
makes 45

¾ cup (120g) sultanas
2 cups (60g) corn flakes
¾ cup (60g) flaked almonds, toasted
½ cup (110g) red glacé cherries
⅔ cup (160ml) sweetened condensed milk
60g white eating chocolate, melted
60g dark eating chocolate, melted

1 Preheat oven to moderate (180°C/160°C fan-forced). Line two oven trays with baking paper.
2 Combine sultanas, corn flakes, nuts, cherries and milk in medium bowl.
3 Drop heaped teaspoons of mixture onto prepared trays, allowing 5cm between each florentine; bake, uncovered, about 6 minutes or until browned lightly. Cool on trays.
4 Spread the base of half the biscuits with white chocolate and remaining half with dark chocolate; run fork through chocolate to make waves. Allow chocolate to set at room temperature.
per florentine 2.1g total fat (0.8g saturated fat); 238kJ (57 cal); 8.9g carbohydrate; 1g protein; 0.3g fibre
TIP One heaped teaspoon is equivalent to 3 level teaspoons.

almond nougat

preparation time 10 minutes (plus standing time)
cooking time 30 minutes
makes 49

2 sheets rice paper
½ cup (175g) honey
1⅓ cups (300g) caster sugar
2 tablespoons water
1 egg white
2 cups (320g) blanched almonds, toasted

1 Lightly grease deep 15cm-square cake pan. Trim one sheet of rice paper into 15cm square; line base of pan.
2 Combine honey, sugar and the water in small saucepan; stir over heat, without boiling, until sugar dissolves. Using pastry brush dipped in hot water, brush down side of pan to dissolve any sugar crystals; bring to a boil. Boil, uncovered, without stirring, about 10 minutes or until syrup reaches 164°C on candy thermometer; remove pan immediately from heat. Place thermometer in pan of boiling water; remove from heat to allow thermometer to gradually decrease in temperature.
3 Beat egg white in small heatproof bowl with electric mixer until soft peaks form. With motor operating, add hot syrup to egg white in thin, steady stream. Stir almonds into egg white mixture.
4 Spoon mixture into prepared pan, pressing mixture firmly into pan. Cut remaining sheet of rice paper large enough to cover top of nougat; press lightly onto nougat. Stand about 2 hours or until cool; cut into 2cm squares.
per piece 3.7g total fat (0.2g saturated fat); 309kJ (74 cal); 9.4g carbohydrate; 1.5g protein; 0.6g fibre
TIP It is important to cool the nougat at room temperature as refrigeration will cause it to soften. Nougat is best kept in an airtight container at room temperature.

Boil syrup, uncovered, without stirring, for about 10 minutes or until the temperature reaches 164°C on a candy thermometer.

Using an electric mixer, beat egg white until soft peaks form; with motor operating, add hot syrup to the bowl in a thin, steady stream.

Stir the almonds into mixture then press the nougat firmly into prepared pan; cover with rice paper. Stand about 2 hours before cutting.

white choc, lemon, lime and coconut truffles

preparation time 40 minutes (plus refrigeration time)
cooking time 5 minutes
makes 30

½ cup (125ml) coconut cream
2 teaspoons finely grated lime rind
2 teaspoons finely grated lemon rind
360g white eating chocolate, chopped coarsely
1¼ cups (85g) shredded coconut

1 Combine coconut cream, rinds and chocolate in small saucepan; stir over low heat until smooth. Transfer mixture to small bowl. Cover; refrigerate 3 hours or overnight.
2 Working with a quarter of the chocolate mixture at a time (refrigerate remaining mixture until needed), roll rounded teaspoons into balls; place on ungreased oven tray. Refrigerate truffles until firm.
3 Working quickly, roll truffles in coconut, return to tray; refrigerate until firm.
per truffle 6.7g total fat (4.9g saturated fat); 376kJ (90 cal); 6.9g carbohydrate; 1.1g protein; 0.5g fibre

dark chocolate and ginger truffles

preparation time 40 minutes (plus refrigeration time)
cooking time 5 minutes
makes 30

⅓ cup (80ml) thickened cream
200g dark eating chocolate, chopped coarsely
½ cup (115g) glacé ginger, chopped finely
¼ cup (25g) cocoa powder

1 Combine cream and chocolate in small saucepan, stirring over low heat until smooth; stir in ginger. Transfer to small bowl. Cover; refrigerate 3 hours or overnight.
2 Working with a quarter of the chocolate mixture at a time (refrigerate remaining mixture until needed), roll rounded teaspoons into balls; place on ungreased oven tray. Refrigerate truffles until firm.
3 Working quickly, roll balls in cocoa, return to tray; refrigerate truffles until firm.
per truffle 3g total fat (1.9g saturated fat); 197kJ (47 cal); 4.6g carbohydrate; 0.6g protein; 0.2g fibre

glossary

AIOLI See Essential Ingredients, page 8.

ALLSPICE Also known as pimento or Jamaican pepper, allspice is so-named because it tastes like a combination of nutmeg, cumin, clove and cinnamon. It is available whole (a pea-sized dark-brown berry) or ground, and used in both sweet and savoury dishes. Available from most supermarkets and specialty spice stores.

ALMONDS

Blanched Brown skins removed.

Essence Often interchangeable with extract; made with almond oil and alcohol or another agent.

Meal Also known as ground almonds; nuts are powdered to a coarse flour-like texture, for use in baking or as a thickening agent. Flourless cakes use a nut meal as a substitute for flour.

Slivered Small pieces cut lengthways.

Vienna Toffee-coated almonds available from some supermarkets, gourmet food and specialty confectionery stores.

AMARETTI Small Italian-style macaroons (biscuit or cookie) made with almond meal.

ANCHOVY FILLETS Salty, strong-flavoured small fish; most commonly available canned. Used in salads, vegetable dishes, pasta and on pizza.

ANISEED Also called anise or sweet cumin; the seeds are the fruit of an annual plant native to Greece and Egypt. Dried, they have a strong licorice flavour. Whole and ground seeds are available.

APPLES, GREEN The Granny Smith apple is crisp and juicy with a rich green skin; good to eat and ideal for cooking.

APRICOTS Used in sweet and savoury dishes, they have a velvety, golden-orange skin and aromatic sweet flesh. Also available dried.

ASPARAGUS These fragile shoots are a member of the lily family; cook with care to avoid damaging the tips.

AVOCADO A fruit with a soft, buttery flesh and a mild flavour. Best eaten raw, when ripe; usually added to salads or made into a dip, such as the famous guacamole. Test for ripeness by gently pressing the stem end; it should feel tender or give slightly.

BACON RASHERS Also known as bacon slices; made from cured and smoked pork side.

BAHARAT An aromatic all-purpose spice blend, baharat is often sold as Lebanese seven-spice, and can be found at Middle-Eastern food stores, some delicatessens and specialty spice stores. Make your own by combining 1 tablespoon ground cumin, 1 tablespoon ground coriander, 2 teaspoons paprika, 1 crushed clove and ½ teaspoon ground nutmeg.

BALMAIN BUGS Crustacean; a type of crayfish.

BAMBOO SHOOTS The tender shoots of bamboo plants harvested before they are two weeks old. Crisp in texture, they are often used in Asian cooking. Available fresh from Asian food stores and canned from supermarkets. Where possible, use fresh shoots as their flavour far outweighs the canned variety. Rinse canned shoots well to rid them of all traces of the canning liquid.

BANANA LEAVES Although they are not edible, banana leaves are used to wrap ingredients which are then baked, roasted, grilled or steamed, imparting an aromatic flavour to the food they enclose. One leaf is usually a couple of metres long so is generally sold cut into large pieces. Cut into smaller pieces, if desired, with a sharp knife close to the main stem then immerse in hot water so leaves will be pliable. They can be ordered from most greengrocers.

BASIL An aromatic herb; there are many types, but the most commonly used is sweet basil.

BAVETTE Similar in appearance to tagliatelle, however, is an all-wheat pasta containing no egg. The length and flatness of this noodle-like pasta contribute to making a little sauce go a long way. Available from some supermarkets and delicatessens.

BEANS

Black See Essential Ingredients, page 8.

Broad See Essential Ingredients, page 8.

Cannellini Small white bean similar in appearance and flavour to great northern and navy or haricot beans. Sometimes sold as butter beans.

Green Sometimes called french or string beans (although the tough string they once had has generally been bred out), this long fresh bean is consumed pod and all.

Salted black Also known as chinese black beans; are fermented and salted soy beans available in cans and jars. Used most often in Asian cooking; chop before, or mash during, cooking to release flavour. Available from Asian food stores.

Snake Long (about 40cm), thin, round, fresh green beans, Asian in origin, with a taste similar to green or french beans. Often used in stir-fries, they are also called yard-long beans because of their length. Available from most greengrocers.

Sprouts Also known as bean shoots; tender new growths of assorted beans and seeds germinated for consumption. The most readily available are mung bean, soy bean, alfalfa and snow pea sprouts.

BEEF

Blade steak From the shoulder blade.

Eye fillet Tenderloin, fillet.

Skirt steak Cut from the underside of the centre.

T-bone steak Sirloin steak with the bone in and fillet eye attached; also known as porterhouse.

BEER Beverage brewed from malted barley and other cereals, yeast and water and flavoured with hops. Usually 5% alcohol or lower.

BEETROOT Also known as beets or red beets; firm, round root vegetable.

BETEL LEAVES See Essential Ingredients, page 8.

BICARBONATE OF SODA Also known as baking soda.

BISCOTTI In Italian, 'bis' means twice and 'cotto' means cooked, hence the name. Their purpose-built dry texture means that biscotti will last well if kept airtight... not that there will be any to last after you sample a few. These delicious biscuits go well with after-dinner coffee and are also available ready-made from most supermarkets and delicatessens.

BLIND BAKING A cooking term describing a pie shell or pastry case baked before filling is added. To bake blind, ease pastry into pan or dish, place on oven tray; cover pastry with baking paper, fill with dried beans, rice or proper baking 'beans' (also called pie weights). Bake in moderately hot (200°C/180°C fan-forced) oven 10 minutes, remove paper and beans; bake for another 10 minutes or until browned lightly. Cool before adding filling. Dried beans and rice used to weigh down the pastry are not suitable for eating; cool after use, then store in an airtight jar and reuse each time you bake blind.

BLOOD ORANGE Are thought to have occurred in nature by accident in 17th-century Sicily. In season for all too short a time in winter, blood oranges, with their red-streaked, salmony-coloured flesh, have a sweet, non-acidic pulp and juice with a slight strawberry or raspberry taste; even the skin is not as bitter as other citrus. Available in autumn and winter from greengrocers.

BOK CHOY Also known as bak choy, pak choi or chinese chard; has a fresh, mild mustard taste. Stems and leaves can be stir-fried, braised or stirred through soup. **Baby bok choy**, also known as pak kat farang, shanghai bok choy or chinese chard, is small and more tender than bok choy. It has a mildly acrid, distinctively appealing taste and is one of the most commonly used Asian greens. Available from supermarkets and greengrocers.

BRANDY Spirit distilled from wine.

BREADCRUMBS

Packaged Fine-textured, crunchy, purchased, white breadcrumbs.

Stale One- or two-day-old pieces of bread made into crumbs by grating, blending or processing.

BRIOCHE Rich French yeast-risen bread made with butter and eggs. Available from pâtisseries or specialty bread shops.

BROCCOLINI A cross between broccoli and chinese kale, broccolini is milder and sweeter than broccoli. Each long stem is topped by a loose floret that closely resembles broccoli, and is completely edible. Available from some supermarkets and greengrocers.

BRUSCHETTA This Tuscan appetiser, pronounced broos-ke-tah, is traditionally made by rubbing slices of toasted Italian bread with garlic then drizzling them with extra virgin olive oil and seasoning with salt and pepper. Today, there are many variations to the classic bruschetta.

BUCATINI Prized for its combination of long pasta because of its length and short pasta due to the hole through its centre, bucatini is wonderful with dense-flavoured sauces as it allows the flavours and fragrances to be prominent.

BURGHUL Also known as bulgur wheat; hulled steamed wheat kernels, once dried are crushed into various size grains. Used in Middle-Eastern dishes.

BUTTER Use salted or unsalted (sweet) butter; 125g is equal to 1 stick butter.

CABBAGE

Chinese Also known as peking cabbage, wong bok or petsai. Elongated in shape with pale green, crinkly leaves; is the most common cabbage in South-East Asia. Can be shredded or chopped and eaten raw or braised, steamed or stir-fried. Available from supermarkets and greengrocers.

Savoy Large, heavy head with crinkled dark-green outer leaves with a mild taste.

CAJUN SEASONING Used to give an authentic USA Deep South spicy Cajun flavour to food, this packaged blend of assorted herbs and spices can include paprika, basil, onion, fennel, thyme, cayenne and tarragon.

CAPERBERRIES See Essential Ingredients, page 8.

CAPERS The grey-green buds of a warm climate (usually Mediterranean) shrub; sold either dried and salted or pickled in vinegar brine. Baby capers also are available.

CAPSICUM Also called bell pepper or, simply pepper; available red, green, yellow or orange or purplish black. Seeds and membranes should be discarded before use.

CARDAMOM Native to India and used extensively in its cuisine, cardamom is a member of the ginger family and attains a sweet yet spicy flavour. This spice can be purchased in pod, seed or ground form from most supermarkets and spice stores.

CARAWAY SEEDS A member of the parsley family, caraway seeds have a nutty, anise-like flavour and are used in many Hungarian and German dishes. Available from most supermarkets and spice stores.

CAYENNE PEPPER A hot powder made from the dried pods of pungent chillies, cayenne pepper has little aroma but a fiery taste. Available from most supermarkets and spice stores.

CELERIAC A member of the celery family, celeriac is a tuberous brown-skinned root with white flesh; tastes like an earthy, more pungent celery. Sometimes called knob celery, celeriac is the cooking celery of Northern Europe. Peeled and diced, it can be used raw in salads; steamed or boiled, it can be mashed like potato or diced and served as a cooked vegetable. At its best in winter, it is available from most greengrocers.

CELERY Grows as a cluster of long stalks; eaten raw or cooked.

CHEESE

Blue Mould-treated cheeses mottled with blue veining. Varieties include firm and crumbly Stilton-types to mild, creamy brie-like cheeses.

Bocconcini Fresh, walnut-sized baby mozzarella; a delicate, semi-soft, white cheese traditionally made in Italy from buffalo milk. Spoils rapidly so must be kept refrigerated, in brine, for 1 or 2 days at most.

Fetta Greek in origin; a crumbly textured goats- or sheep-milk cheese with a sharp salty taste.

Fontina A smooth, semi-soft cheese with a nutty taste and a brown or red rind. This creamy, rich cheese is an exceptional table cheese as well as a wonderful cooking cheese. Available from some supermarkets and delicatessens.

Goat Made from goat milk, goat cheese has an earthy, strong taste. Can be purchased in both soft and firm textures, in various shapes and sizes, sometimes rolled in ash or herbs. Available from most supermarkets and delicatessens.

Gorgonzola A creamy Italian blue cheese with a mild, sweet taste. Gorgonzola is as good an accompaniment to fruit as it is when used in cooking. Available from some supermarkets and delicatessens.

Gruyere A firm, cow-milk Swiss cheese having small holes and a nutty, slightly salty flavour. Emmental or appenzeller can be used as a substitute. Available from some supermarkets and delicatessens.

Haloumi A firm, cream-coloured sheep-milk cheese matured in brine; has a minty, salty fetta flavour. It can be grilled or fried, briefly, without breaking down. Available from most supermarkets and Middle-Eastern food stores.

Parmesan Also known as parmigiano; is a hard, grainy, cow-milk cheese. The curd is salted in brine for a month before being aged for up to two years in humid conditions.

Pecorino The generic Italian name for cheeses made from sheep milk. It's a hard, white to pale yellow cheese, usually matured for eight to 12 months. If unavailable, use parmesan.

Provolone A mild Italian cheese when young, similar to mozzarella. Golden yellow in colour, with a smooth shiny skin and a mild smoky flavour. Available from some supermarkets and delicatessens.

Ricotta Soft white cow-milk cheese; roughly translates as 'cooked again'; made from whey, a by-product of other cheese making, to which fresh milk and acid are added. Ricotta is a sweet, moist cheese with a fat content of around 8.5% and a slightly grainy texture.

CHERMOULLA See Essential Ingredients, page 9.

CHERRIES Soft stone fruit varying in colour from yellow to dark red. Sweet cherries are eaten whole and in desserts while sour cherries such as the bitter Morello variety are used in jams, preserves, pies and savoury dishes, particularly as an accompaniment to game birds and meats.

CHERVIL While this aromatic feathery green herb tastes somewhat like a blend of fennel and celery, it is a member of the carrot family. Traditionally used for its leaves alone, the roots are also edible. Available both fresh and dried but has the best flavour when fresh; like coriander and parsley, its delicate flavour diminishes the longer it is cooked. Chervil goes well with cream and eggs, and in white fish and chicken dishes.

CHICKEN
Breast With skin and bone intact.

Breast fillets Breast halved, skinned and boned.

Mince Also called ground chicken.

Tenderloins Thin strip of meat lying under the breast.

Thigh Has skin and bone intact.

Thigh cutlets Thigh with skin and centre bone intact; sometimes known as a chicken chop.

CHICKPEAS Also known as hummus, garbanzos or channa; an irregularly round, sandy-coloured legume.

CHILLI
Dried flakes Deep-red, dehydrated chilli slices and whole seeds.

Thai red Small, hot and red in colour.

CHINESE BARBECUED DUCK
Traditionally cooked in special ovens, it has a sweet-sticky coating made from soy sauce, sherry, five-spice and hoisin sauce. Available from Asian food stores.

CHINESE COOKING WINE A clear distillation of fermented rice, water and salt, it's about 29.5% alcohol by volume. Used for marinades and as a sauce ingredient, it can be purchased from most Asian food stores.

CHINESE WATER SPINACH
See Essential Ingredients, page 9.

CHIPOTLE See Essential Ingredients, page 9.

CHIVES Related to the onion and leek; has a subtle onion flavour.

Garlic Also known as chinese chives, are strongly flavoured, have flat leaves and are eaten as a vegetable.

CHOCOLATE
Compound For dipping and coating.

Dark cooking We used premium quality dark cooking chocolate rather than compound.

Dark eating Made of cocoa liquor, cocoa butter and sugar.

Milk Primarily for eating.

Milk melts Discs of compound milk chocolate ideal for melting and moulding.

White Eating chocolate.

White melts Discs of compound white chocolate ideal for melting or moulding.

CHOCOLATE HAZELNUT SPREAD
Also known as Nutella.

CHORIZO A salami-like sausage of Spanish origin, chorizo is made of coarsely ground pork and highly seasoned with garlic and chillies. Available from most delicatessens.

CHOY SUM See Essential Ingredients, page 9.

CIABATTA In Italian, it means 'slipper', which is the traditional shape of this crisp-crusted wood-fired bread. Available from most supermarkets or bakeries.

CINNAMON STICK Dried inner bark of the shoots of the cinnamon tree.

CLOVES Dried flower buds of a tropical tree, cloves can be used whole or in ground form. Has a distinctively pungent and 'spicy' scent and flavour and can be purchased from most supermarkets and spice stores.

COCOA POWDER Also called cocoa; dried, unsweetened, roasted then ground cocoa beans.

COCONUT
Cream Is obtained commercially from the first pressing of the coconut flesh alone, without the addition of water; the second pressing (less rich) is sold as the milk. Available in cans and cartons at supermarkets.

Desiccated Unsweetened, concentrated, dried finely shredded coconut flesh.

Flaked Dried flaked coconut flesh.

Milk Not the juice found inside the fruit, which is known as coconut water, but the diluted liquid from the second pressing from the white flesh of a mature coconut. Available in cans and cartons at supermarkets.

Shredded Thin strips of dried coconut.

CORELLA PEAR Also called forelle, corella pears are small in size and wonderful eaten fresh or in a salad. Available from autumn to spring, from some supermarkets and greengrocers.

CORIANDER Also known as cilantro or chinese parsley; bright-green-leafed herb with a pungent flavour. Often stirred into or sprinkled over a dish just before serving for maximum impact. Also available ground.

Root and stem mixture Roots and stems of a bunch of coriander can be cleaned, chopped and used in various dishes, most notably, Thai curry pastes.

CORN KERNELS Also called niblets; available canned from supermarkets.

CORNBREAD An American quick bread using cornmeal as all or most of the flour. Often flavoured with other ingredients such as cheese, bacon and green onions.

CORNFLOUR Also called cornstarch; used as a thickening agent in cooking.

CORNICHONS French word for 'gherkin'; minuscule pickled gherkins used to accompany pâtés or as a condiment to salads. Available from most supermarkets and delicatessens.

COUSCOUS A fine, grain-like cereal product, originally from North Africa, made from semolina. Couscous can be used in salads, as a base for stews or, as the Egyptians do, as a dessert mixed with sugar, nuts and dried fruit. Available from most supermarkets and Middle-Eastern food stores.

CRAB

Blue swimmer Also known as sand crab or Atlantic blue crab.

Meat Flesh of fresh crabs. Use canned if fresh is not available.

Mud Also known as mangrove crab; native to the tropical regions of the Bay of Bengal and the Pacific and Indian Oceans.

CRAISINS Sweetened, dried cranberries often used in salads, muesli or muffins. Available from most supermarkets.

CREAM We used fresh pouring cream, also known as pure cream. It has no additives, and contains a minimum fat content of 35%.

Thickened A whipping cream that contains a thickener. Has a minimum fat content of 35%.

CREAM CHEESE Commonly known as Philadelphia or Philly cheese. A soft, cow-milk cheese with a fat content of at least 33%. Available from supermarkets.

CREME FRAICHE A French variation of sour cream; is a mildly acidic, high fat, slightly nutty tasting thick cream. Crème fraîche and sour cream can be used interchangeably with sour cream in some

recipes, but the former can also be whipped like cream and does not split or curdle when boiled. Available from most supermarkets and delicatessens.

CUCUMBER, LEBANESE Short, slender and thin-skinned; this variety is also known as the European or burpless cucumber.

CUMIN Also known as zeera or comino; is the dried seed of a plant related to the parsley family having a spicy, nutty flavour. Available in seed form or dried and ground from supermarkets.

CURRANTS, DRIED Tiny, almost black raisins so-named after a grape variety that originated in Corinth, Greece.

CURRY POWDER A blend of ground spices used for convenience when making Indian food. Can consist of some of the following spices in varying proportions: dried chilli, cinnamon, cumin, coriander, fennel, fenugreek, mace, cardamom and turmeric. Available in mild or hot varieties.

CUSTARD POWDER Instant mixture used to make pouring custard; similar to North American instant pudding mixes.

DAIKON See Essential Ingredients, page 9.

DASHI See Essential Ingredients, page 9.

DILL Green-coloured herb with feathery leaves and tiny green-yellow flowers. Commonly used in fish and egg dishes or finely chopped in salads.

DRIED SHRIMP Also known as goong hang, salted sun-dried prawns ranging in size from not much larger than a rice seed to 'big' ones measuring about 1cm in length. Are sold packaged, shelled as a rule, in all Asian grocery stores.

DUKKAH An Egyptian nut, seed and spice mixture. It adds exotically complex, uniquely aromatic flavours to various grilled, baked or barbecued seafood, meat and poultry dishes. Dukkah can also be used in a dip or sprinkled over a finished dish just before serving. Available from some delicatessens and specialty spice stores.

EGGPLANT Also known as aubergine; belongs to the same family as tomatoes, chillies and potatoes. Ranging in size from tiny to very large and in colour from pale green to deep purple; eggplant has

an equally wide variety of flavours.

Pea Also known as makeua puong, slightly larger than a green pea and of similar shape and colour; sold fresh, in bunches like grapes, or pickled in jars. More bitter than the slightly larger Thai eggplant, which can be substituted in many Thai recipes; both can be found in Asian grocery stores.

FENNEL Also known as finocchio, bulb or Florence fennel, is also the name given to dried licorice-flavoured seeds. Eaten raw, braised, fried, roasted or stewed, it is mildly sweet and has a subtle licorice-like flavour. Fronds and top shoots are usually discarded (unless used as a garnish) and the bulb trimmed at the base to extract the fibrous core. A large fennel bulb can be as big as a grapefruit, while baby fennel can be slightly flat and weigh as little as 100g.

FIG Small, soft, pear-shaped fruit with a sweet pulpy flesh full of tiny edible seeds. Also available dried.

FIRM WHITE FISH Means non-oily fish. This category includes bream, flathead, whiting, snapper, jewfish and ling. Redfish also comes into this category.

FIVE-SPICE POWDER A fragrant ground mixture of cassia, clove, star anise, sichuan pepper and fennel seeds, five-spice, also known as chinese five-spice, can be used as a seasoning for stir-fries or as a rub for meats. Available from most supermarkets, Asian food stores or specialty spice stores.

FLOUR

Besan A fine, powdery flour made from dried ground chickpeas. Available from Asian and health food stores.

Plain An all-purpose wheat flour.

Self-raising Plain flour sifted with baking powder in the proportion of 1 cup flour to 2 teaspoons baking powder.

FRANGELICO Hazelnut-flavoured liqueur.

FRESH HERBS We have specified when to use fresh or dried (not ground) herbs in the proportion of one to four for fresh herbs; use 1 teaspoon dried herbs instead of 4 teaspoons (1 tablespoon) chopped fresh herbs.

FRIED SHALLOTS Served as a condiment or sprinkled over just-cooked food, fried shallots provide an extra crunchy finish to a salad, stir-fry or curry. Once opened, they will keep for months if stored in a tightly sealed glass jar. Available from Asian food stores.

GAI LARN See Essential Ingredients, page 10.

GALANGAL See Essential Ingredients, page 10.

GARAM MASALA A blend of spices, originating in Northern India; consists of cardamom, cinnamon, coriander, cloves, fennel and cumin, in varying proportions, roasted and ground together. Available from some supermarkets, Indian food stores and specialty spice stores.

GELATINE We used powdered gelatine; also available in sheet form known as leaf gelatine.

GHEE A clarified butter with the milk solids removed, this fat can be heated to a high temperature without burning and can be used for deep-frying. Available from Middle-Eastern and Indian food stores.

GINGER

Fresh Also known as green or root ginger; is the thick gnarled root of a tropical plant. Can be kept peeled, covered with dry sherry in a jar and refrigerated, or frozen in an airtight container.

Ground Also called powdered ginger; used as a flavouring in cakes, pies and puddings but not instead of fresh ginger.

Pickled Also known as gari or shouga, pickled ginger is thinly sliced young ginger which is pickled and then usually dyed pink or red. Often eaten with sushi to cleanse the palate. Available from some supermarkets and Asian food stores.

GLUCOSE SYRUP Also called liquid glucose, is made from wheat starch; used in jam and confectionery. Available from health food stores and supermarkets.

GRAPEFRUIT So named because they grow in clusters, it is the largest citrus fruit available. A pink-fleshed version is also available.

GRAPEVINE LEAVES Available from early spring, fresh grapevine leaves can be found in most specialist greengrocers. Alternatively, you can purchase cryovac-packed-in-brine leaves from Middle-Eastern food stores; rinse and dry well before using.

GREMOLATA An Italian gremolata is traditionally a blend of finely chopped lemon rind, parsley and garlic. Sprinkled over osso buco just before serving warms the gremolata, enlivening it just enough to send a sharp aromatic message to the diner's tastebuds.

HARISSA See Essential Ingredients, page 10.

HAZELNUT Also known as filberts; plump, grape-size, rich, sweet nut with a brown inedible skin that is removed by rubbing heated nuts together vigorously in a tea towel.

Meal Also known as ground hazelnuts.

HORSERADISH A plant grown for its pungent, spicy roots; they are generally grated and used as a condiment, particularly with roast beef or fish, or in sauces. Is also available bottled or dried.

JUNIPER BERRIES Dried fruit of the juniper shrub, an evergreen from the Northern Hemisphere. These blue-to-black berries are usually crushed to release their flavour and then used to flavour meats and sauces. Available from specialty herb or health food shops.

KAFFIR LIME LEAVES See Essential Ingredients, page 10.

KALAMATA OLIVES Purplish-black Greek olives cured in vinegar and sometimes preserved in olive oil.

KALONJI Also known as nigella, are angular purple-black seeds, creamy colour inside and possess a sharp, nutty taste. Are available in specialty spice, Middle-Eastern and Asian food stores.

KIRSCH Cherry-flavoured liqueur.

KUMARA Polynesian name of orange-fleshed sweet potato often confused with yam.

LAMB

Backstrap The larger fillet from a row of loin chops or cutlets.

Boned shoulder Boneless section of the forequarter. Also available rolled and secured with string or netting.

Cutlet Small, tender rib chop.

Fillet The smaller piece of meat from a row of loin chops or cutlets.

French-trimmed shanks Also known as drumsticks or Frenched shanks; all the gristle and narrow end of the bone

is discarded then the remaining meat trimmed from the forequarter leg.

Leg Cut from the hindquarter.

Rack Row of cutlets.

Trim Boneless cuts free from external fat.

LAVASH See Essential Ingredients, page 11.

LEEK A member of the onion family, with a mild flavour. Its thick white stem must be washed thoroughly before use; separate its layers and rinse away any trapped dirt. Leeks can be boiled, steamed or braised; is most famously used in vichyssoise.

LEMONADE A carbonated soft drink.

LEMON GRASS See Essential Ingredients, page 11.

LENTILS Dried pulses often identified by and named after their colour (red, brown, yellow). Also known as dhal.

Puy Originally from the region of the same name in France, these are a small, dark-green, fast-cooking lentil with a delicate flavour.

LETTUCE

Butter Have small, round, loosely formed heads with soft, buttery-textured leaves ranging from pale green on the outer leaves to pale yellow-green on the inner leaves. Has a sweet flavour.

Cos Also known as romaine lettuce; is the traditional Caesar salad lettuce.

Curly endive Also known as frisée, curly endive is a curly-leafed green vegetable having a prickly texture and bitter taste. Mainly used in salads, it is available from most greengrocers.

Iceberg A heavy, firm round lettuce with tightly packed leaves and crisp texture.

Lamb's Also called mâche, corn salad or lamb tongue, has a mild, almost nutty flavour and tender narrow dark-green leaves. Available from most greengrocers.

Mesclun Is a salad mix of assorted young lettuce and other green leaves, including baby spinach leaves, mizuna and curly endive.

Mizuna Often found in mesclun, mizuna is a wispy, feathered green salad leaf that originated in Japan. Available from most supermarkets and greengrocers.

Radicchio An Italian lettuce with dark burgundy leaves and a strong bitter taste.

LYCHEES See Essential Ingredients, page 11.

MACADAMIA Native to Australia, a rich and buttery nut; store in refrigerator because of its high oil content.

MALIBU Coconut-flavoured rum.

MANDARIN Small, loose-skinned citrus fruit also known as tangerine. Segments are also available canned in a light syrup.

MANGO, GREEN Sour and crunchy, green mangoes are just immature fruit that can be eaten as a vegetable in salads, curries and stir-fries. They will keep, wrapped in plastic, in the refrigerator up to two weeks. Available from most greengrocers.

MAPLE SYRUP A thin syrup distilled from the sap of the maple tree. Maple-flavoured syrup is not an adequate substitute for the real thing.

MARJORAM Strong-flavoured herb traditionally used in Italian and Greek cooking; use sparingly.

MARSALA A sweet fortified wine.

MASCARPONE A cultured cream product made in much the same way as yogurt, is whitish to creamy yellow in colour, with a soft, creamy texture. This Italian fresh soft cheese can be used in sweet dishes, such as tiramisu, and savoury. Available from most supermarkets and delicatessens.

MERGUEZ A small, spicy sausage that originated in Tunisia, but was quickly claimed by cooks throughout North Africa and Spain. Traditionally made with lamb, and is easily recognised because of its chilli-red colour, merguez can be fried, grilled or roasted. Available from most butchers, delicatessens and sausage specialty shops.

MILK

Buttermilk Sold alongside fresh milk products in supermarkets; is commercially made similarly to yogurt. It is low in fat and is a good substitute for dairy products such as cream or sour cream; good in baking and in salad dressings.

Evaporated Unsweetened canned milk from which water has been extracted by evaporation. Also available skim with a fat content of 0.3%.

Sweetened condensed From which 60% of the water has been removed; the remaining milk is sweetened with sugar.

MIRIN A Japanese champagne-coloured cooking wine made of glutinous rice and alcohol expressly for cooking and should not be confused with sake. There is a seasoned sweet mirin called manjo mirin made of water, rice, corn syrup and alcohol. Available from some supermarkets and Asian food stores.

MISO See Essential Ingredients, page 11.

MIXED SPICE A blend of ground spices usually consisting of cinnamon, allspice, cloves and nutmeg. Available from most supermarkets and specialty spice stores.

MORTAR AND PESTLE See Essential Equipment, page 18.

MUSHROOMS

Button Sometimes called champignons, are the youngest variety, and usually the smallest. The body of this mushroom is firm and tightly closed against the stem, with none of the gill-like 'veil' exposed.

Cup Slightly bigger and darker in colour than the button, with its veil (or velum) just starting to open. Cups are among the most versatile, having a distinctive flavour without being overpowering. Perfect for soups, stir-fries and sauces, and delicious sautéed in a frying pan.

Flat Large, flat mushrooms with a rich earthy flavour and meaty texture; ideal for filling and barbecuing as a meal on its own rather than just another ingredient.

Oyster Also called abalone mushrooms, available in a wide variety of colours, have a subtle, delicate flavour and work well with veal, seafood and poultry.

Shiitake See Essential Ingredients, page 14.

Swiss brown Also known as cremini or Roman mushrooms, are light to dark brown mushrooms with full-bodied flavour. They hold their shape upon being cooked. Button or cups can be substituted.

MUSSELS Buy from a fish market where there is reliably fresh fish. Must be tightly closed when bought, indicating they are alive. Before cooking, scrub shells with a strong brush and remove 'beards'. Discard any shells that do not open after cooking.

MUSTARD

American Usually served with hot dogs, is mild with a smooth texture and is often flavoured with sugar and spices.

Black seeds Also known as brown mustard seeds, are more pungent than the white (or yellow) seeds and are used in most prepared mustards.

Dijon Is a pale-yellow to brown French mustard often flavoured with white wine.

Wholegrain Also known as seeded mustard, is a coarse-grain mustard made from black and yellow mustard seeds and dijon-style mustard.

NAAN Leavened bread associated with tandoori dishes of Northern India; there, it is baked pressed against the inside wall of a heated tandoor or clay oven.

NAM JIM Is a generic term for a Thai dipping sauce; most versions include fish sauce and chillies, but the remaining ingredients are up to the individual cook.

NASHI See Essential Ingredients, page 11.

NOODLES

Bean thread See Essential Ingredients, page 12.

Fried Also called crispy noodles; used in chow mein and sang choy bow, are packaged (commonly in 100g packets) already deep-fried. Available from supermarkets and Asian food stores.

Hokkien Also known as stir-fry noodles; are fresh wheat noodles resembling thick, yellow-brown spaghetti needing no pre-cooking before being used.

Rice See Essential Ingredients, page 12.

Rice stick Also known as sen lek, ho fun or kway teow; come in different widths. Dried noodles made from rice flour and water; available flat and wide or very thing (vermicelli). Should be soaked in boiling water to soften.

Soba See Essential Ingredients, page 12.

NUTMEG See Essential Ingredients, page 12.

OCEAN TROUT A farmed fish with pink, soft flesh, it is from the same family as the Atlantic salmon.

OIL

Olive Made from ripened olives. Extra virgin and virgin are the best; extra light or light refers to the taste not fat levels.

Peanut Pressed from ground peanuts; most commonly used oil in Asian cooking because of its high smoke point (capacity to handle high heat without burning).

Sesame Made from roasted, crushed, white sesame seeds; a flavouring rather than a cooking medium.

Spray We used a cholesterol-free cooking-oil spray made from canola oil.

Vegetable Any number of oils sourced from plants rather than animal fats.

ONION

Green Also known as scallion or, incorrectly, shallot; an immature onion picked before the bulb has formed, having a long, bright-green edible stalk.

Red Also known as Spanish, red Spanish or Bermuda onion; a sweet-flavoured, large, purple-red onion.

Spring Crisp, narrow green-leafed tops and a round sweet white bulb larger than green onions.

ORANGE FLOWER WATER

Concentrated flavouring made from orange blossoms.

ORECCHIETTE

Originally a homemade specialty from the Italian region of Puglia, orecchiette translates as 'little ears', a shape this short pasta resembles. If not available, use any small pasta you like — penne, farfalle or little shells.

OYSTERS

A bivalve mollusc; when buying, look for oysters that are plump and glossy and smell fresh.

PANCETTA

An unsmoked bacon; pork belly cured in salt and spices then rolled into a sausage shape and dried for several weeks. Usually used, either sliced or chopped, as an ingredient rather than eaten on its own. Available from some supermarkets and delicatessens.

PANETTONE

A sweet Italian yeast bread with raisins and candied orange, is usually tall and cylindrical and translates as 'big bread'. Available from some supermarkets and delicatessens.

PAPAYA, **GREEN** Readily available in various sizes; look for one that is very hard and slightly shiny, which indicates that it is freshly picked. For use in Thai cooking, papaya must be totally unripe, the flesh so light green it is almost white. Buy the firmest one you can find; it will soften rapidly it you don't use it within one or two days. Available from most Asian food stores.

PAPPARDELLE A wide, ribbon-like pasta with scalloped sides, pappardelle is sometimes sold as lasagnette or even lasagne. Available from some supermarkets and delicatessens.

PAPRIKA Ground, dried red capsicum (bell pepper), available sweet and hot from supermarkets and specialty spice stores.

PASTE Some recipes in this book call for commercially prepared pastes of various strength and flavours; use whichever one you feel suits your spice-level tolerance best.

Green curry The hottest of the traditional pastes; great in chicken and vegetable curries, and a great addition to stir-fries and noodle dishes.

Laksa A bottled paste containing lemon grass, chillies, onions, galangal, shrimp paste and turmeric used to make the classic soup by the same name. Available from some supermarkets and Asian food stores.

Panang curry Based on curries of Penang, off the northwest coast of Malaysia, close to the Thai border. A complex, sweet and milder variation of red curry paste; good with seafood.

Red curry Probably the most popular curry paste; a hot blend of different flavours that complements the richness of pork, duck and seafood, also works well in marinades and sauces.

Shrimp A strong-scented, almost solid preserved paste made of salted dried shrimp. Used as a pungent flavouring in many South-East Asian soups and sauces. Available from Asian food stores.

PECANS Native to the United States and now grown locally; golden-brown, buttery and rich. Good in savoury and sweet dishes; especially good in salads.

PENNE Translated literally as 'quills'; ridged macaroni cut into short lengths on the diagonal.

PEPITAS Dried pumpkin seeds.

PEPPERCORNS

Pickled green Also known as prik tai ahn, has a fresh 'green' flavour without being extremely pungent; early harvested unripe pepper that needs to be dried or pickled to avoid fermentation. We used pickled Thai green peppercorns, which are canned, still strung in clusters, but an equivalent weight from a bottle of green peppercorns in brine can be substituted.

Sichuan See Essential Ingredients, page 14.

PINE NUTS

Also known as pignoli, pine nuts are not in fact a nut but a small, cream-coloured kernel from pine cones. Used commonly in pesto and salads, pine nuts often appear in Middle-Eastern and Indian cooking. Available from supermarkets and nut stores.

PISTACHIOS

Pale green, delicately flavoured nut inside hard off-white shells. To peel, soak shelled nuts in boiling water 5 minutes; drain, pat dry with absorbent paper. Rub skins with cloth to peel.

PITTA BREAD See Essential Ingredients, page 12.

POLENTA See Essential Ingredients, page 12.

POMEGRANATE Leathery, dark-red-skinned fruit the size of oranges, are filled with hundreds of seeds, each of which is wrapped in the edible lucent-crimson pulp that gives it a unique tangy sweet-sour flavour. Available during autumn and winter from most greengrocers.

Molasses Not to be confused with pomegranate syrup or grenadine (a sweet red liquid used in cocktails); is made from the juice of pomegranate seeds boiled down to a thick syrup. Brush over grilling or roasting meat, seafood or poultry. Available at Middle-Eastern food stores, specialty food shops and delicatessens.

POPPY SEEDS Small, dried, bluish-grey seeds of the poppy plant. Poppy seeds have a crunchy texture and a nutty flavour. Available whole or ground in most supermarkets.

PORK

American-style ribs Well-trimmed, long mid-loin ribs used in traditional American barbecue spare ribs. Grilling, barbecuing or roasting are the best methods for this cut; wonderful when brushed with a sweet baste for perfect sticky ribs.

Fillet Skinless, boneless eye-fillet cut from the loin.

Loin From pork middle.

Neck Sometimes called pork scotch, boneless cut from the foreloin.

Spare ribs Also known as belly ribs or rashers, pork spare ribs have no bone and an equal proportion of fat and meat.

PORT Fortified wine.

POTATOES

Desiree Oval, smooth and pink-skinned with waxy yellow flesh; good in salads, boiled and roasted.

Kipfler A small, finger-shaped potato with a nutty flavour, this yellow-skinned potato is great baked and in salads. Available all year from most greengrocers.

Lasoda Round, red-skinned with deep eyes, white flesh; good for mashing and roasting.

New Also called chats or baby potatoes; not a different variety but an early harvest potato with very thin skin; good unpeeled steamed, eaten hot or cold in salads.

Pontiac Large, round, red-skinned with deep eyes, white flesh; good grated, boiled and baked.

Russet burbank Also known as Idaho; russet in colour, fabulous baked.

Sebago White skin, oval; good fried, mashed and baked.

PRAWNS Also known as shrimp. To 'peel and devein', remove the head by holding it in one hand and twisting the body with the other; peel away the legs and shell from the body, but leave the tail intact, if you like, for decorative purposes. Remove and discard the centre vein from the back of each prawn, using a small sharp knife or your fingers.

PRESERVED LEMON Lemons preserved in salt and lemon juice. A common ingredient in North African cooking. Available from most Middle-Eastern food stores and delicatessens.

PROSCIUTTO Salted, air-cured and aged, prosciutto is usually eaten uncooked. Available from some supermarkets and delicatessens.

PRUNES Commercially or sun-dried plums.

PUMPKIN Also known as squash; is a member of the gourd family and used as an ingredient or eaten on its own. Various types can be substituted for one another.

Butternut Pear-shaped with golden skin and orange flesh.

QUAIL A small, delicately flavoured, domestically grown game bird ranging in weight from 250g to 300g.

QUINCE A yellow-skinned fruit with hard texture and astringent, tart taste. Once cooked, they turn a deep-pink-ruby-salmon colour. Available during autumn and early winter from greengrocers.

RAMBUTANS Related to the lychee; also known as hairy lychees as they are similar in appearance with the additional feature of long red tendrils.

READY-ROLLED PASTRY Packaged sheets of frozen puff and shortcrust pastry. Available from supermarkets.

REDCURRANT JELLY A preserve made from redcurrants used as a glaze for desserts and meats or in sauces.

RHUBARB Classified as a vegetable, is eaten as a fruit and therefore considered as one. Leaves must be removed before cooking as they contain traces of poision; the edible crisp, pink-red stalks are chopped and cooked.

RICE

Arborio Commonly used for making risottos; a round-grain rice well-suited to absorb a large amount of liquid. Its high starch content help give risottos their creamy texture. It is perfectly cooked when the rice is al dente; tender on the outside, but slightly firm in the centre. Available from most supermarkets.

Basmati From Hindu meaning 'fragrant', this fine, long-grain, highly aromatic rice is grown in the foothills of the Himalayan mountains. When cooked, it has a light, fluffy texture with a nutlike flavour; goes well with curries. Available from most supermarkets and Indian food stores.

Brown Natural whole grain.

Jasmine Sometimes sold as Thai fragrant rice, Jasmine rice is so-named due to its sweet aroma. Available from supermarkets and Asian food stores.

White Is hulled and polished, can be short- or long-grained.

Wild See Essential Ingredients, page 17.

RICE PAPER

Confectionery Imported from Holland, this variety is white and looks more like a grainy sheet of paper. It is used in confectionary making and baking, and eaten uncooked.

Vietnamese Commonly used, softened in hot water, as a wrapper for fresh spring rolls, generally served at room temperature. This variety is made from ground rice flour, salt and water. Imported from South-East Asia, it is sold packaged in 375g batches in either round or square pieces from Asian food stores.

RISONI Risoni, like orzo, is a very small rice-shaped pasta. It is great added to soups, baked in a casserole or as a side dish when served with a main course. Available from supermarkets.

ROCKET Also called arugula; a pepper-tasting green leaf used similarly to baby spinach leaves, eaten raw in salad or used in cooking.

Baby leaves Are both smaller and less peppery than the larger variety.

SAFFRON See Essential Ingredients, page 12.

SAKE Japan's favourite rice wine, sake is used in cooking, marinating and as part of dipping sauces. If unavailable, dry sherry, vermouth or brandy can be used as a substitute. When consumed as a drink, it can be served cold or warm. Available from liquor stores.

SALMON ROE Also called red caviar; makes a wonderful hors d'oeuvre. Sold fresh, it is extremely perishable and should be consumed within 3 days. Always keep, covered, in refrigerator. Available from most fishmongers.

SAMBAL OELEK See Essential Ingredients, page 13.

SASHIMI Japanese method of slicing raw fish. When purchasing fish for sashimi, ensure it has a firm texture and a pleasant (but not 'fishy') sea-smell.

SAUCE

Char sui Also called chinese barbecue sauce, is paste-like, dark-red-brown in colour and sweet and spicy in flavour. Made with fermented soybeans, honey and various spices, can also be diluted and used as a marinade. Available from most supermarkets and Asian food stores.

Cranberry A packaged product made of cranberries cooked in sugar syrup. Goes well with roast poultry and meats.

Fish Also called nam pla or nuoc nam, fish sauce is made from pulverised salted fermented fish, most often anchovies. It has a pungent smell and strong taste, so use sparingly. Available from supermarkets and Asian food stores.

Hoisin A thick, sweet Chinese barbecue sauce, hoisin is made from salted fermented soy beans, onions and garlic. It can be used as a marinade or a baste, or as a flavouring for stir-fried, braised or roasted foods. Available from supermarkets and Asian food stores.

Kecap manis An Indonesian sweet, thick soy sauce made with palm sugar, used in marinades, dips, sauces and dressings, as well as a table condiment. Depending on the brand, the soy's sweetness comes from either molasses or palm sugar. Available from supermarkets and Asian food stores.

Oyster Made from oysters and their brine, cooked with salt and soy sauce then thickened; available from most supermarkets and Asian food stores. Vegetarian oyster sauce, made from water, mushroom extract, soya beans, salt, sugar and starch, is available from most Asian food stores.

Plum A thick, sweet and sour dipping sauce made from plums, vinegar, sugar, chillies and spices.

Soy Also known as sieu, is made from fermented soy beans. Several variations are available in most supermarkets and Asian food stores.

Sweet chilli The comparatively mild, thin sauce made from red chillies, sugar, garlic and vinegar; often used as a condiment.

Tabasco Brand name of extremely fiery sauce made from vinegar, hot red peppers and salt.

Tomato Also called ketchup; flavoured condiment made from tomatoes, vinegar and spices.

Worcestershire A thin, dark-brown spicy sauce used as a seasoning for meat, gravies and cocktails and as a condiment.

SAVOIARDI SPONGE FINGER BISCUITS
Italian-style crisp sponge fingers made from sponge-cake mixture.

SCALLOPS
A bivalve mollusc with fluted shell valve; we use scallops having the coral (roe) attached.

SEAWEED

Kombu See Essential Ingredients, page 13.

Nori See Essential Ingredients, page 13.

Wakame See Essential Ingredients, page 13.

SEMOLINA
Made from crushed durum wheat hearts, ground to a very fine flour, semolina flour is used for making pasta and breads. Available at most supermarkets and health food stores.

SESAME SEEDS
The most common are black and white; a good source of calcium. To toast, spread seeds evenly on oven tray, toast briefly in moderate (180°C/160°C fan-forced) oven.

SHALLOTS
Also called French shallots, golden shallots or eschalots; small, elongated, brown-skinned member of the onion family. Grows in tight clusters similar to garlic.

SILVERBEET
Also known as swiss chard; has fleshy white stalks and large, dark green leaves. Prepared in the same way as spinach.

SNOW PEAS
Also called mange tout ('eat all'). Snow pea tendrils, the growing shoots of the plant, are available from most supermarkets and greengrocers.

SOUR CREAM
Thick, smooth and slightly acidic cream; used to add richness to soups and stews, also dolloped on potatoes and soups.

SOURDOUGH BREAD
Has been around since ancient times and is the 'real' French bread but it became universally known when Isidore Boudin, a French baker in San Francisco, added a local starter (or levain or mother) to his native breadmaking traditions. The name refers not to the taste, which is slightly sweet, but to the bread's singularly natural fermentation process. Available from some supermarkets and bakeries.

SPATCHCOCK
Also called poussin; a small chicken, no more than six weeks old, weighing a maximum of 500g. Also, a cooking technique where a small chicken is split open, then flattened and grilled.

SILVER CACHOUS
Small, round, cake-decorating sweets, also available in gold or various colours.

SPINACH
Also known as english spinach and, incorrectly, silverbeet. Its tender green leaves are good uncooked in salads or added to soups, stir-fries and stews just before serving. **Baby spinach leaves**, young leaves mostly used raw in salads, are also available.

SPLIT PEAS
Also known as field peas; green or yellow pulse grown especially for drying, split in half along a centre seam. Used in soups, stews and, occasionally, spiced and cooked on their own.

SQUID HOOD
A type of mollusc; also known as calamari. Buy squid hoods to make preparation easier.

STAR ANISE
See Essential Ingredients, page 14.

STAR FRUIT
Also known as carambola, five-corner fruit or chinese star fruit, this pale green or yellow colour fruit has a clean, crisp texture. The flavour may be either sweet or sour, depending on variety and when picked. There is no need to peel or seed it and they're slow to discolour. Available all year round from most supermarkets and greengrocers.

STOCK
Available in cans or tetra packs. Stock cubes or powder can be used. As a guide, 1 teaspoon of stock powder or 1 small crumbled stock cube mixed with 1 cup (250ml) water will give a fairly strong stock. Be aware of the salt and fat content of stock cubes, powders and prepared stocks.

SUGAR

Brown A very soft, fine granulated sugar retaining molasses for its characteristic colour and flavour.

Caster Also known as superfine or finely granulated table sugar.

Demarara Small-grained golden-coloured crystal sugar.

Icing Also known as confectioners' sugar or powdered sugar; granulated sugar crushed together with a small amount (about 3%) cornflour added.

Palm Also called nam tan pip, jaggery, jawa or gula melaka; made from the sap of the sugar palm tree. Light brown to black in colour; usually sold in rock-hard cakes. If unavailable, use brown sugar. Available from some supermarkets and Asian food stores.

Raw Natural brown granulated sugar.

SUGAR SNAP PEAS Also called honey snap peas; fresh small pea that can be eaten whole, pod and all, similarly to snow peas. Available autumn to spring from supermarkets and greengrocers.

SUMAC See Essential Ingredients, page 14.

TAHINI See Essential Ingredients, page 15.

TAMARI A thick, dark soy sauce made mainly from soy beans without the wheat used in standard soy sauce. Used in dipping sauces and as a baste. Available from supermarkets and Asian food stores.

TAMARIND See Essential Ingredients, page 15.

TAPENADE A thick, black paste consisting of black olives, olive oil, capers, anchovies and Mediterranean herbs. Used as an ingredient in dressings and sauces, or eaten on its own as a spread or dip. Available from most supermarkets and delicatessens.

TAT SOI See Essential Ingredients, page 15.

THAI BASIL See Essential Ingredients, page 15.

TOFU See Essential Ingredients, page 15.
Firm Made by compressing bean curd to remove most of the water. Used in stir-fries as it can be tossed without falling apart.

Fried puffs Packaged pieces of soft bean curd which have been deep-fried until the surface is brown and crusty and the inside almost dry.

TOMATOES

Canned Peeled tomatoes in natural juice. Available whole, crushed and diced.

Cherry Also known as Tiny Tim or Tom Thumb tomatoes; are small and round.

Egg Also called plum or roma, these are smallish, oval-shaped tomatoes much used in Italian cooking or salads.

Grape Baby egg tomatoes.

Paste Triple-concentrated tomato puree used to flavour soups, stews, sauces and casseroles.

Semi-dried Partially dried tomato pieces in olive oil; softer and juicier than sun-dried, these are not a preserve so don't keep as long as sun-dried.

Sun-dried We used sun-dried tomatoes packaged in oil, unless otherwise specified.

TORTILLA Pronounced tor-tee-yah; are made either of wheat flour or ground corn meal, and can be purchased fresh, frozen or vacuum-packed. Available from supermarkets.

TREVALLY Also known as blue-eye, blue-eye cod and deep sea trevalla; thick, moist, white-fleshed fish.

TURKISH BREAD Also known as pide; turkish bread comes in long (about 45cm) flat loaves as well as individual rounds. Made from wheat flour and sprinkled with sesame or black onion seeds. Available from most supermarkets and Middle-Eastern bakeries.

TURKISH DELIGHT A gel-like Middle-Eastern sweet coated in icing sugar. Commonly flavoured with rosewater or orange flower water, can also contain pistachios or almonds.

TURMERIC See Essential Ingredients, page 16.

VANILLA BEAN See Essential Ingredients, page 16.

VEAL Meat from a young calf, identified by its creamy pink flesh, fine texture and delicate taste.
Chop From the rib and loin (back).

Cutlets Choice chop from the mid-loin (back) area.

Shin Usually cut into 3cm- to 5cm-thick slices; also called osso buco and used in the famous Italian slow-cooked casserole of the same name.

VIETNAMESE MINT See Essential Ingredients, page 16.

VINEGAR

Apple cider Made from fermented apples.

Balsamic Originally from Modena, Italy, there are now many balsamic vinegars on the market ranging in pungency and quality depending on how, and how long, they have been aged. Quality can be determined up to a point by price; use the most expensive sparingly.

Malt Made from fermented malt and beech shavings.

Raspberry See Essential Ingredients, page 16.

Red wine Based on fermented red wine.

Rice See Essential Ingredients, page 16.

Sherry Natural vinegar aged in oak according to traditional Spanish system; mellow wine vinegar named for its colour.

White Made from spirit of cane sugar.

WALNUTS A rich, buttery and flavourful nut. Should be stored in the refrigerator because of its high oil content.

WASABI See Essential Ingredients, page 16.

WATER CHESTNUTS See Essential Ingredients, page 17.

WATERCRESS See Essential Ingredients, page 17.

WINE The adage is that you should never cook with wine you wouldn't drink; we use good-quality dry white and red wines in our recipes.

WITLOF See Essential Ingredients, page 17.

WONTON WRAPPERS Also known as wonton skins; made of flour, eggs and water they come in varying thicknesses. Usually sold packaged in large amounts and found in the refrigerated section of Asian grocery stores and some supermarkets; gow gee, egg or spring-roll pastry sheets can be substituted.

YEAST Allow 2 teaspoons (7g) dried granulated yeast to each 15g fresh yeast.

YOGURT We used plain, unflavoured yogurt, unless otherwise specified.

ZA'ATAR See Essential Ingredients, page 17.

ZUCCHINI Also known as courgette.
Flowers are also edible and are usually stuffed before being baked or fried; available at specialty greengrocers.

index

conversion chart

MEASURING EQUIPMENT

The difference between one country's measuring cups and another's is within a 2 or 3 teaspoon range. Metric measures in Australia: 1 cup holds (approximately) 250ml, 1 tablespoon holds 20ml and 1 teaspoon holds 5ml. North America, NZ and the UK use 15ml tablespoons.

HOW TO MEASURE

The most accurate way of measuring dry ingredients is to weigh them. When using graduated metric measuring cups, shake dry ingredients loosely into the appropriate cup. Do not tap the cup on a bench or tightly pack the ingredients unless directed to do so. Level top of measuring cups and spoons with a knife. When measuring liquids, place a clear glass or plastic jug with metric markings on a flat surface to check accuracy at eye level.

We use large eggs having an average weight of 60g.

DRY MEASURES

METRIC	IMPERIAL
15g	½oz
30g	1oz
60g	2oz
90g	3oz
125g	4oz (¼lb)
155g	5oz
185g	6oz
220g	7oz
250g	8oz (½lb)
280g	9oz
315g	10oz
345g	11oz
375g	12oz (¾lb)
410g	13oz
440g	14oz
470g	15oz
500g	16oz (1lb)
750g	24oz (1½lb)
1kg	32oz (2lb)

LIQUID MEASURES

METRIC	IMPERIAL
30ml	1 fluid oz
60ml	2 fluid oz
100ml	3 fluid oz
125ml	4 fluid oz
150ml	5 fluid oz (¼ pint/1 gill)
190ml	6 fluid oz
250ml	8 fluid oz
300ml	10 fluid oz (½ pint)
500ml	16 fluid oz
600ml	20 fluid oz (1 pint)
1000ml (1 litre)	1¾ pints

LENGTH MEASURES

METRIC	IMPERIAL
3mm	⅛in
6mm	¼in
1cm	½in
2cm	¾in
2.5cm	1in
5cm	2in
6cm	2½in
8cm	3in
10cm	4in
13cm	5in
15cm	6in
18cm	7in
20cm	8in
23cm	9in
25cm	10in
28cm	11in
30cm	12in (1ft)

OVEN TEMPERATURES

These oven temperatures are only a guide for conventional ovens. For fan-forced ovens, check the manufacturer's manual.

	°C (CELSIUS)	°F (FAHRENHEIT)	GAS MARK
Very slow	120	250	½
Slow	150	275-300	1-2
Moderately slow	170	325	3
Moderate	180	350-375	4-5
Moderately hot	200	400	6
Hot	220	425-450	7-8
Very hot	240	475	9